CW00500369

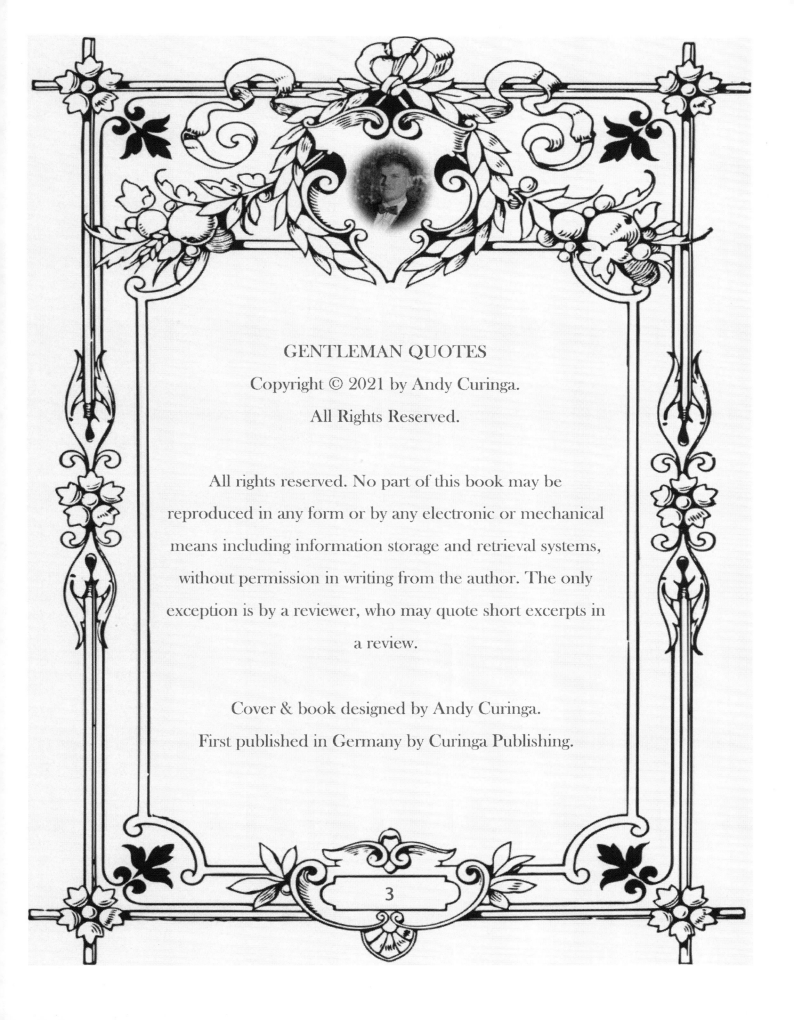

GENTLEMAN QUOTES

Copyright © 2021 by Andy Curinga.

All Rights Reserved.

All rights reserved. No part of this book may be reproduced in any form or by any electronic or mechanical means including information storage and retrieval systems, without permission in writing from the author. The only exception is by a reviewer, who may quote short excerpts in a review.

Cover & book designed by Andy Curinga.

First published in Germany by Curinga Publishing.

WHO IS A GENTLEMAN?

Although you'll recognize in this book that there are many different views and statements on what traits a gentleman must have, there are some similarities.

Generally, a gentleman is strong in his mind, which includes patience, commitment, communication, strong in body (personal health and fitness), and being respectful.

Character – A gentleman should have high moral character. He should be generous, understanding, empathetic, respectful, and genuine.

However, check it for yourself!

"Courtesy is as much a mark of a gentleman as courage."

Theodore Roosevelt

7

"The word of a gentleman is as

good as his bond;

and sometimes better."

Charles Dickens

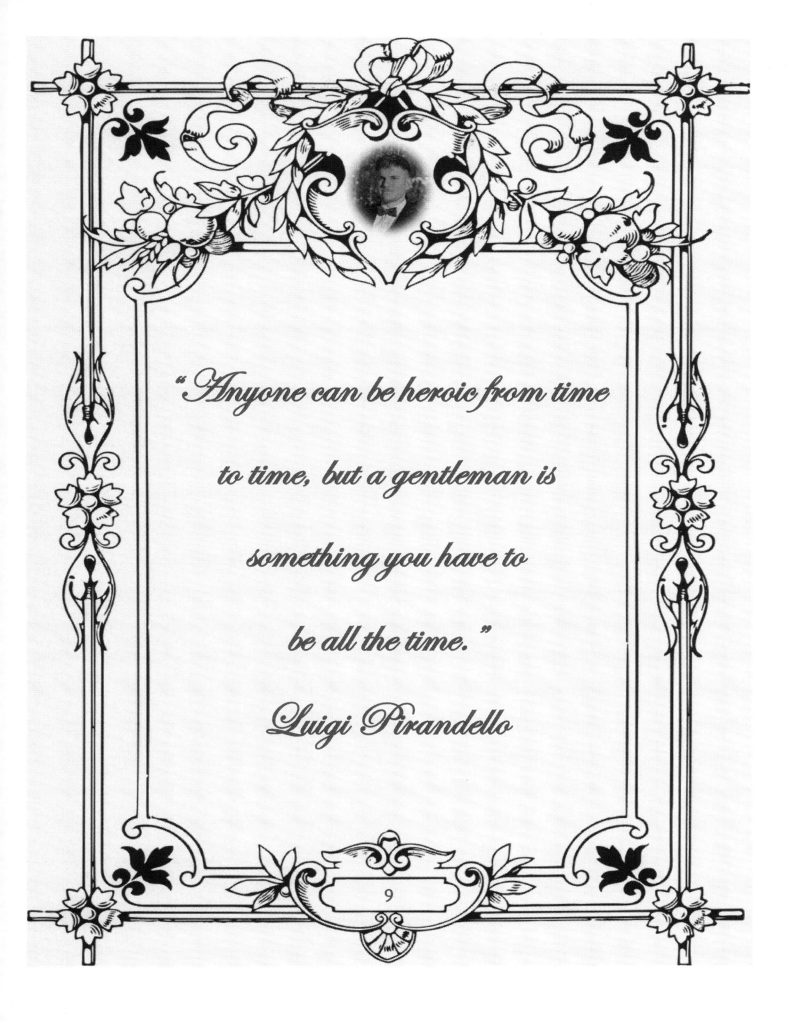

"Anyone can be heroic from time to time, but a gentleman is something you have to be all the time."

Luigi Pirandello

"A gentleman is someone who

does not what he wants to do, but

what he should do."

Haruki Murakami

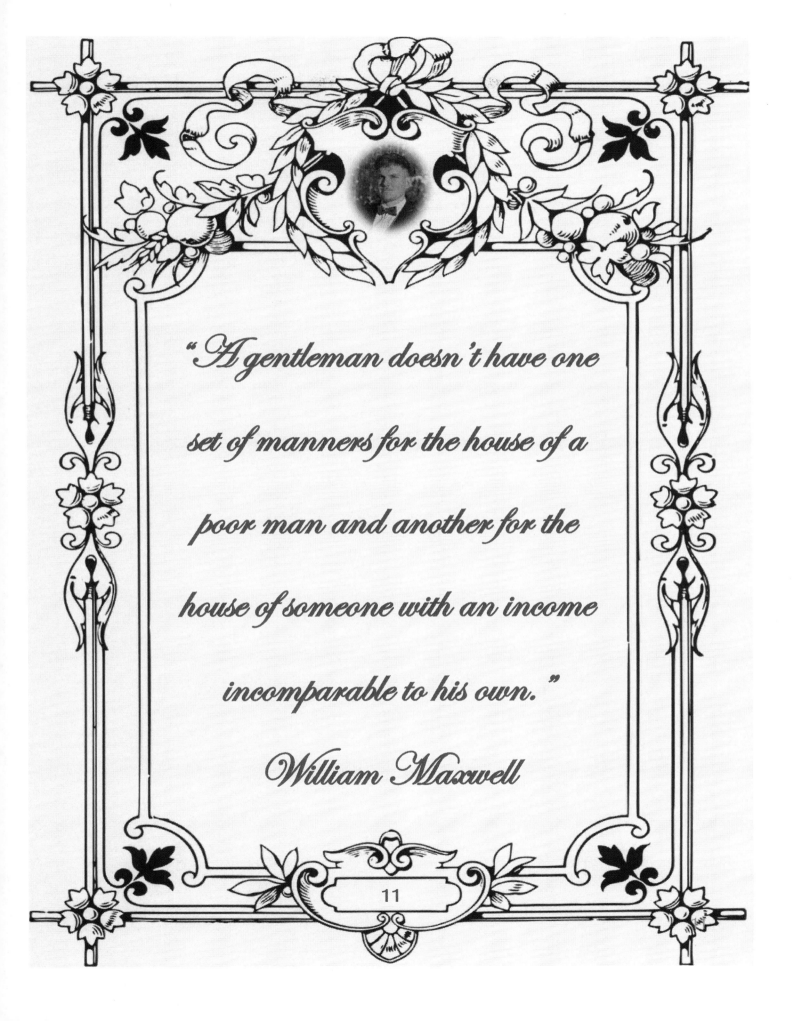

"A gentleman doesn't have one set of manners for the house of a poor man and another for the house of someone with an income incomparable to his own."

William Maxwell

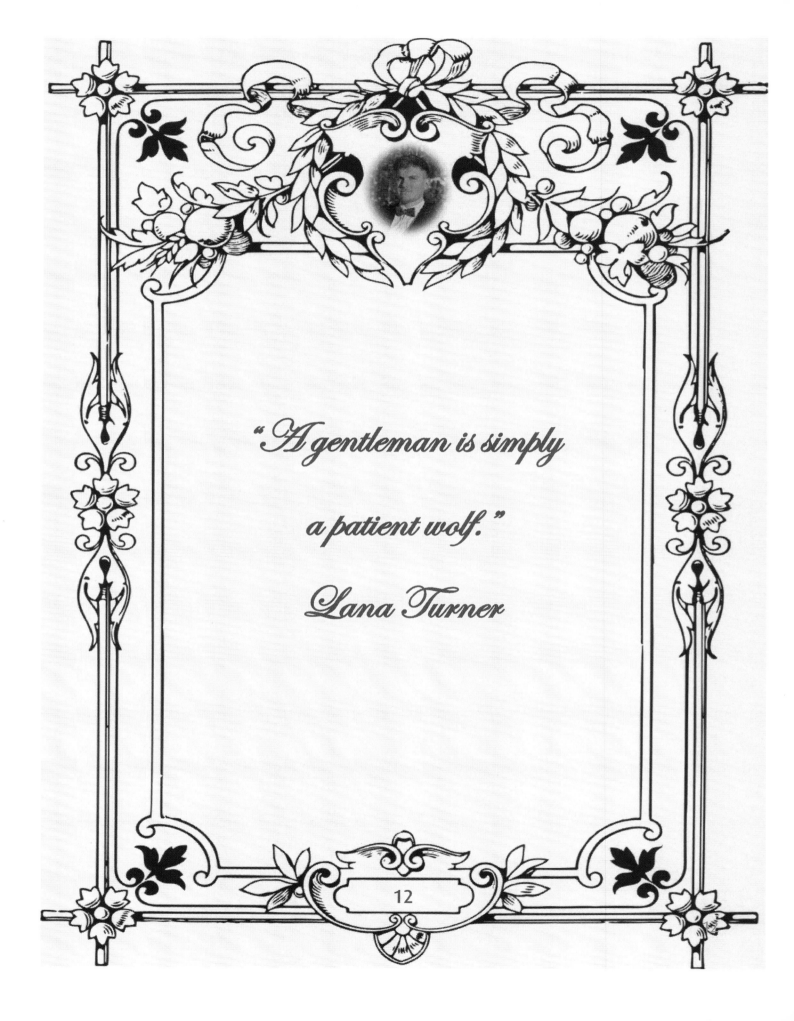

"A gentleman is simply

a patient wolf."

Lana Turner

"*I have always loved things*

that are timeless and

get better with age."

Ralph Lauren

13

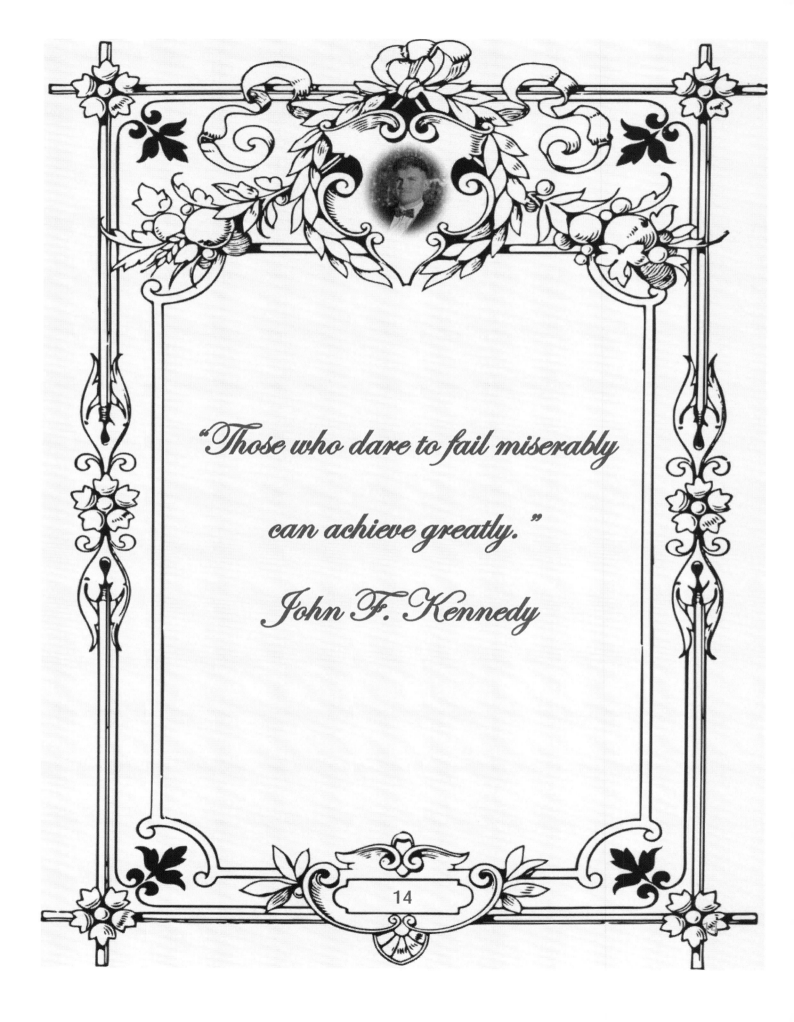

"Those who dare to fail miserably

can achieve greatly."

John F. Kennedy

14

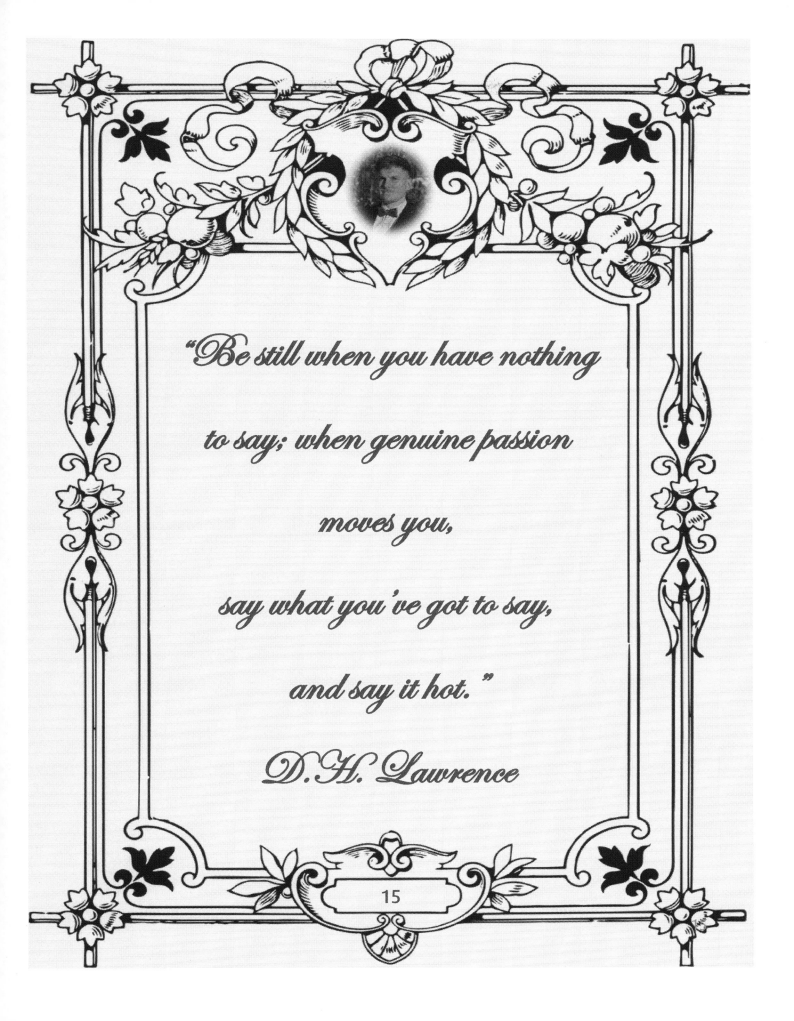

"Be still when you have nothing

to say; when genuine passion

moves you,

say what you've got to say,

and say it hot."

D.H. Lawrence

"A gentleman is one who puts

more into the world

than he takes out."

George Bernard Shaw

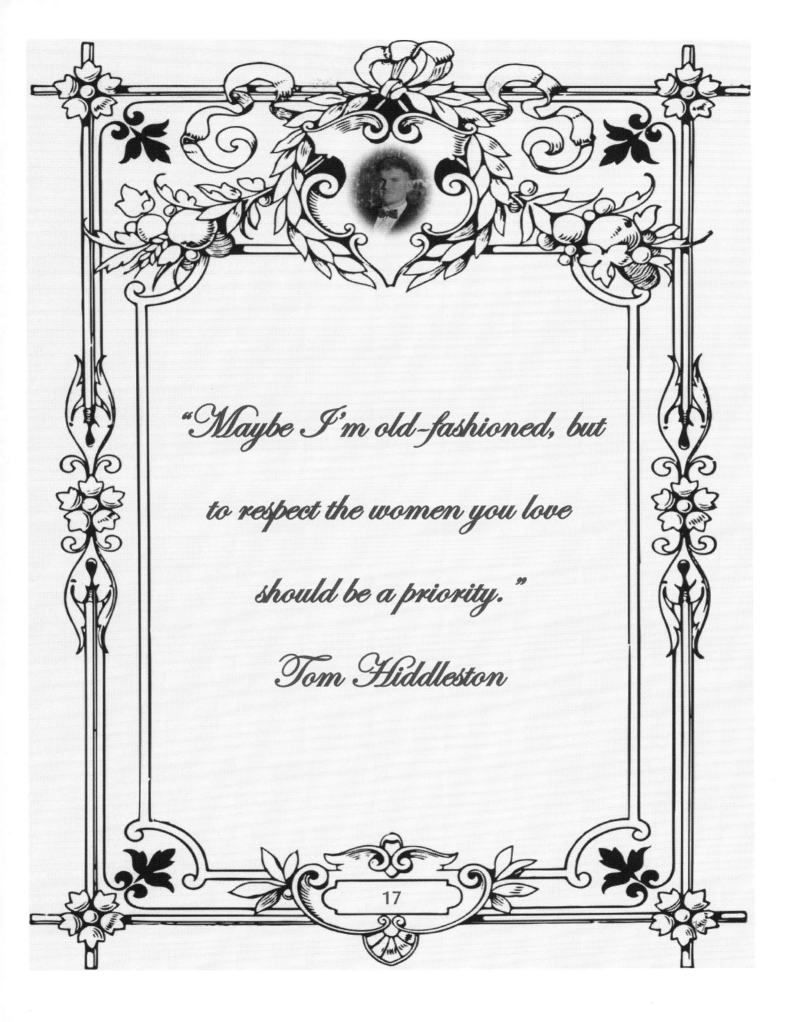

"Maybe I'm old-fashioned, but

to respect the women you love

should be a priority."

Tom Hiddleston

"*A true gentleman is one who is*

never unintentionally rude."

Oscar Wilde

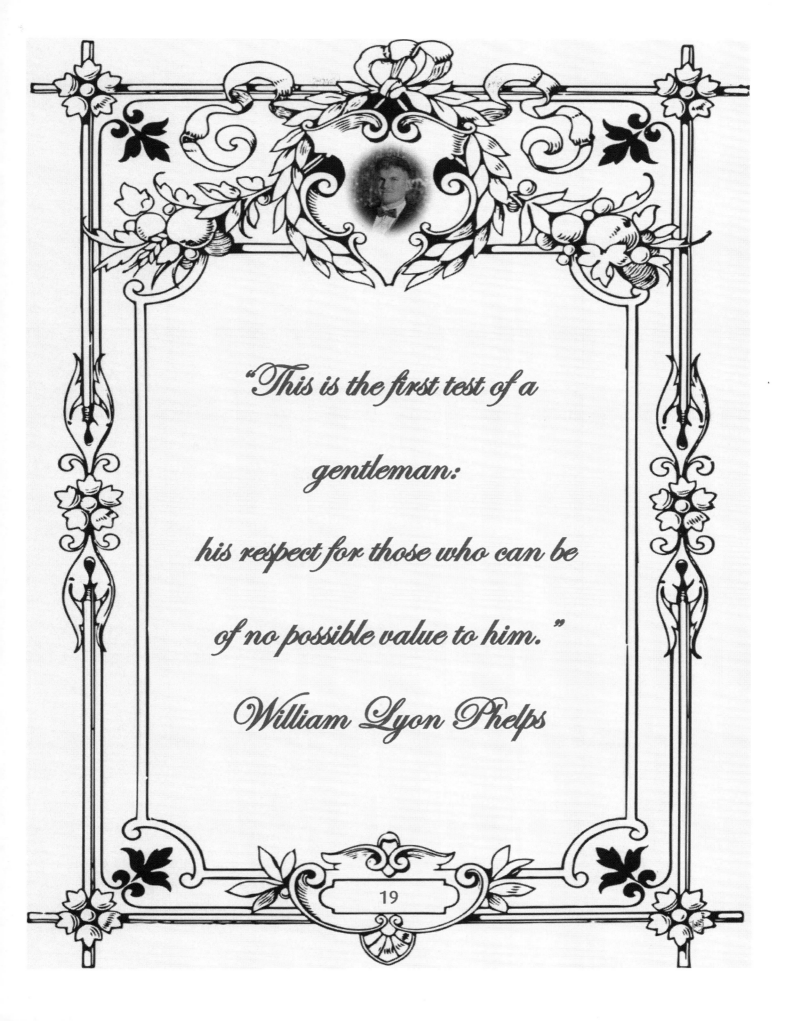

"This is the first test of a

gentleman:

his respect for those who can be

of no possible value to him."

William Lyon Phelps

19

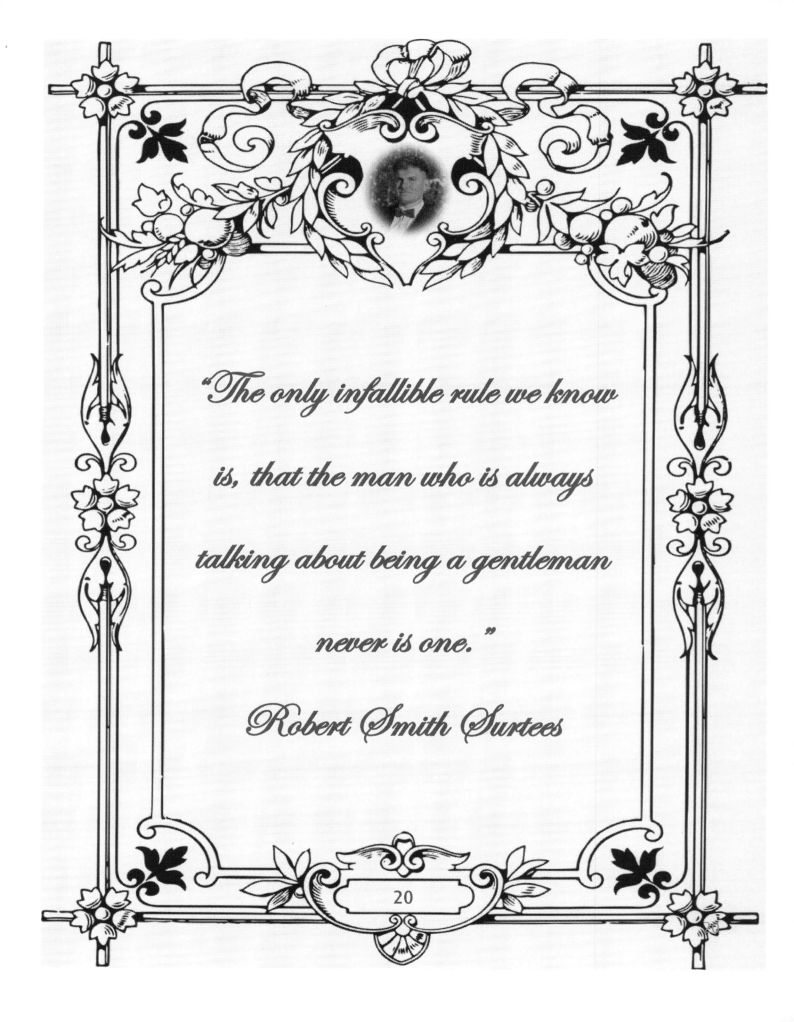

"The only infallible rule we know is, that the man who is always talking about being a gentleman never is one."

Robert Smith Surtees

20

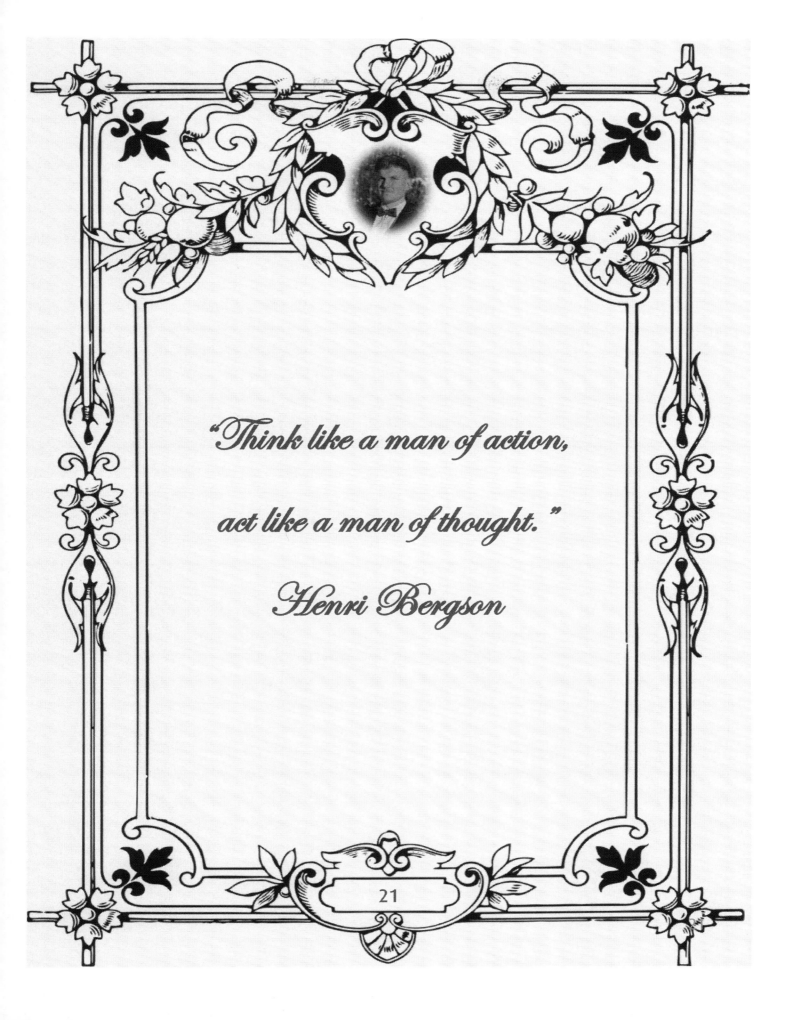

"Think like a man of action,

act like a man of thought."

Henri Bergson

21

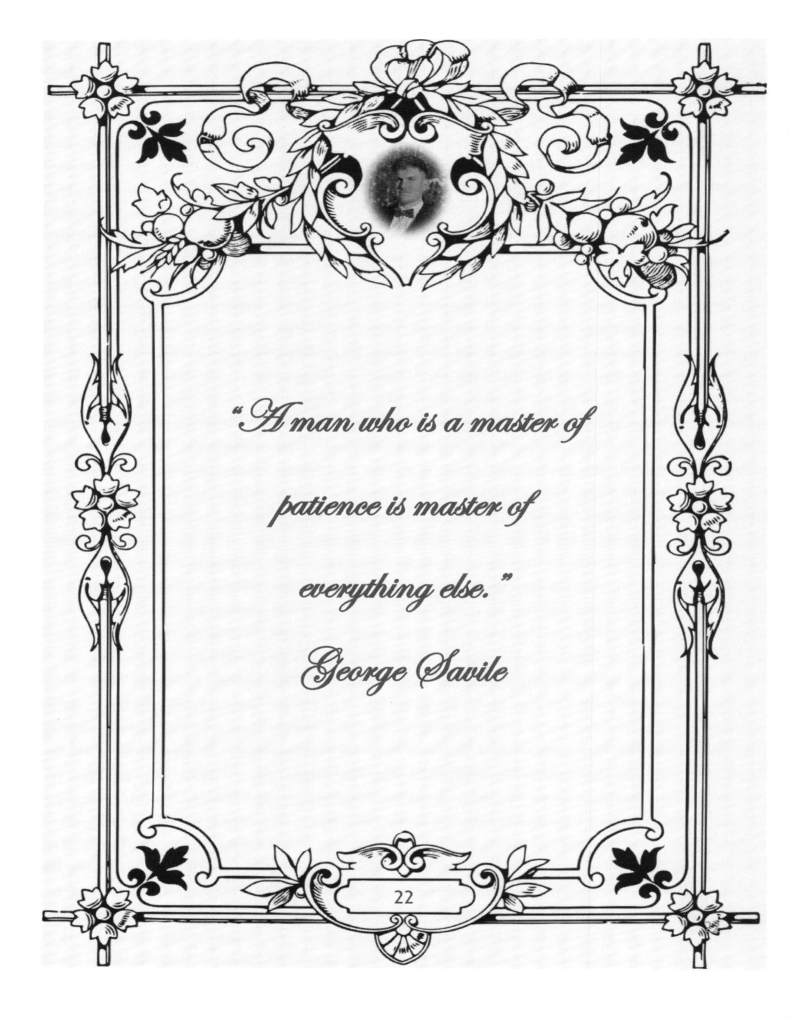

"A man who is a master of

patience is master of

everything else."

George Savile

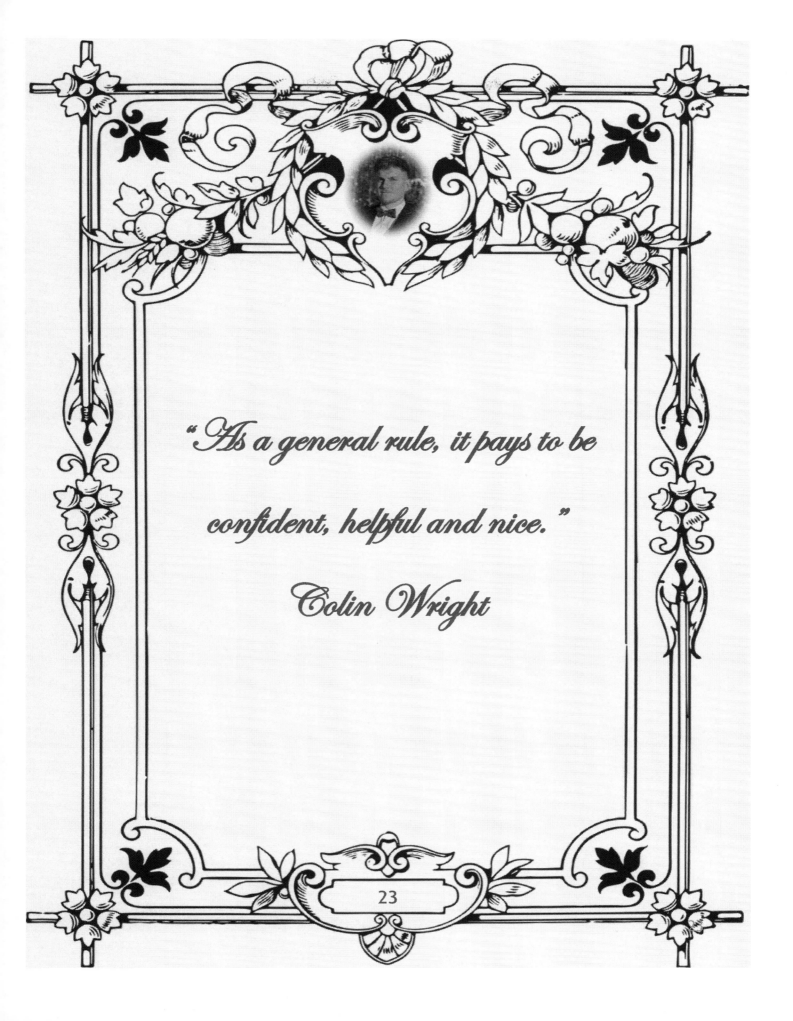

"As a general rule, it pays to be

confident, helpful and nice."

Colin Wright

"Being a gentleman

is a worthy goal."

Orlando Bloom

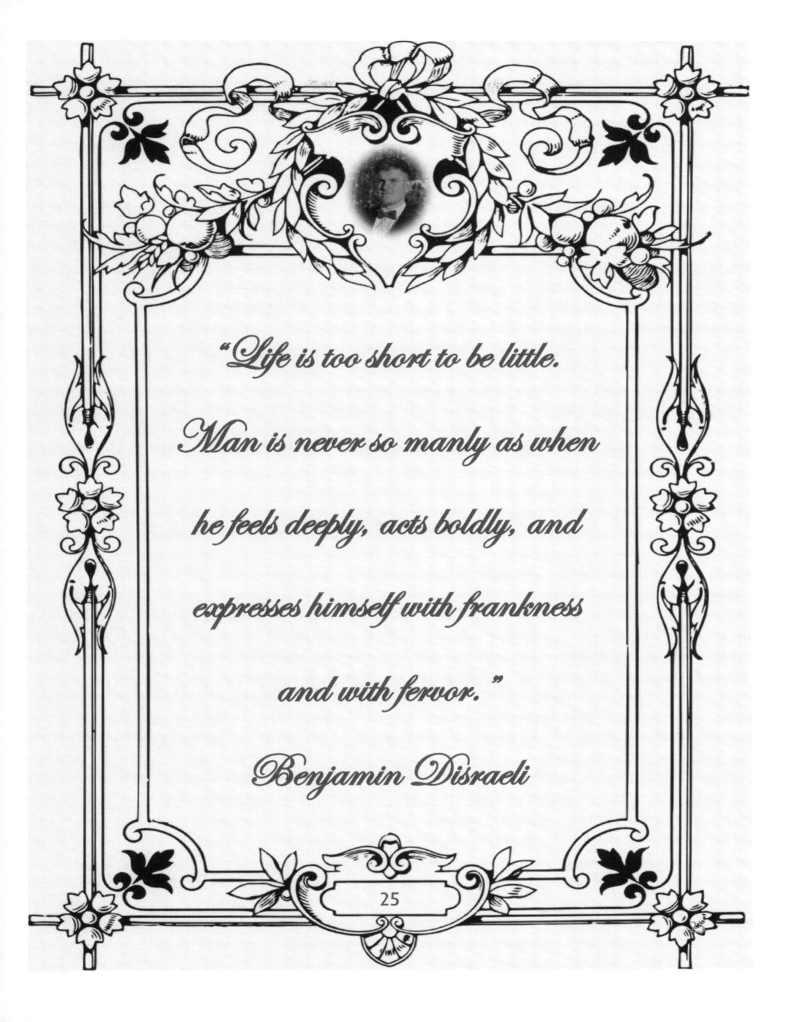

"Life is too short to be little.

Man is never so manly as when

he feels deeply, acts boldly, and

expresses himself with frankness

and with fervor."

Benjamin Disraeli

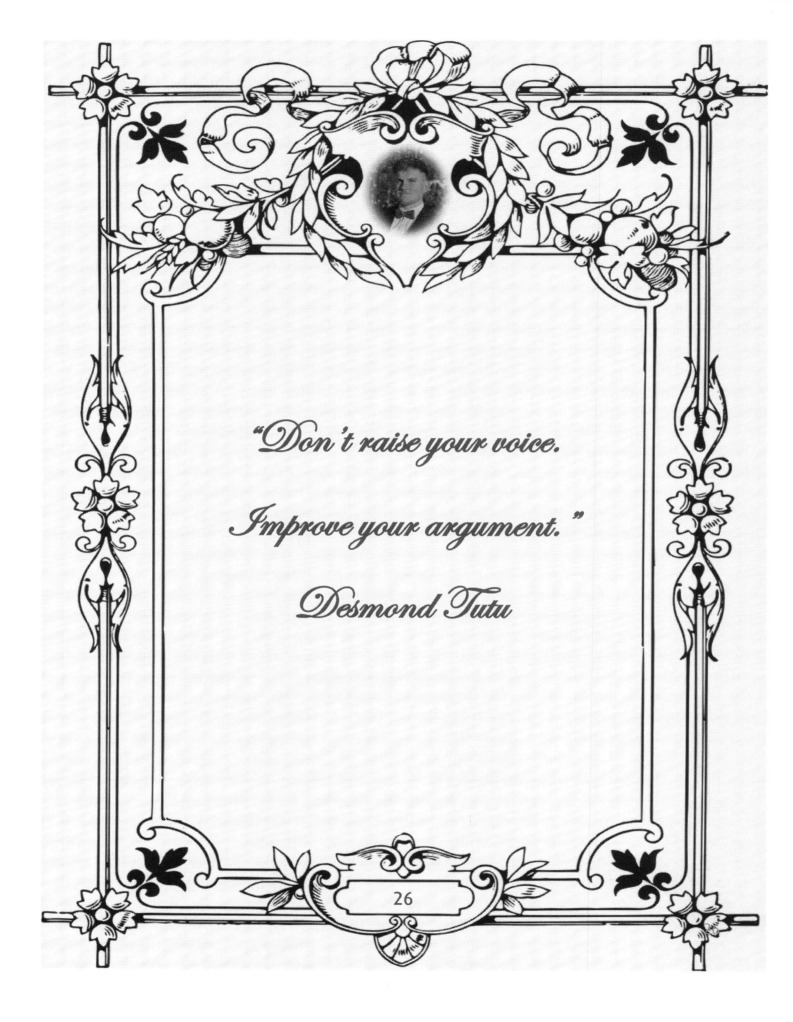

"*Don't raise your voice.*

Improve your argument."

Desmond Tutu

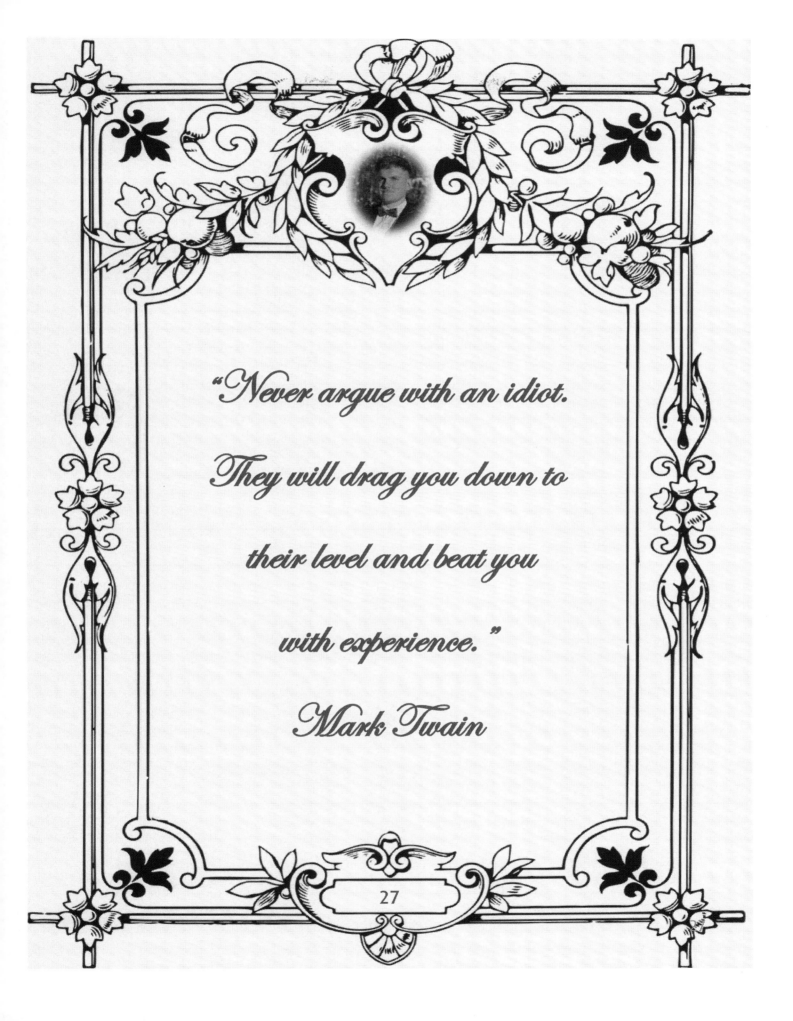

"Never argue with an idiot.

They will drag you down to

their level and beat you

with experience."

Mark Twain

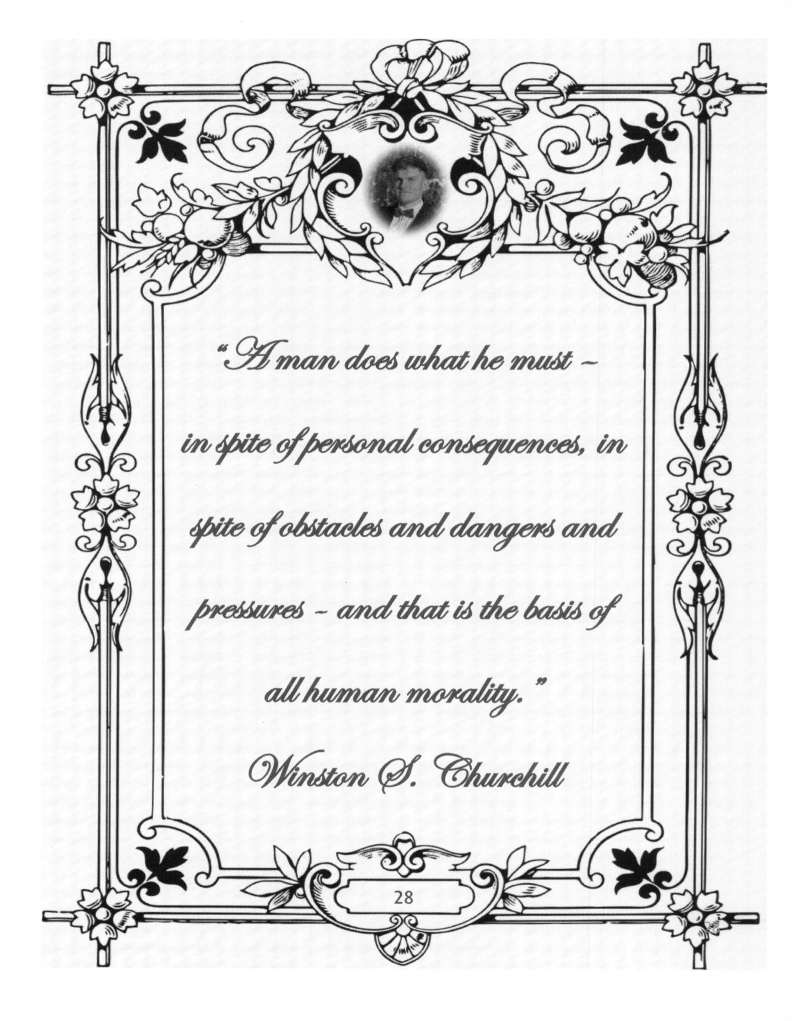

"A man does what he must – in spite of personal consequences, in spite of obstacles and dangers and pressures – and that is the basis of all human morality."

Winston S. Churchill

"Education begins the

gentleman,

but reading, good company and

reflection must finish him."

John Locke

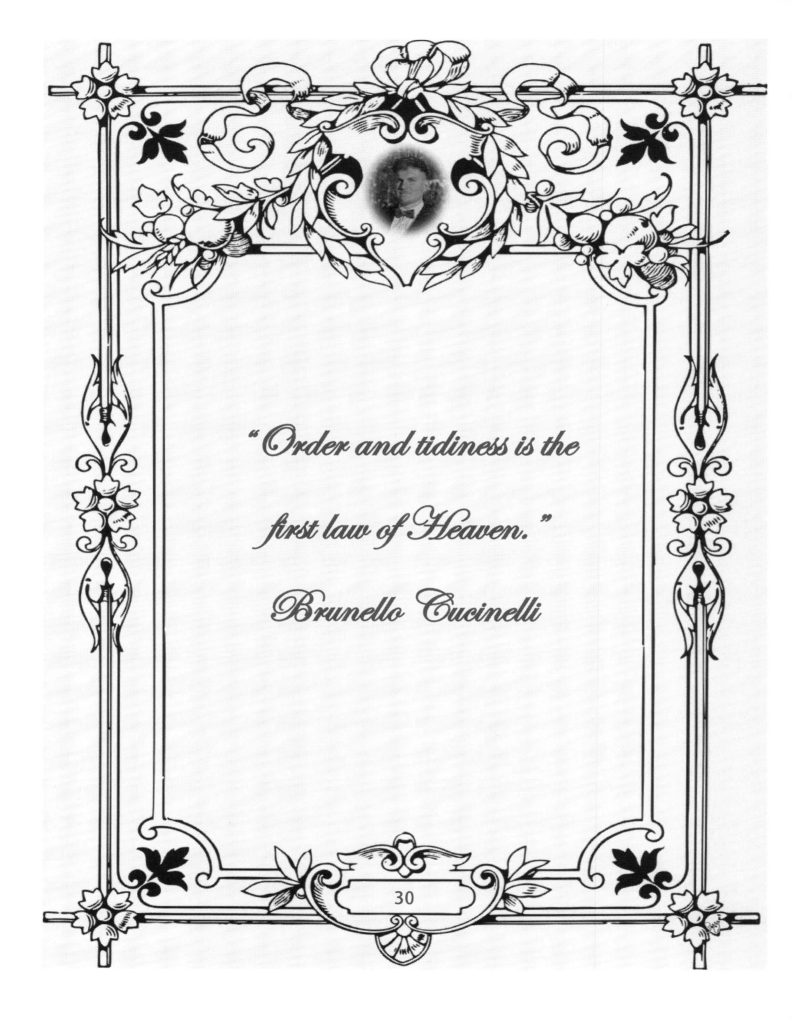

" *Order and tidiness is the*

first law of Heaven. "

Brunello Cucinelli

30

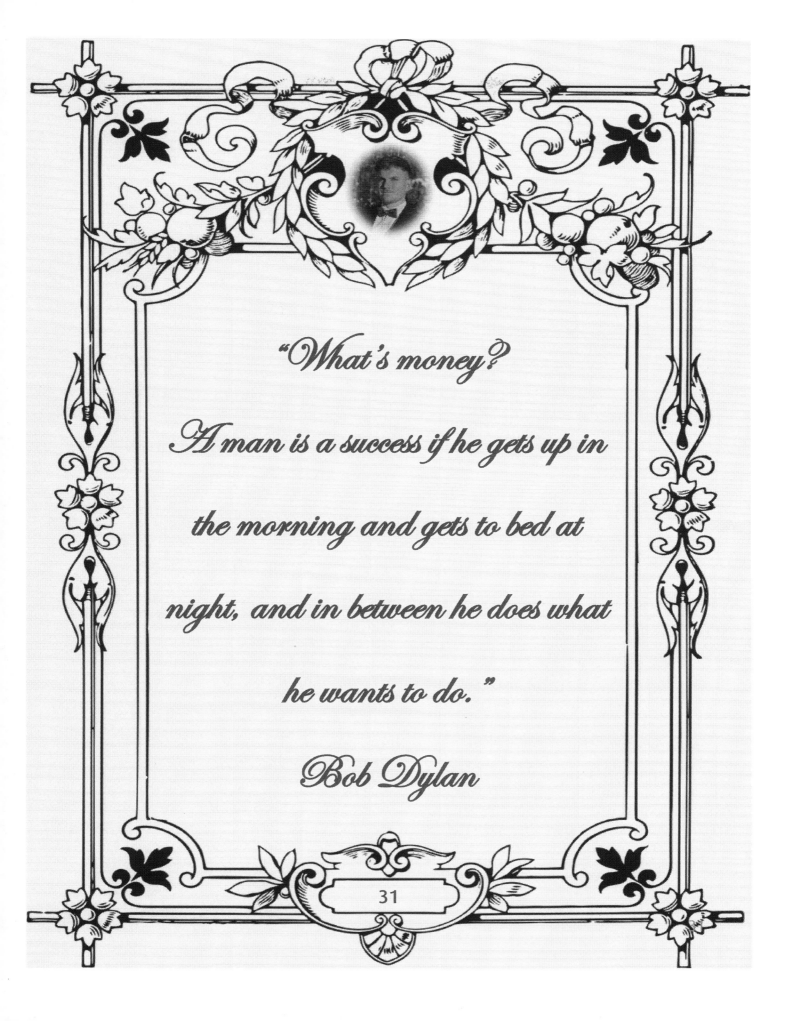

"What's money?

A man is a success if he gets up in

the morning and gets to bed at

night, and in between he does what

he wants to do."

Bob Dylan

"Be kind, for everyone you meet

is fighting a hard battle."

Ian Maclaren

"A person who never made a

mistake never tried

anything new."

Albert Einstein

33

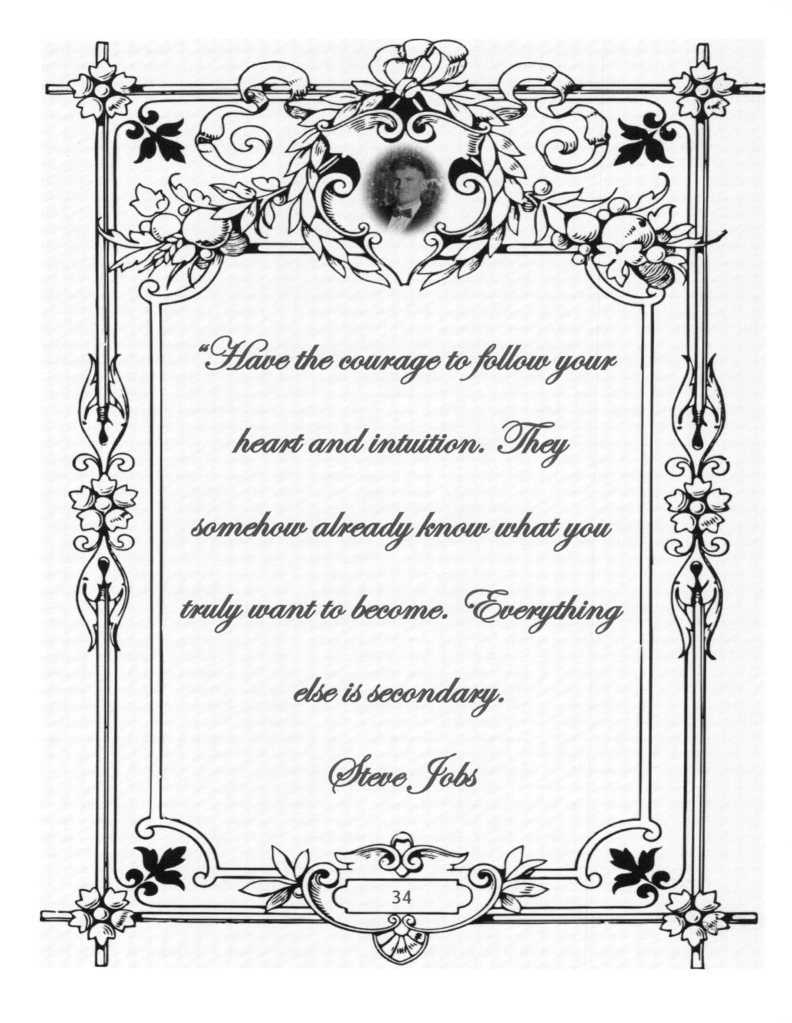

"Have the courage to follow your heart and intuition. They somehow already know what you truly want to become. Everything else is secondary.

Steve Jobs

34

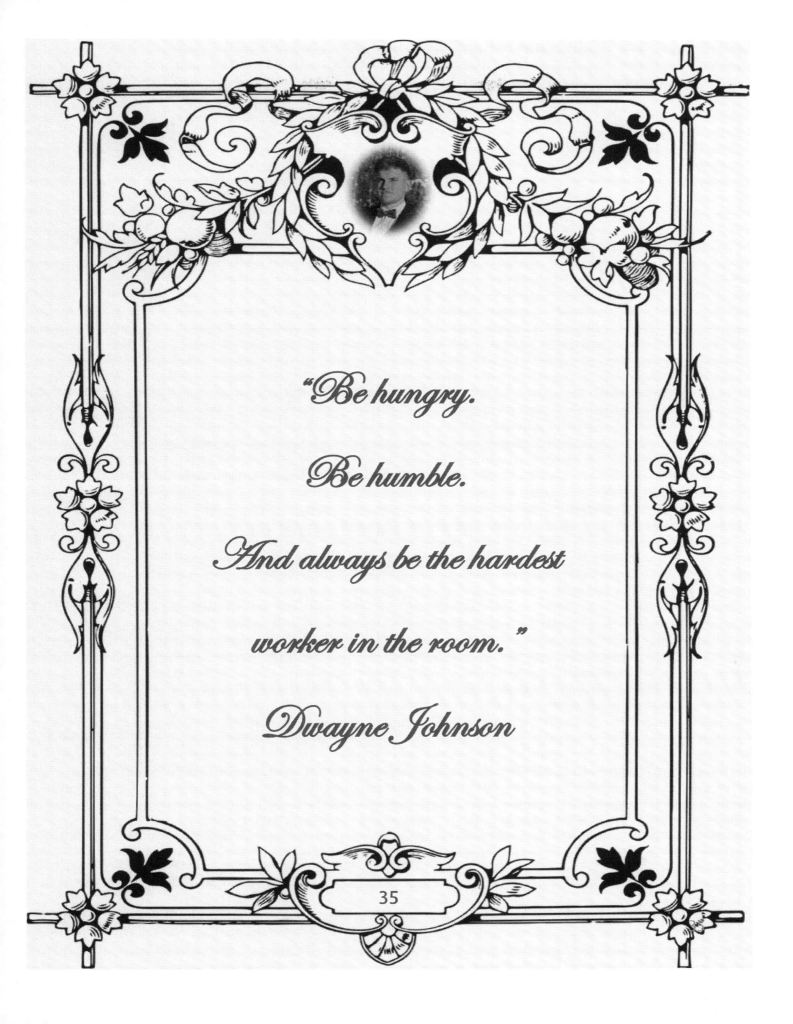

"Be hungry.

Be humble.

And always be the hardest

worker in the room."

Dwayne Johnson

"Celebrate the effort, for it is in the

trying that you discover you."

Sima Dahl

"Don't hide your scars,

they make you who you are."

Frank Sinatra

37

"Courage is what it takes to stand

up and speak; courage is also what

it takes to sit down and listen."

Winston S. Churchill

38

"Choose being kind over being

right and you'll be

right every time."

Richard Carlson

"We are still in the position of

waking up and having a choice.

Do I make the world better

today somehow, or do

I not bother?

Tom Hanks

"Excellence is not a skill,

it's an attitude."

Ralph Marston

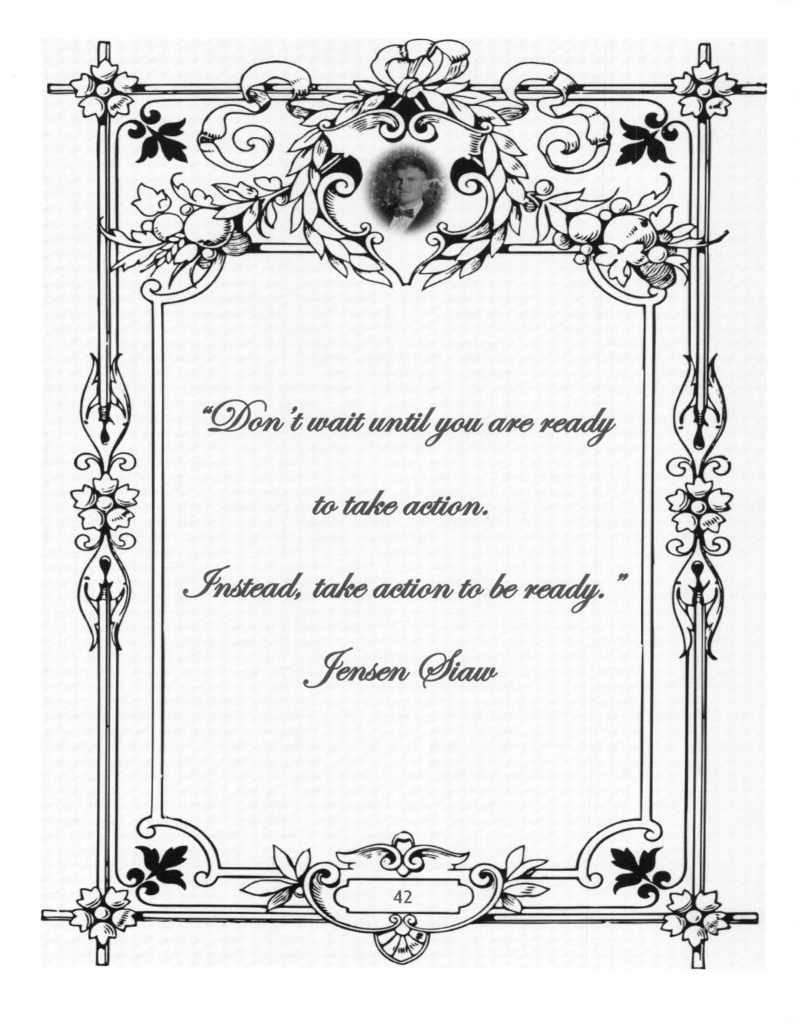

"*Don't wait until you are ready*

to take action.

Instead, take action to be ready."

Jensen Siaw

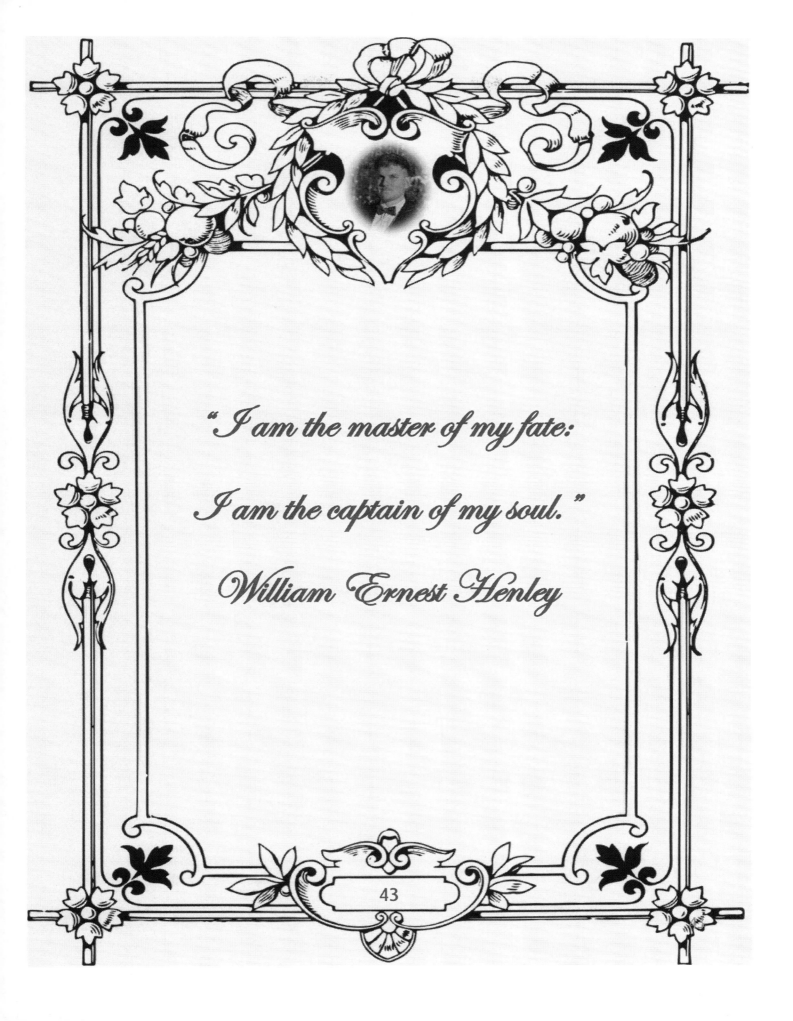

"I am the master of my fate:

I am the captain of my soul."

William Ernest Henley

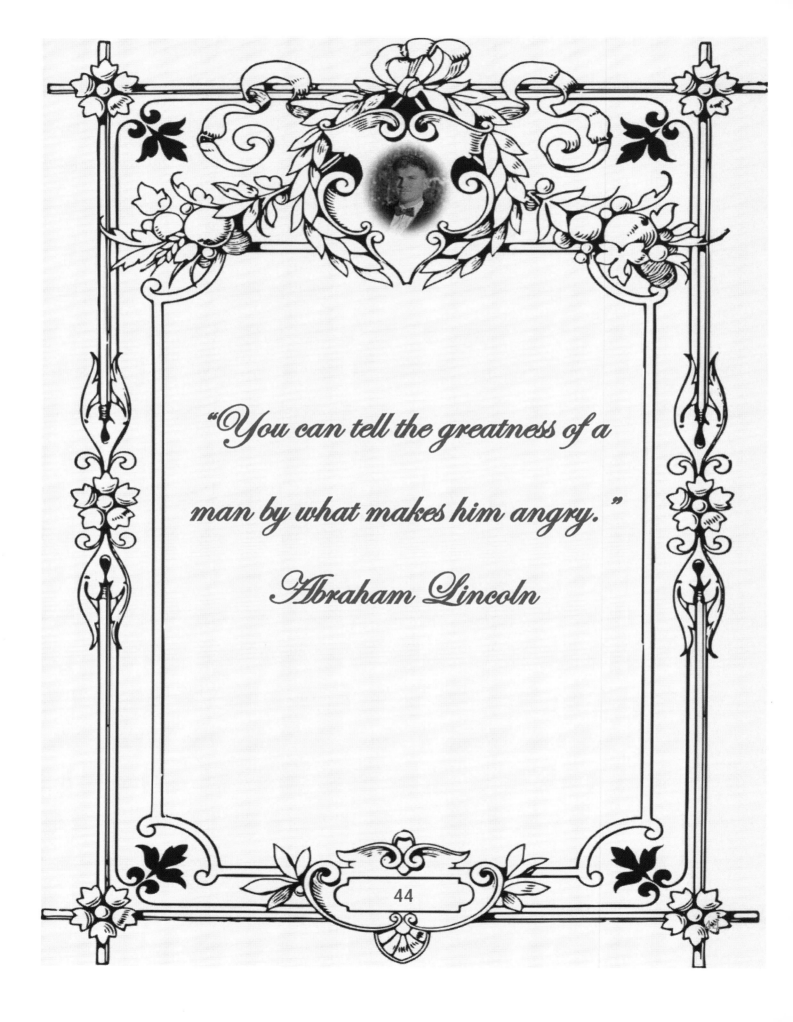

"You can tell the greatness of a

man by what makes him angry."

Abraham Lincoln

44

"Hard work doesn't guarantee success, but improves its chances."

B.J. Gupta

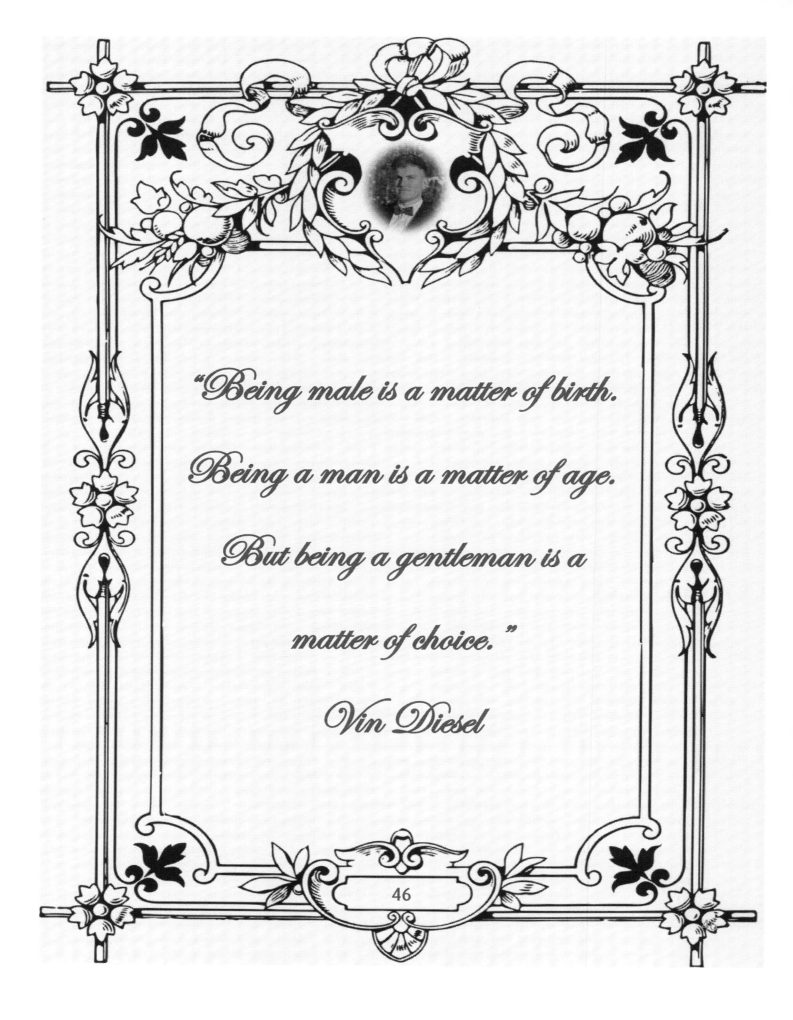

"Being male is a matter of birth.

Being a man is a matter of age.

But being a gentleman is a

matter of choice."

Vin Diesel

46

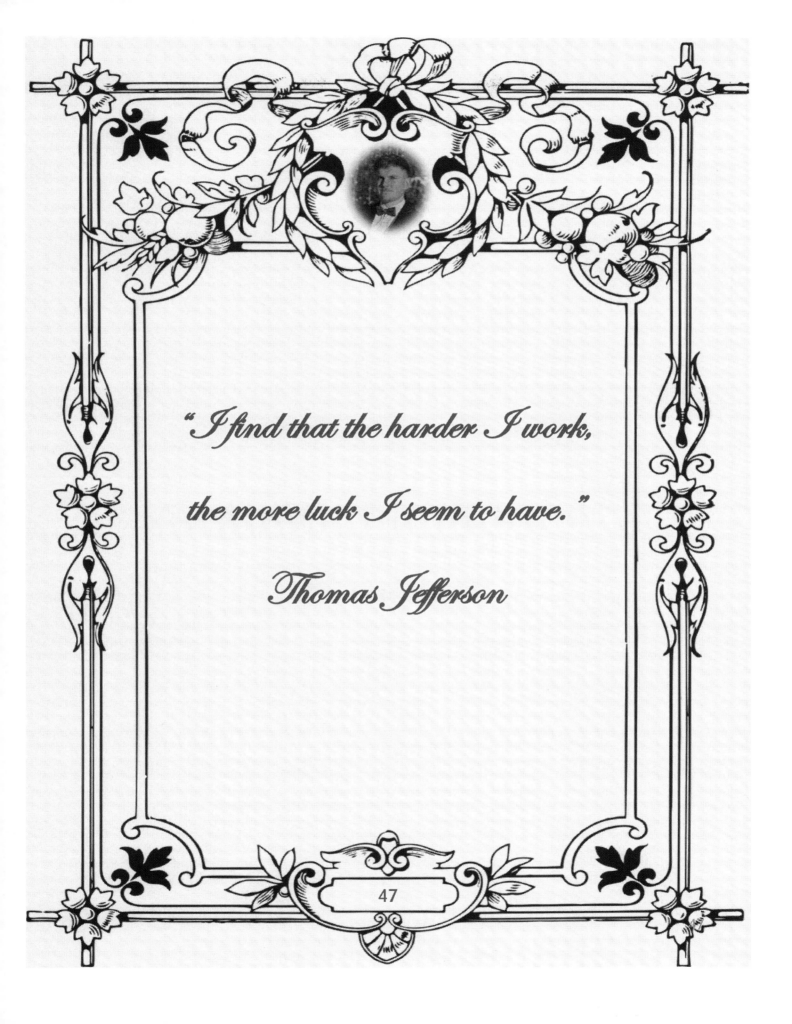

"I find that the harder I work,

the more luck I seem to have."

Thomas Jefferson

47

"*If you cannot do great things,*

do small things in a great way."

Napoleon Hill

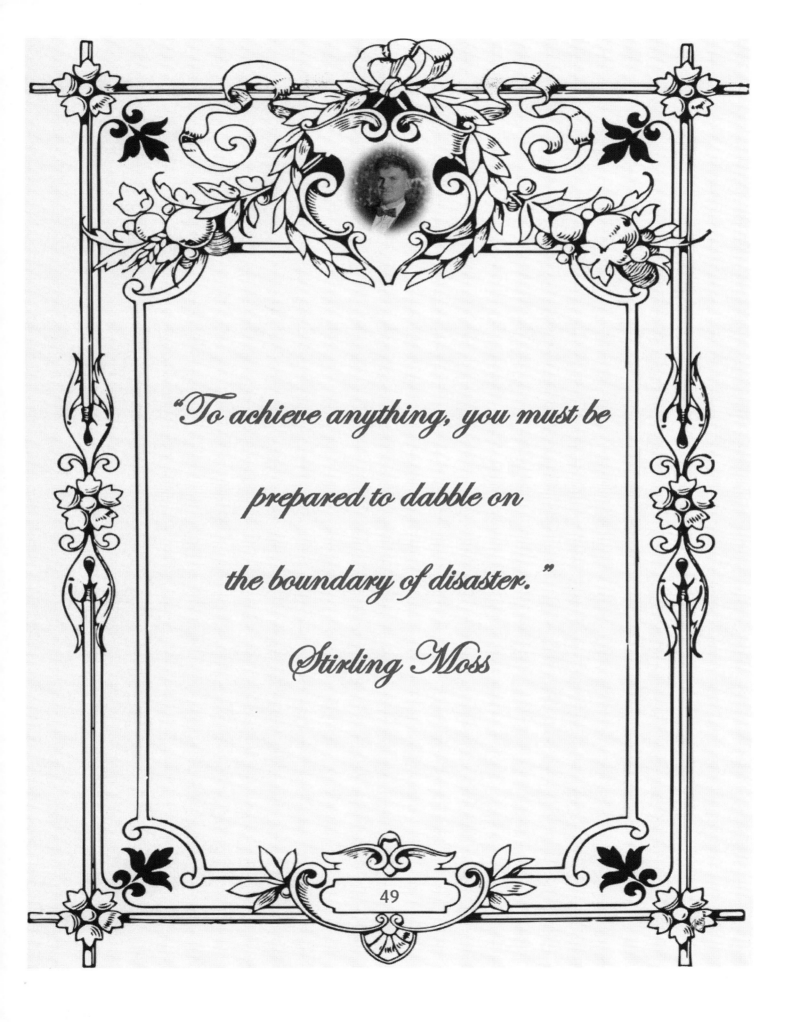

"To achieve anything, you must be

prepared to dabble on

the boundary of disaster."

Stirling Moss

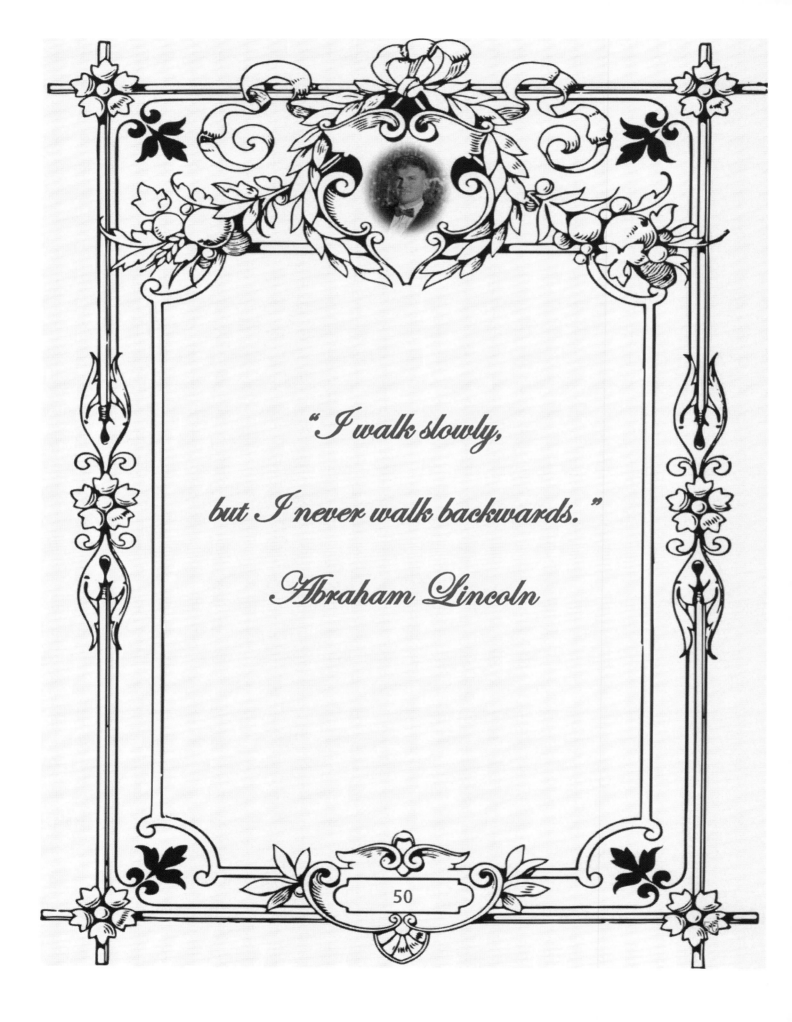

"I walk slowly,

but I never walk backwards."

Abraham Lincoln

50

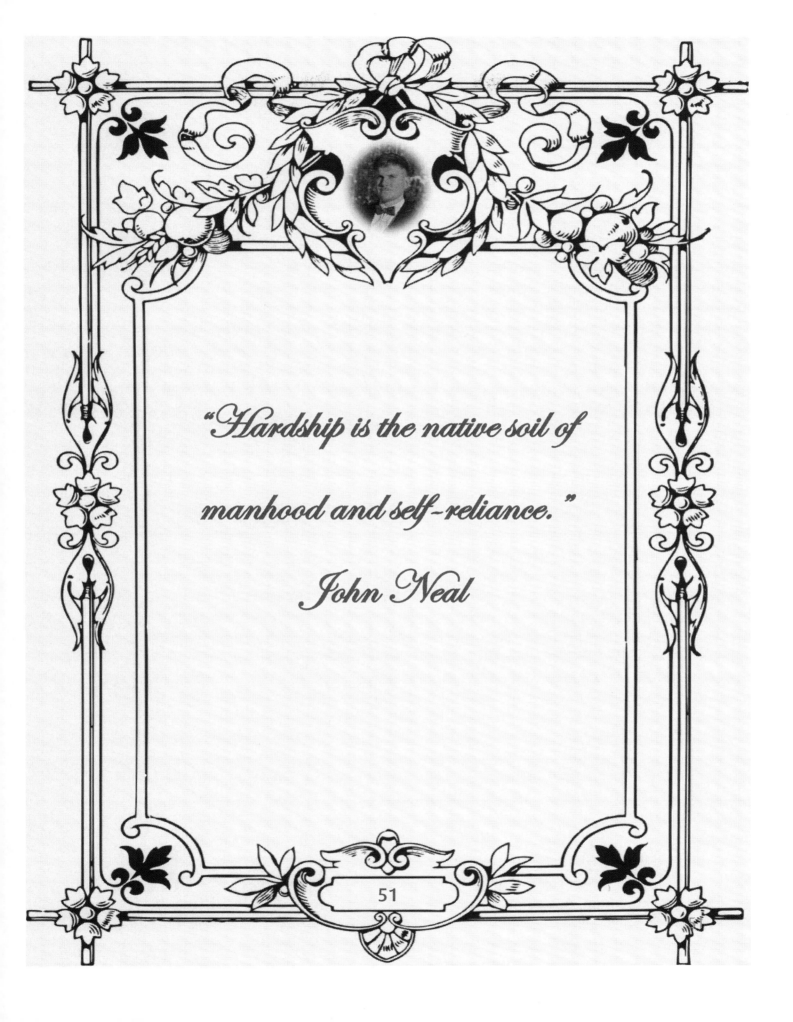

"Hardship is the native soil of

manhood and self-reliance."

John Neal

"*If you work really hard and*

you're kind,

amazing things will happen."

Conan O'Brien

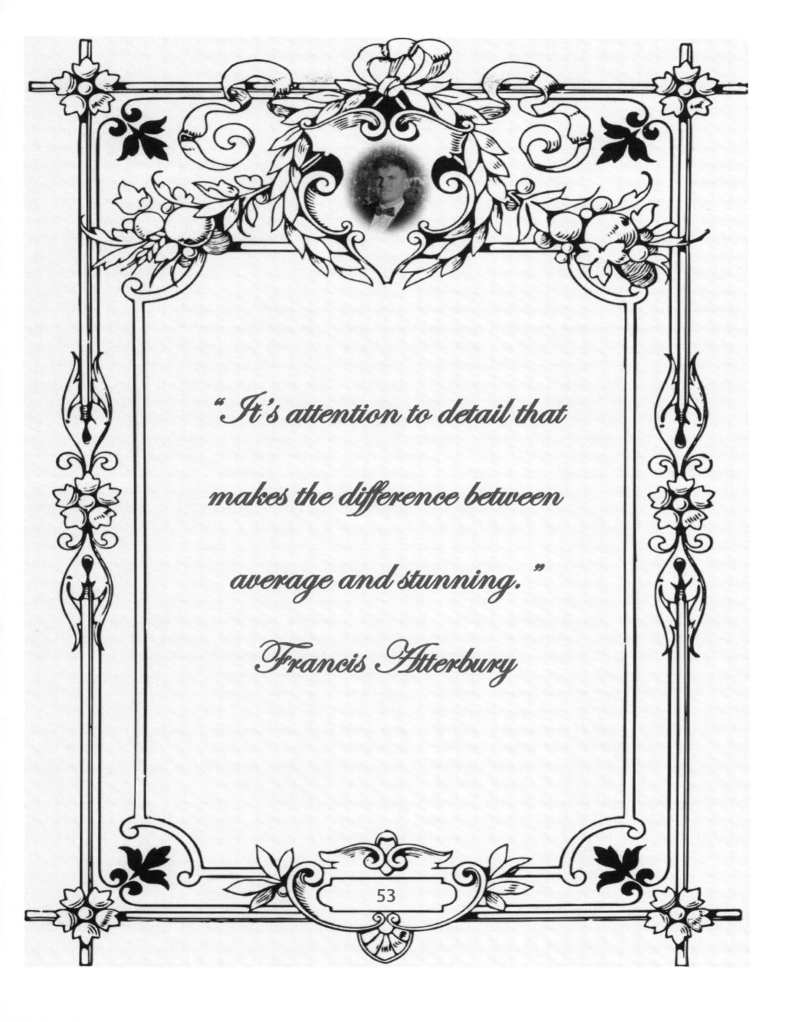

"It's attention to detail that

makes the difference between

average and stunning."

Francis Atterbury

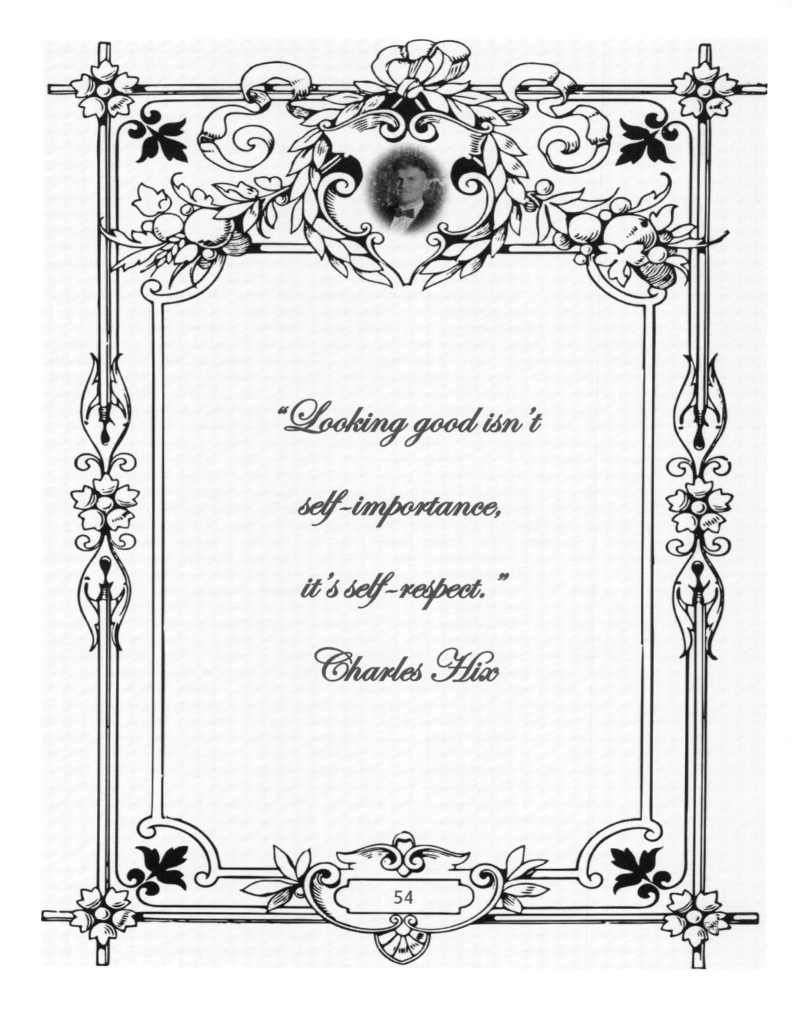

"Looking good isn't self-importance, it's self-respect."

Charles Hix

54

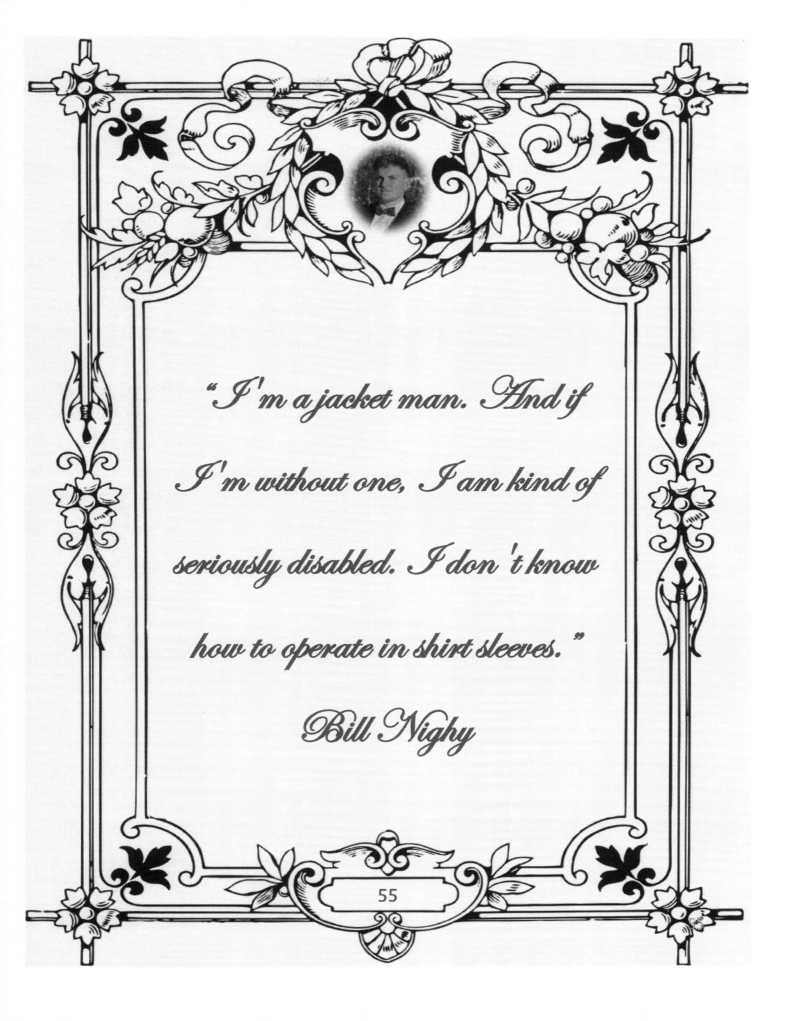

"I'm a jacket man. And if I'm without one, I am kind of seriously disabled. I don't know how to operate in shirt sleeves."

Bill Nighy

"Make it simple,

but significant."

Don Draper

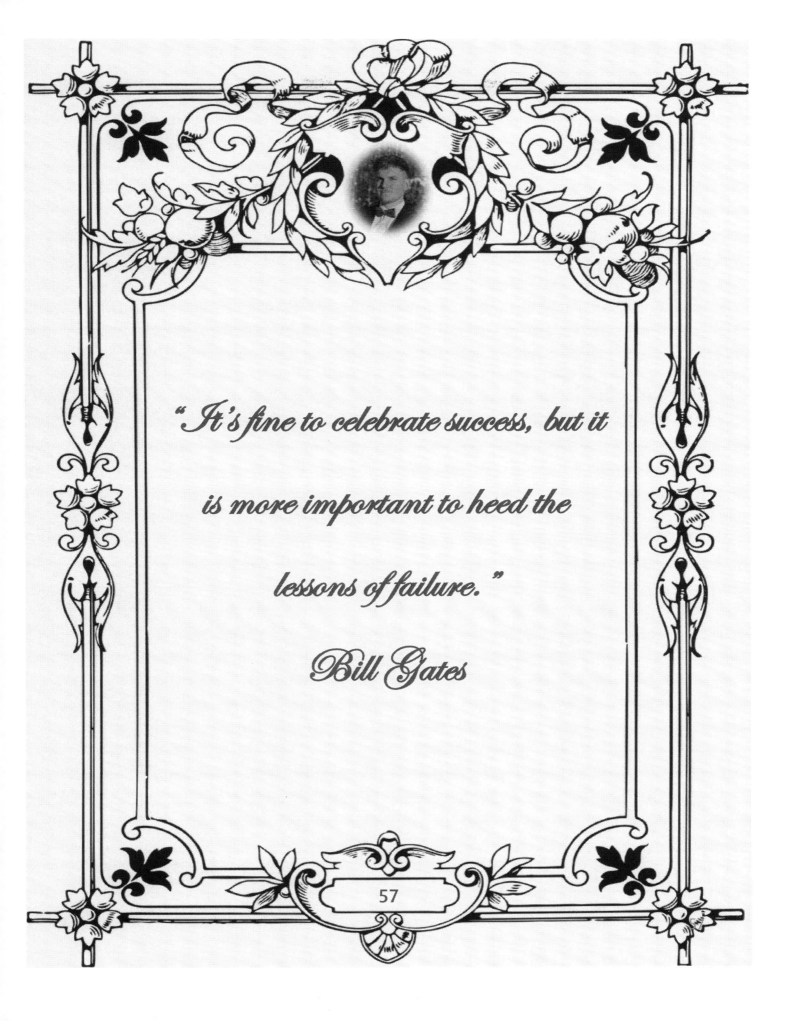

"It's fine to celebrate success, but it

is more important to heed the

lessons of failure."

Bill Gates

"*It's hard to beat a person who*

never gives up."

Babe Ruth

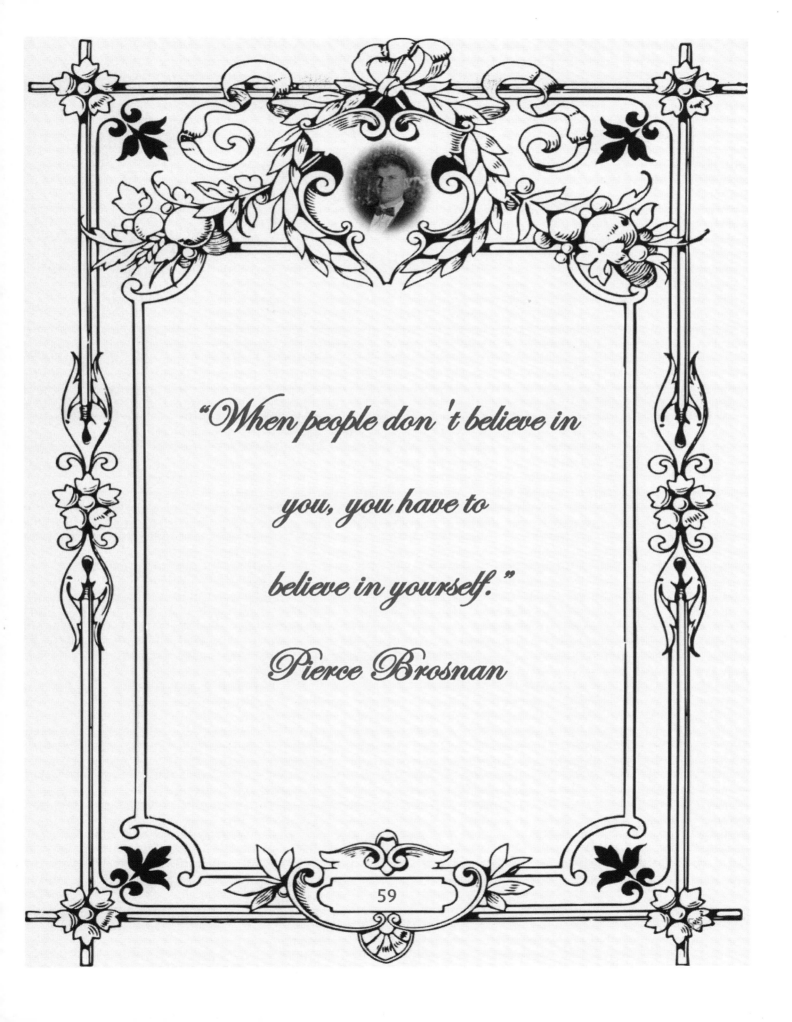

"When people don't believe in

you, you have to

believe in yourself."

Pierce Brosnan

59

"Only the gentle are

ever really strong."

James Dean

"*All successes begin with*

self-discipline.

It starts with you."

Dwayne Johnson

61

"The big lesson in life, baby, is

never be scared of

anyone or anything."

Frank Sinatra

"Don't be different just for

different's sake.

If you see it differently,

function that way.

Follow your own muse, always."

Morgan Freeman

"You have to create something

from nothing."

Ralph Lauren

64

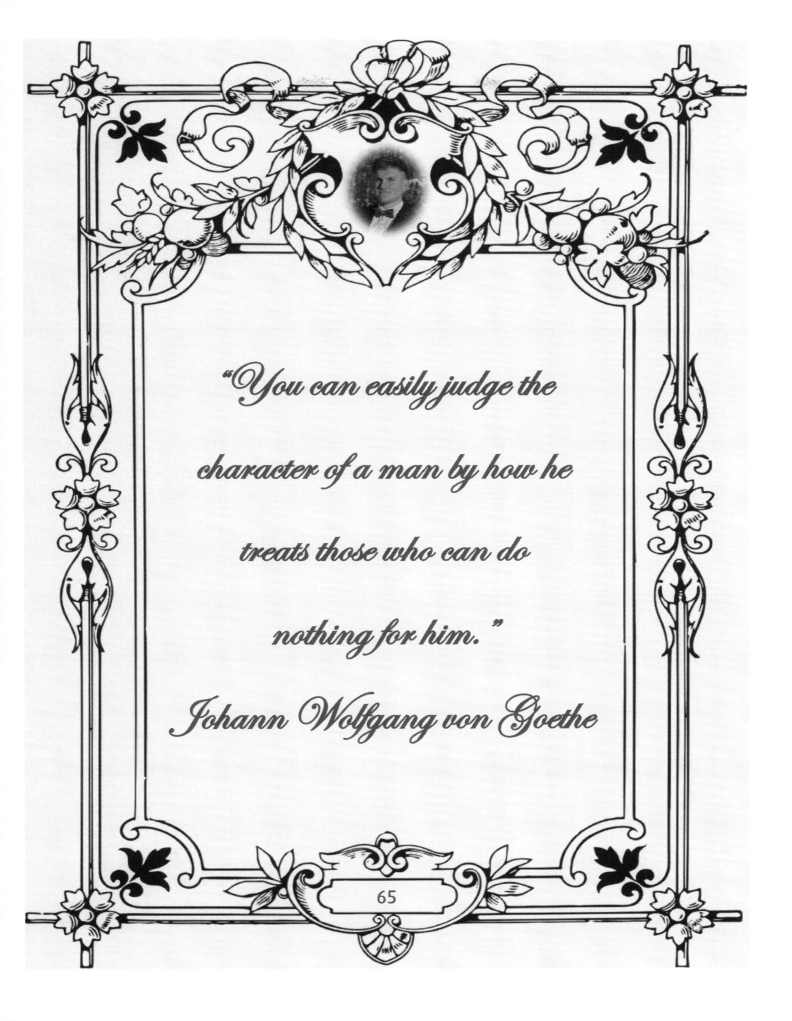

"You can easily judge the

character of a man by how he

treats those who can do

nothing for him."

Johann Wolfgang von Goethe

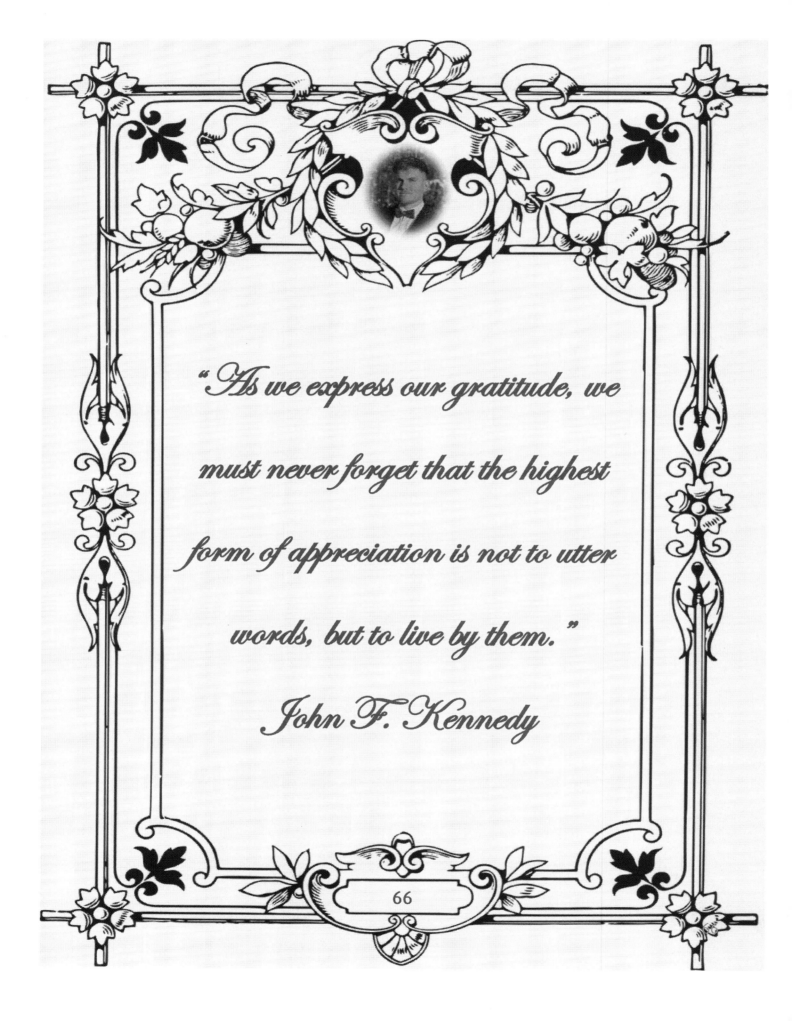

"As we express our gratitude, we must never forget that the highest form of appreciation is not to utter words, but to live by them."

John F. Kennedy

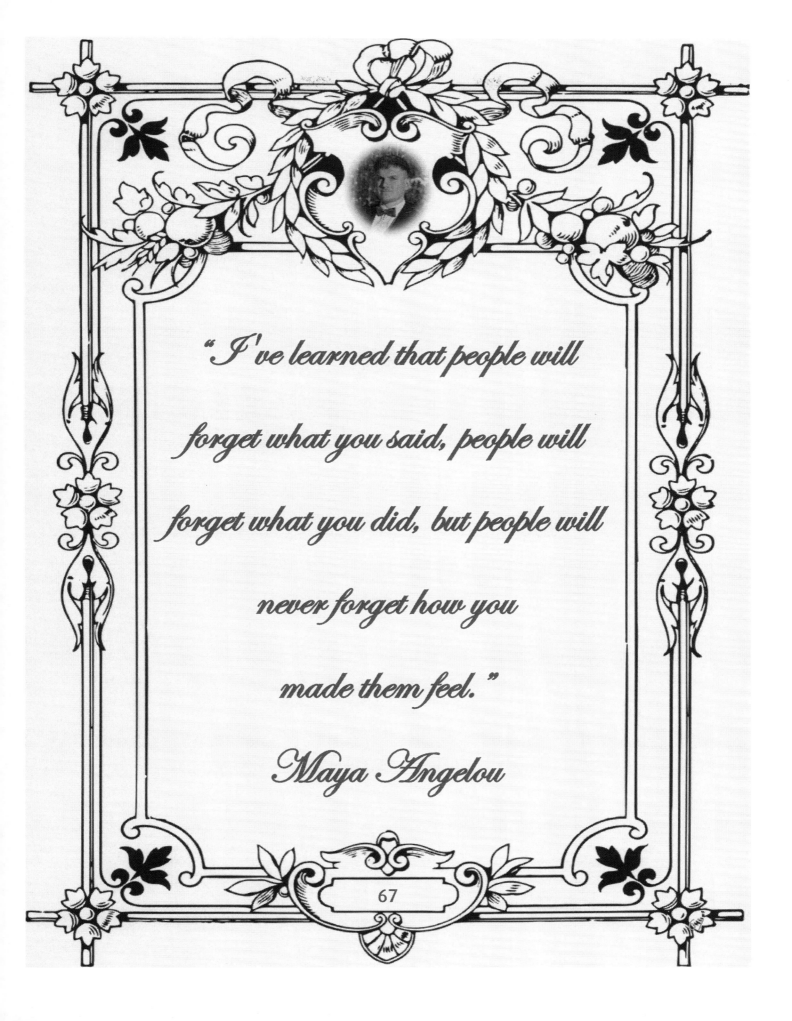

"I've learned that people will forget what you said, people will forget what you did, but people will never forget how you made them feel."

Maya Angelou

67

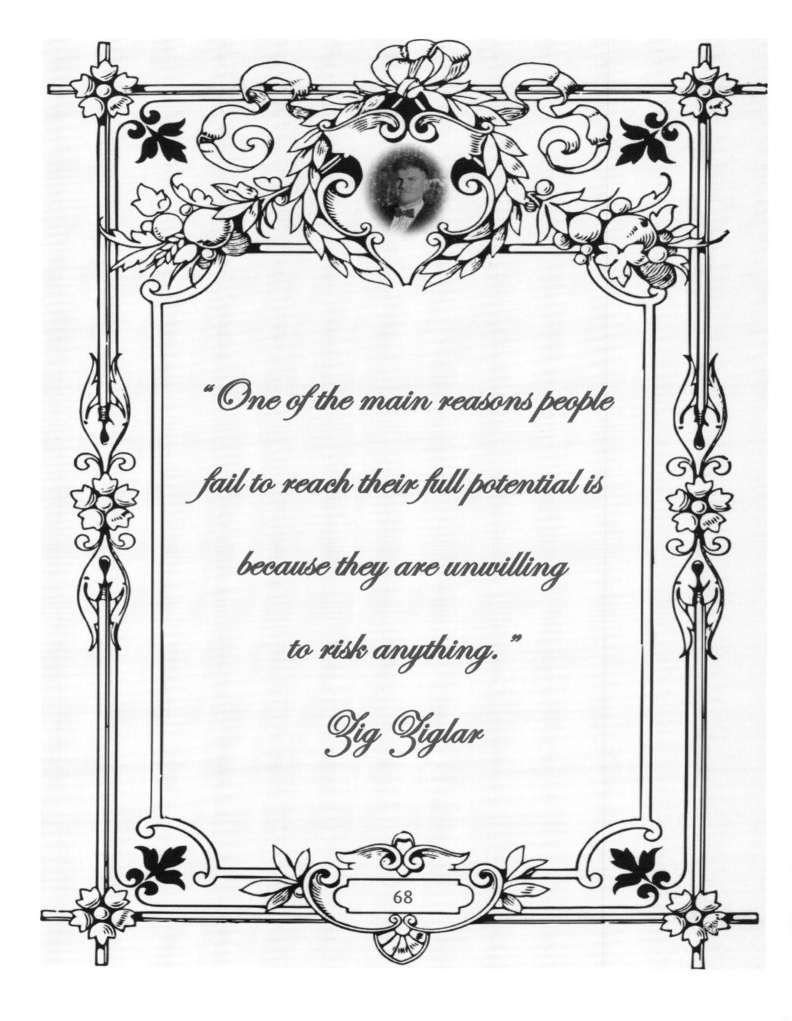

"One of the main reasons people

fail to reach their full potential is

because they are unwilling

to risk anything."

Zig Ziglar

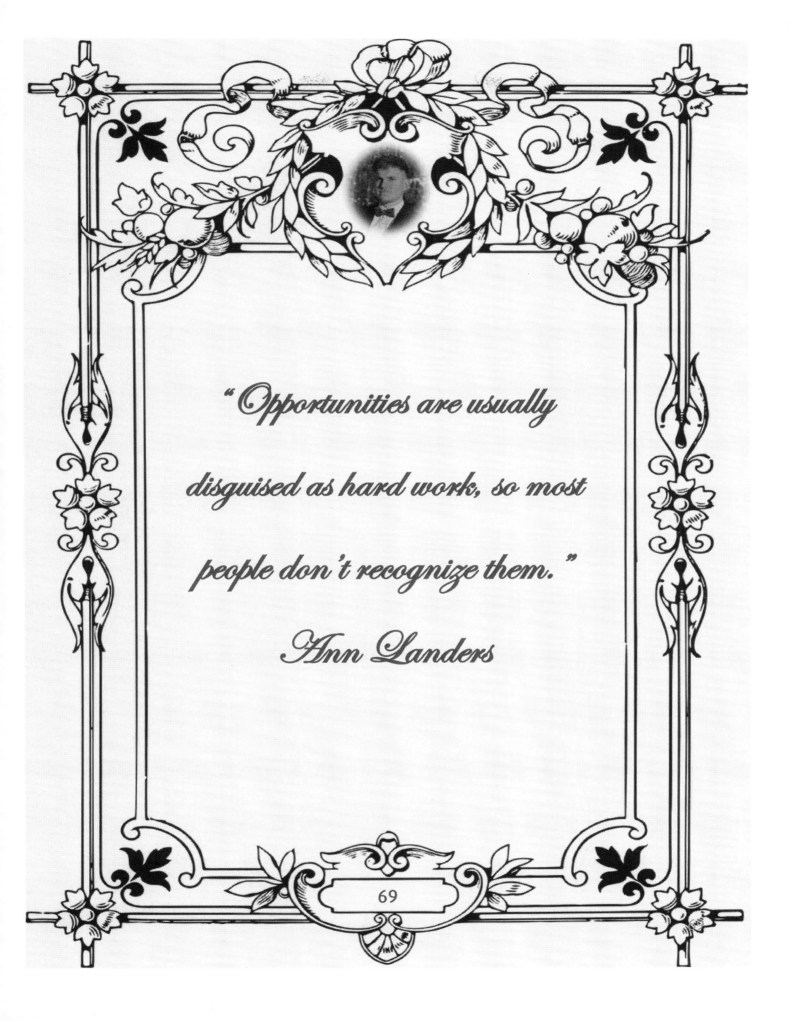

" *Opportunities are usually disguised as hard work, so most people don't recognize them.* "

Ann Landers

"Our attitude towards life

determines life's attitude

towards us."

John N. Mitchell

70

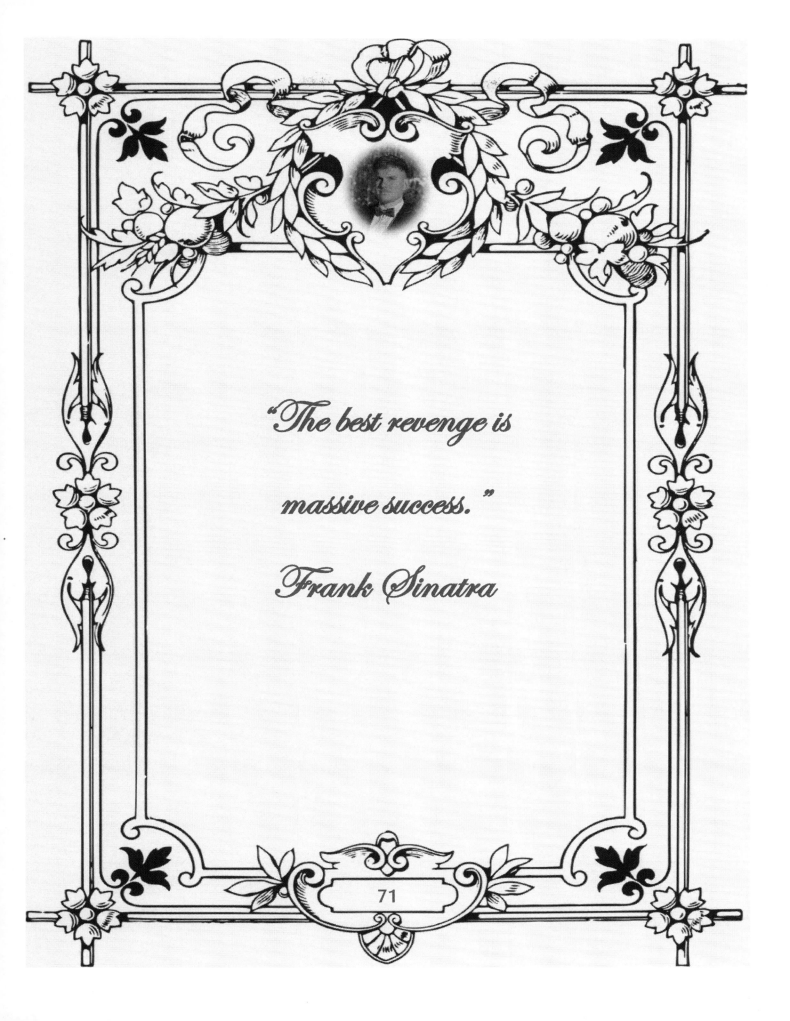

"The best revenge is

massive success."

Frank Sinatra

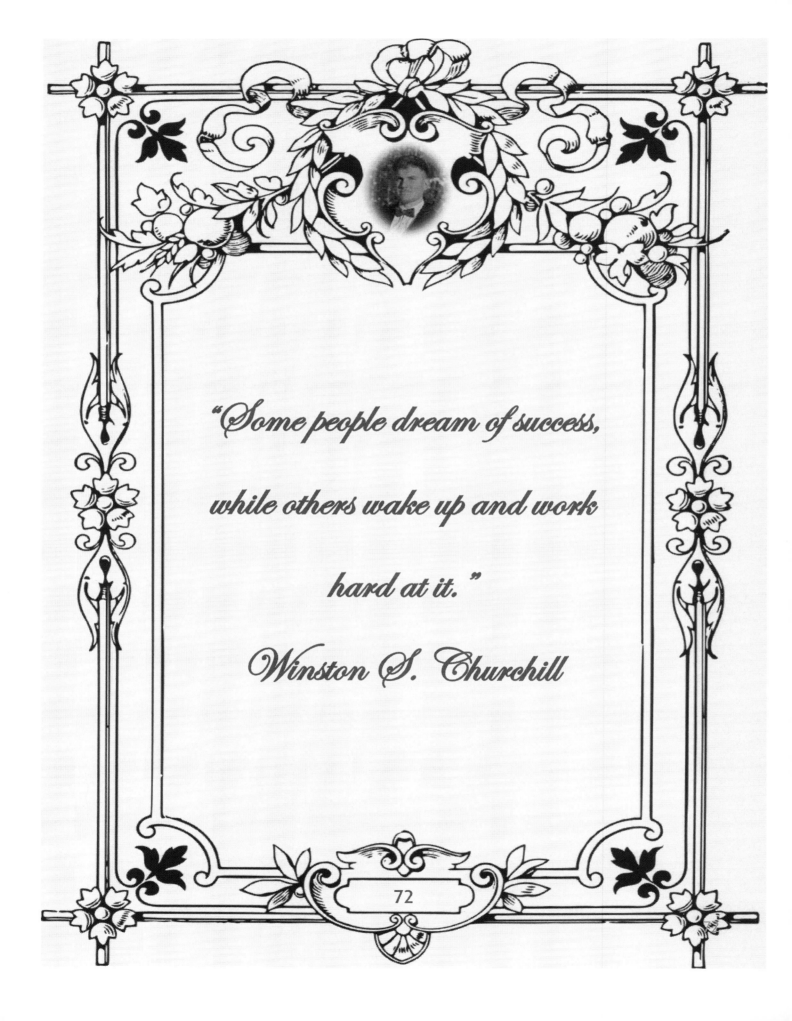

"Some people dream of success,

while others wake up and work

hard at it."

Winston S. Churchill

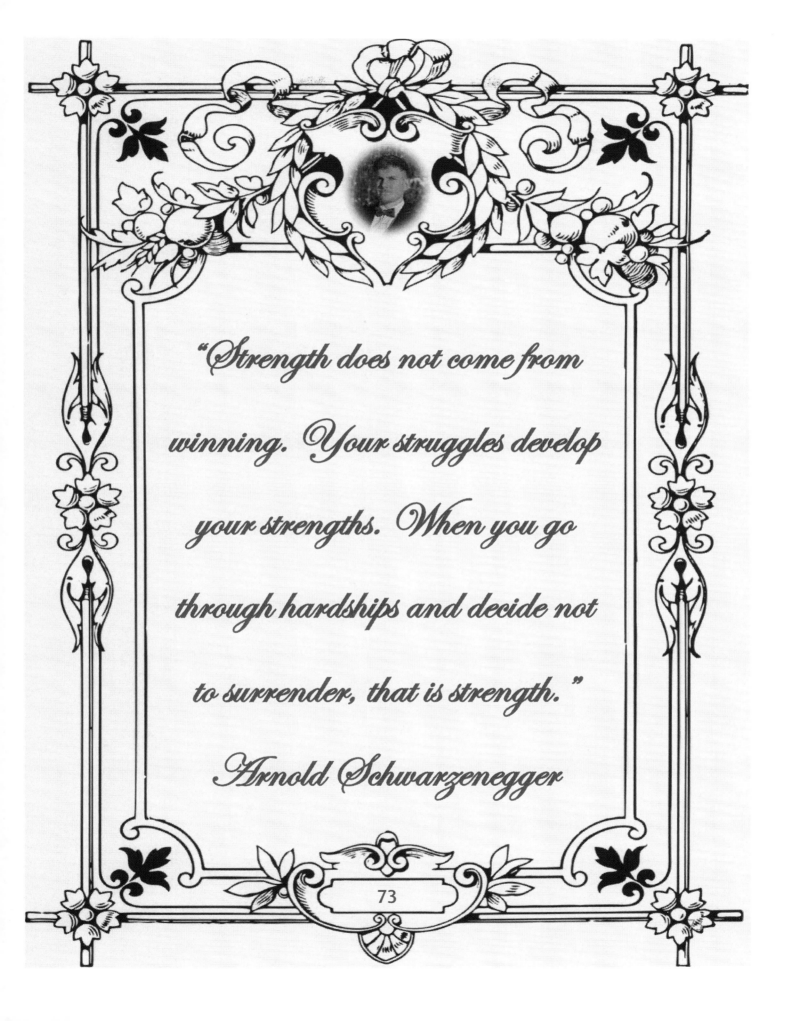

"Strength does not come from winning. Your struggles develop your strengths. When you go through hardships and decide not to surrender, that is strength."

Arnold Schwarzenegger

73

"The measure of intelligence is the

ability to change."

Albert Einstein

74

"*Making an effort is polite,*

and getting ready

and looking after yourself

makes an event more fun."

Jude Law

"The most important things in life

are the connections you

make with others."

Tom Ford

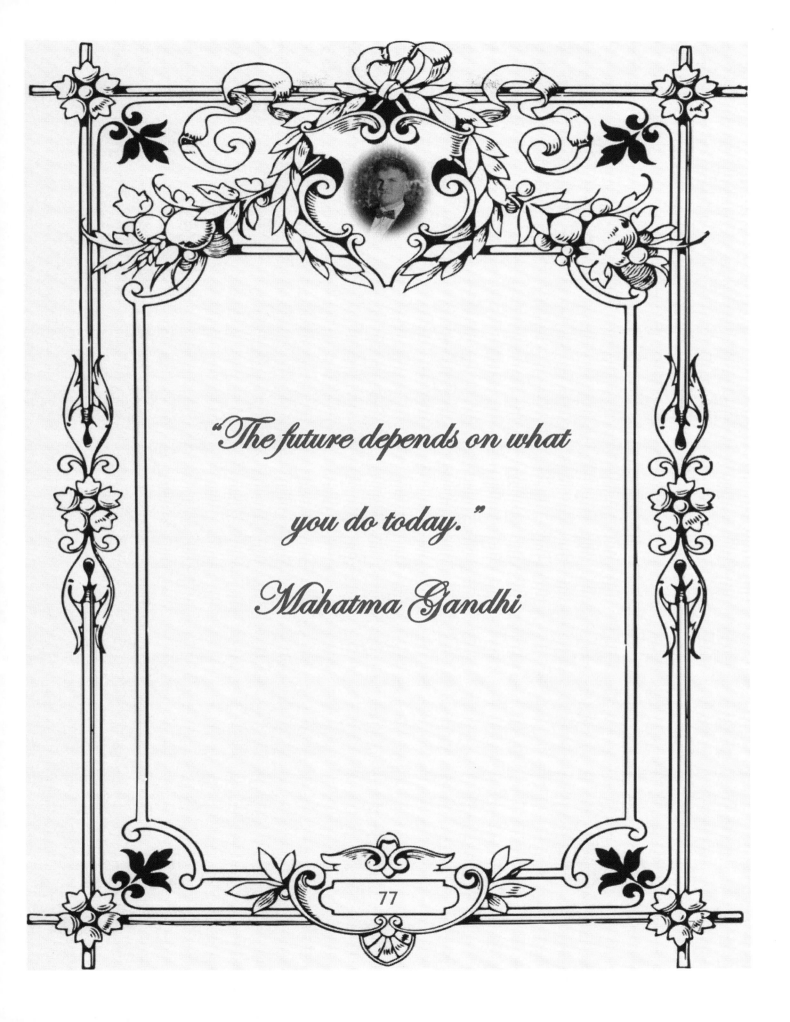

"The future depends on what

you do today."

Mahatma Gandhi

"Those who spend their time

looking for the faults in others

usually make no time to correct

their own."

Art Jonak

78

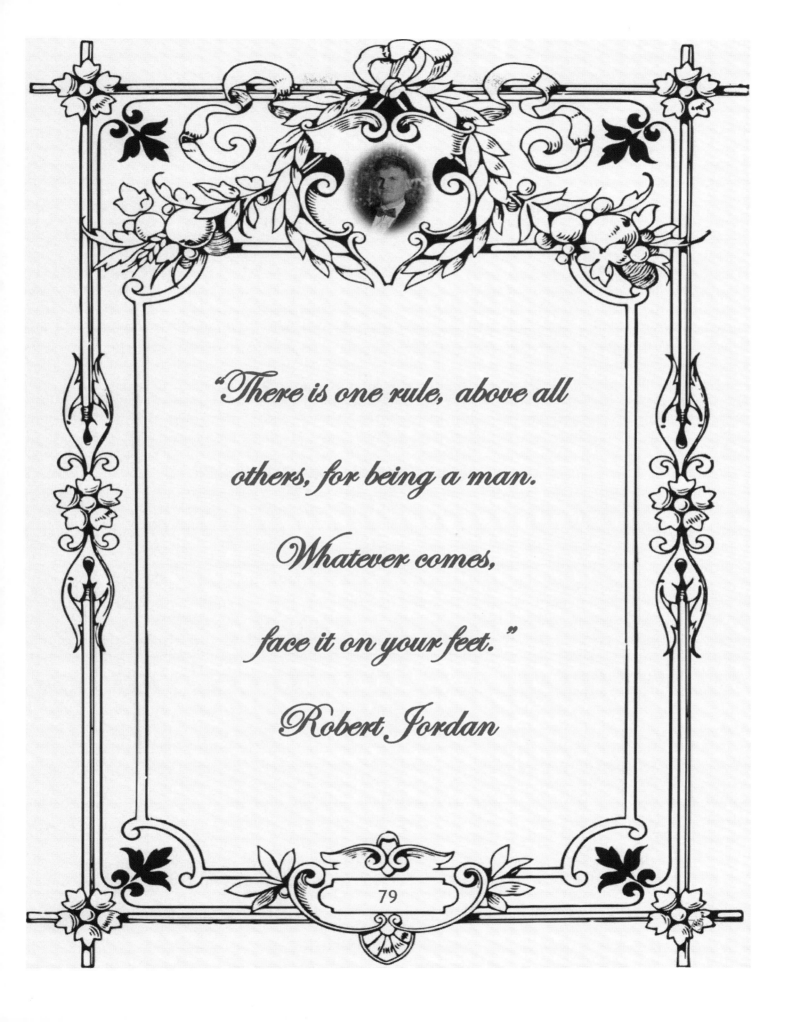

"There is one rule, above all

others, for being a man.

Whatever comes,

face it on your feet."

Robert Jordan

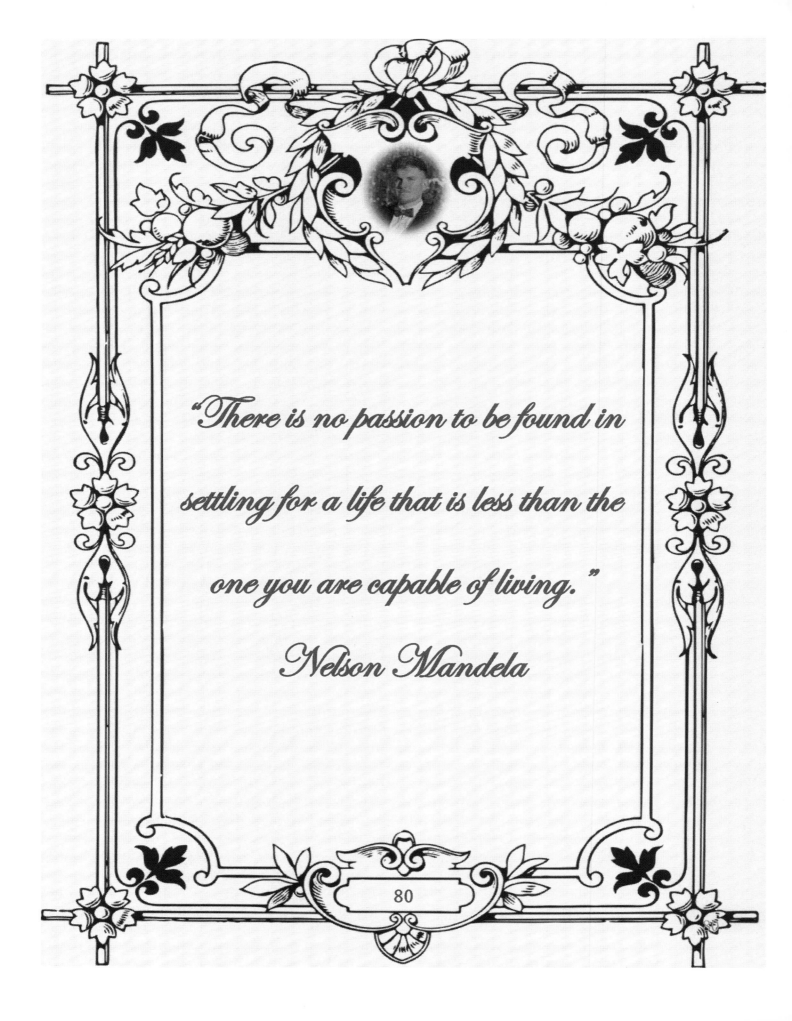

"There is no passion to be found in settling for a life that is less than the one you are capable of living."

Nelson Mandela

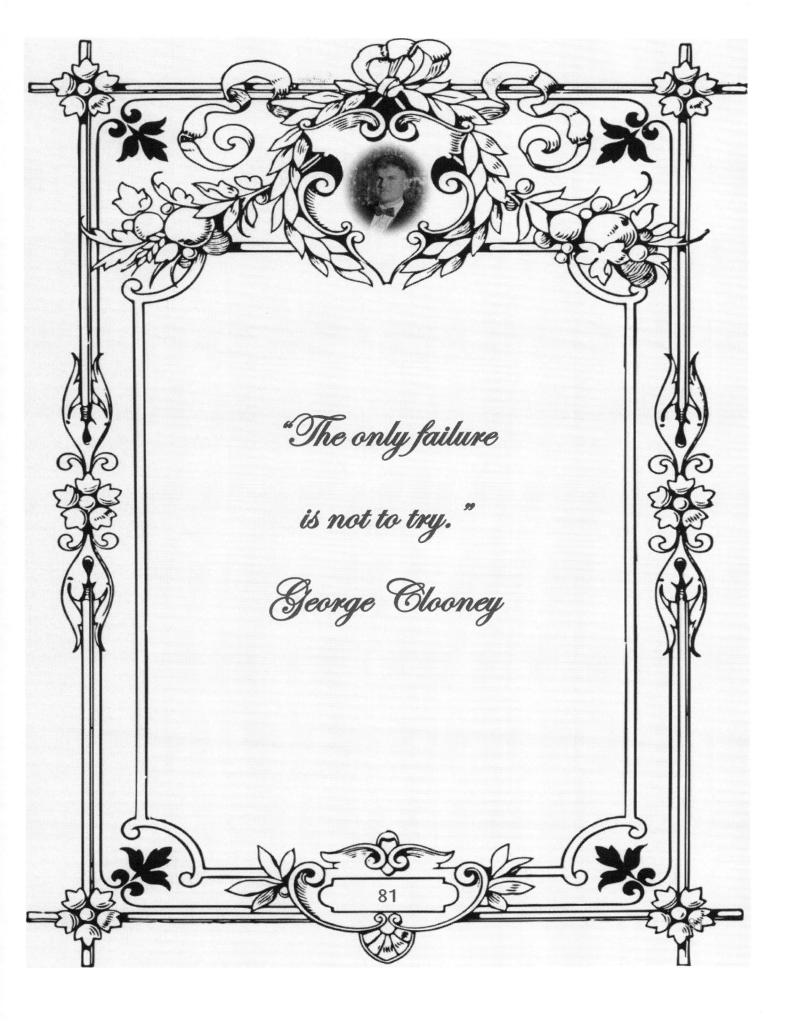

"The only failure

is not to try. "

George Clooney

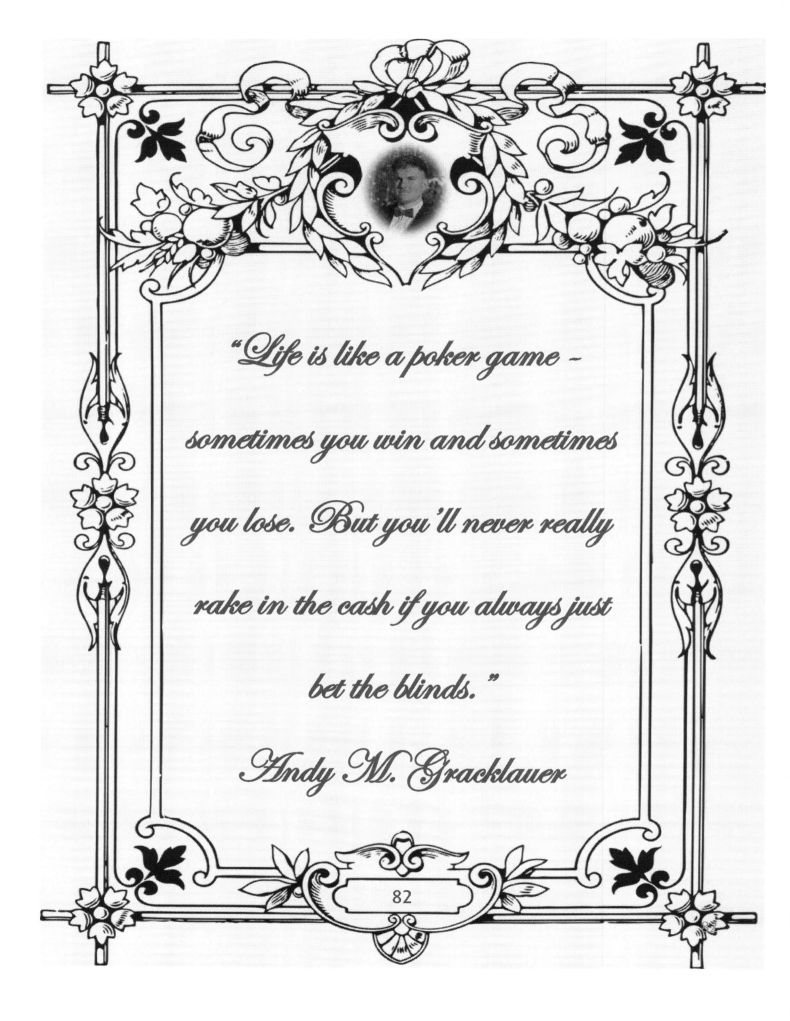

"Life is like a poker game -

sometimes you win and sometimes

you lose. But you'll never really

rake in the cash if you always just

bet the blinds."

Andy M. Gracklauer

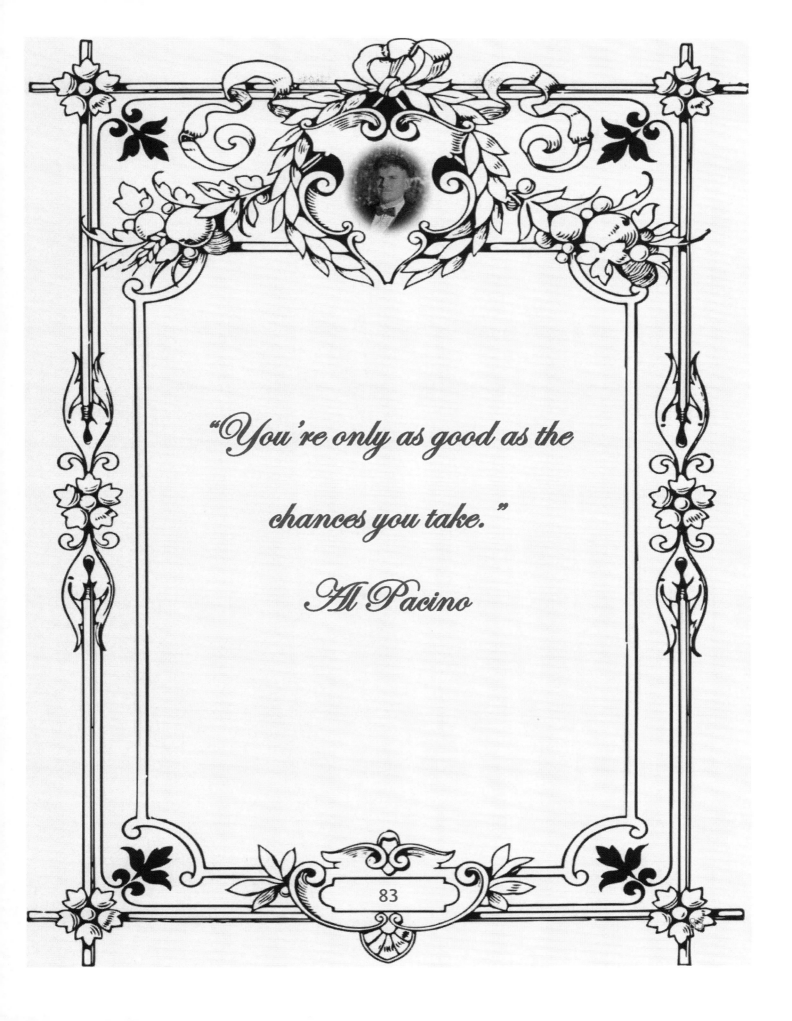

"You're only as good as the chances you take."

Al Pacino

83

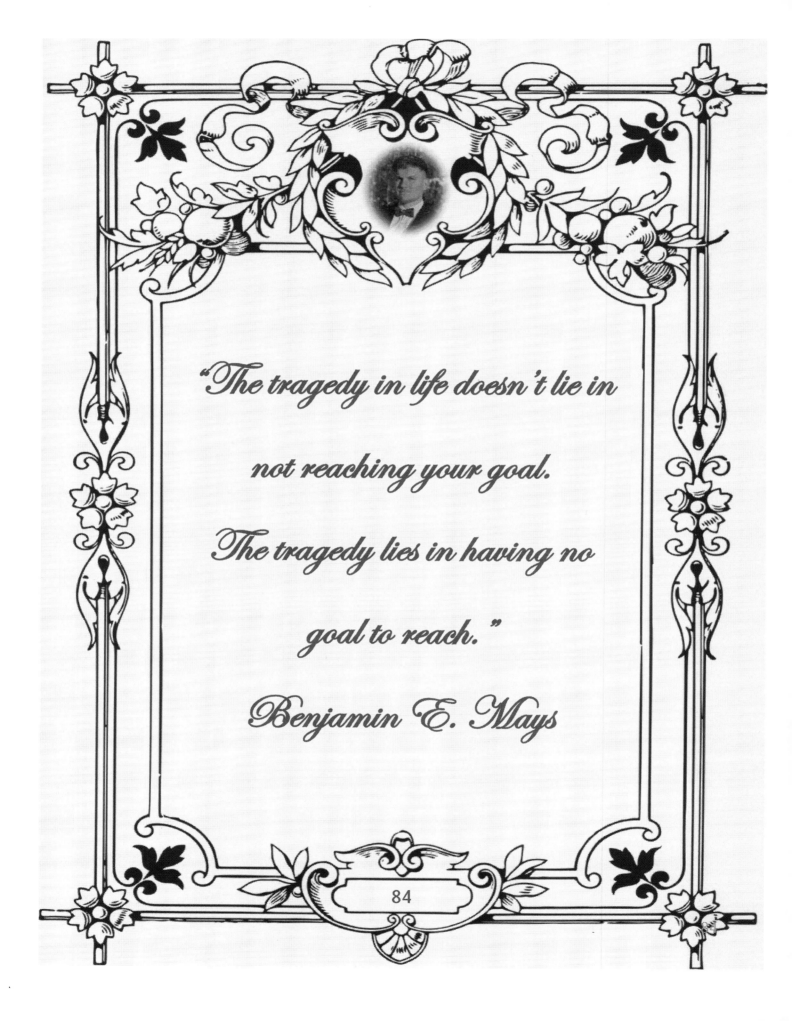

"The tragedy in life doesn't lie in

not reaching your goal.

The tragedy lies in having no

goal to reach."

Benjamin E. Mays

84

"*Be curious,*

not judgmental."

Walt Whitman

"*You're only given one*

spark of madness.

You must not lose it."

Robin Williams

"*Work hard in silence,*

let success be your noise."

Frank Ocean

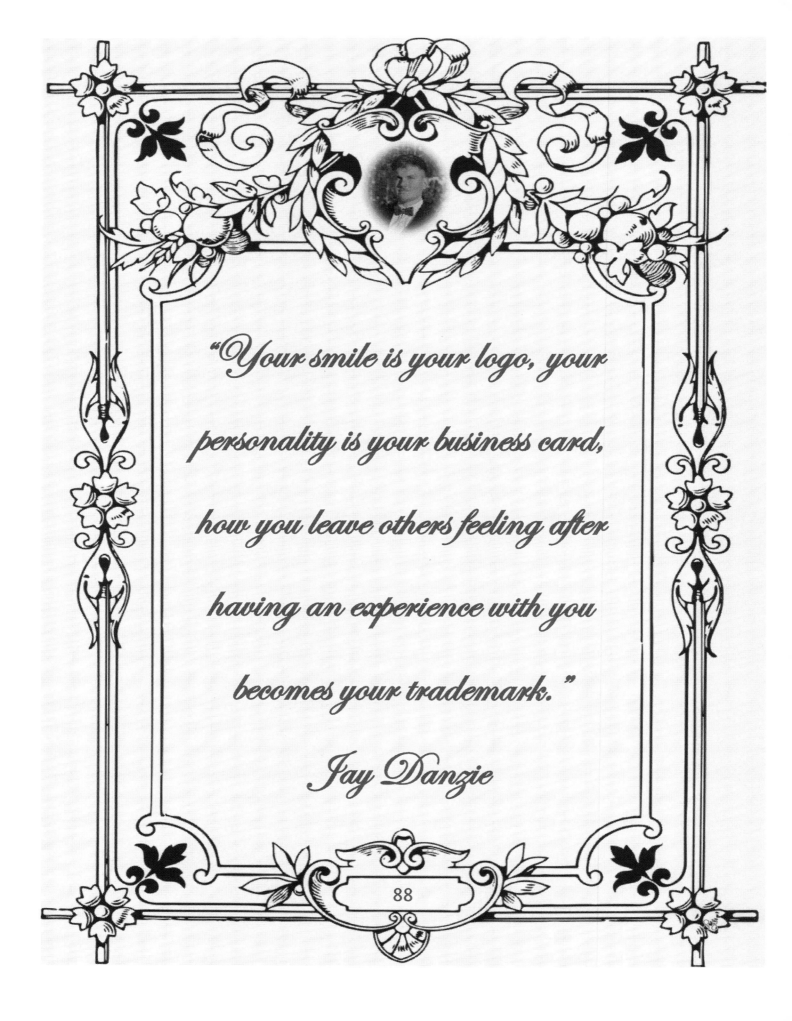

"*Your smile is your logo, your personality is your business card, how you leave others feeling after having an experience with you becomes your trademark.*"

Jay Danzie

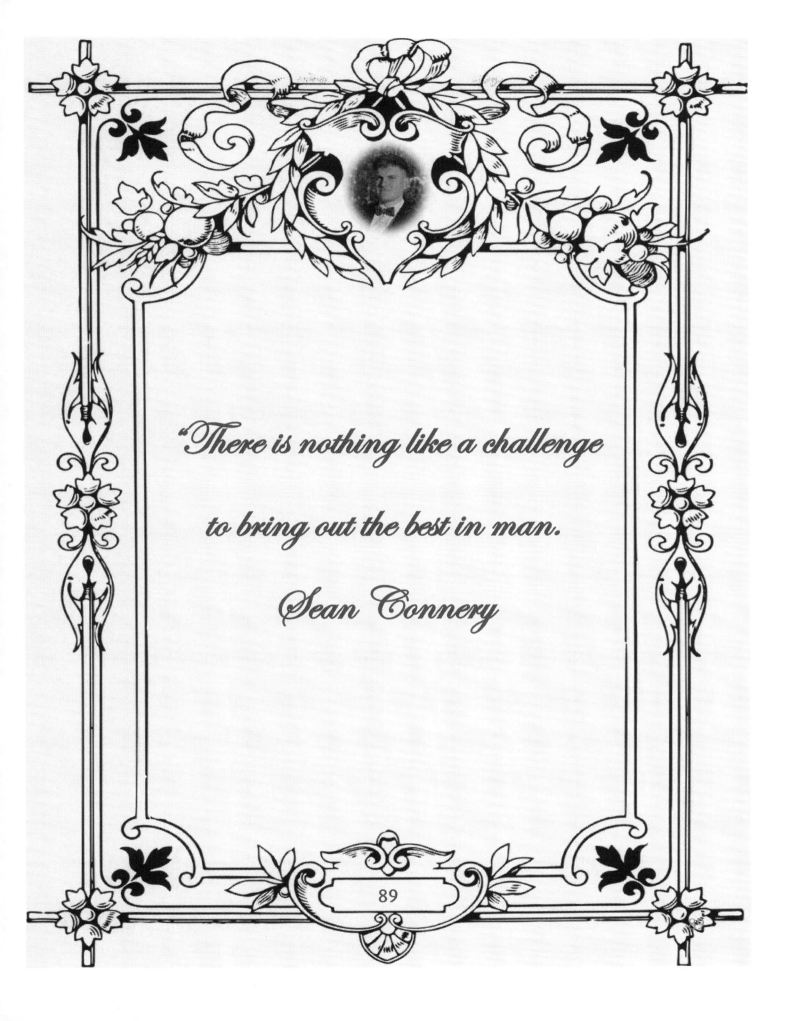

"There is nothing like a challenge
to bring out the best in man.

Sean Connery

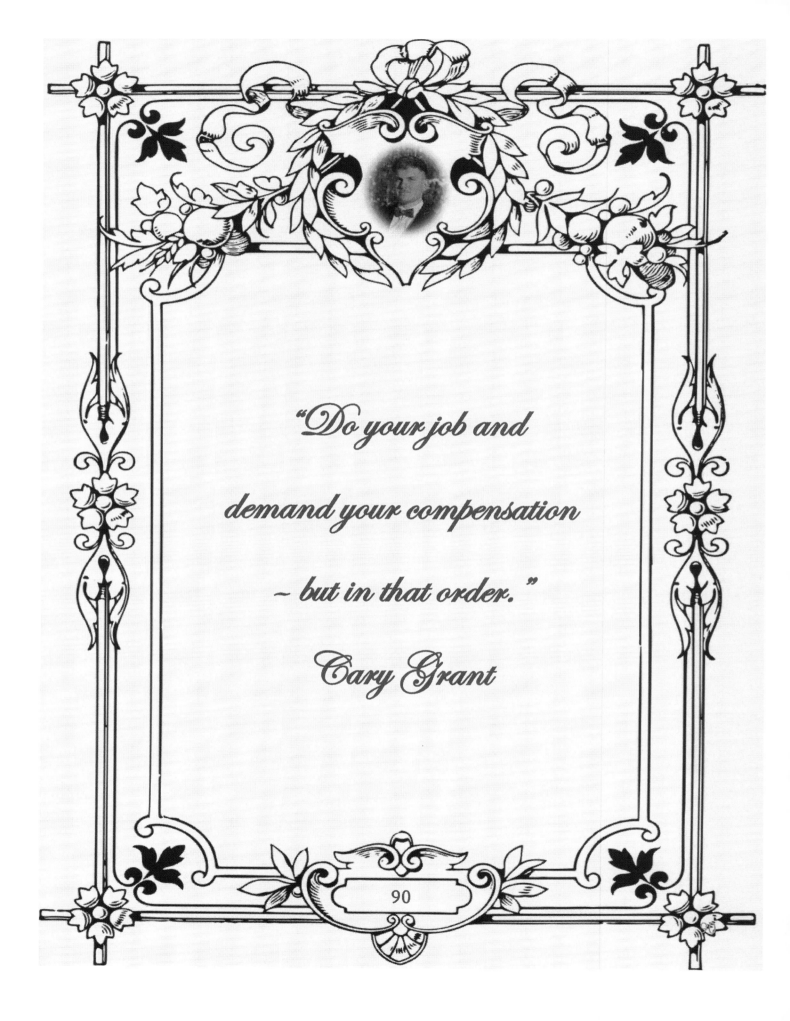

"Do your job and

demand your compensation

~ but in that order."

Cary Grant

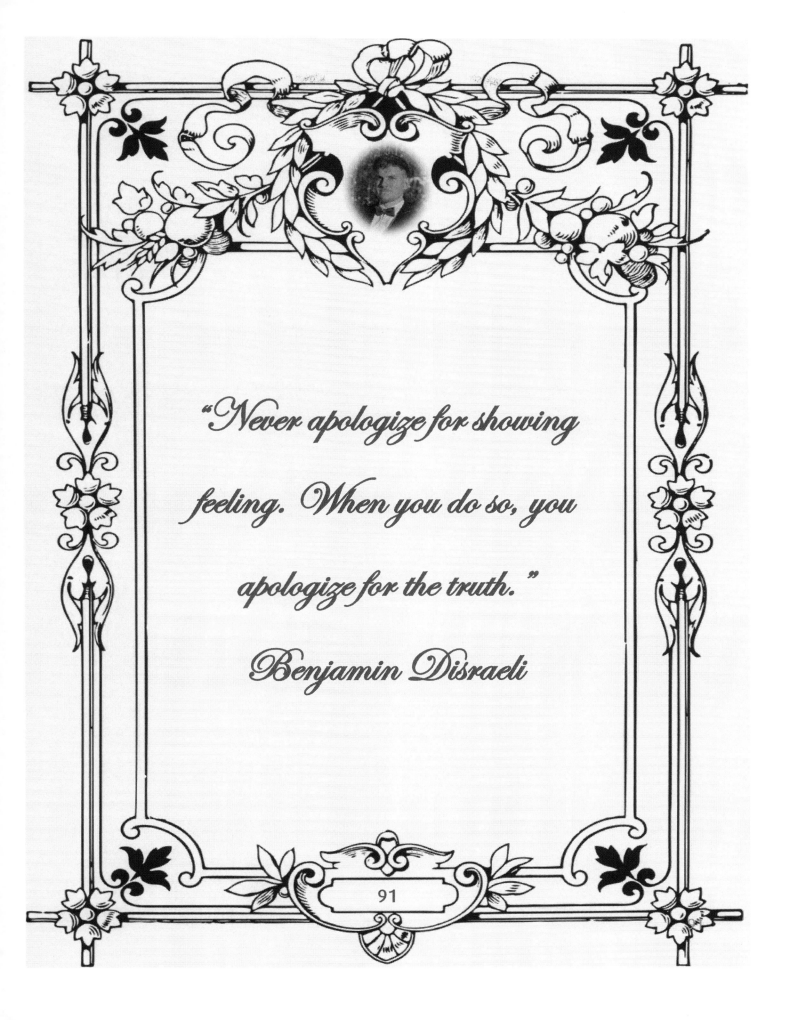

"*Never apologize for showing feeling. When you do so, you apologize for the truth.*"

Benjamin Disraeli

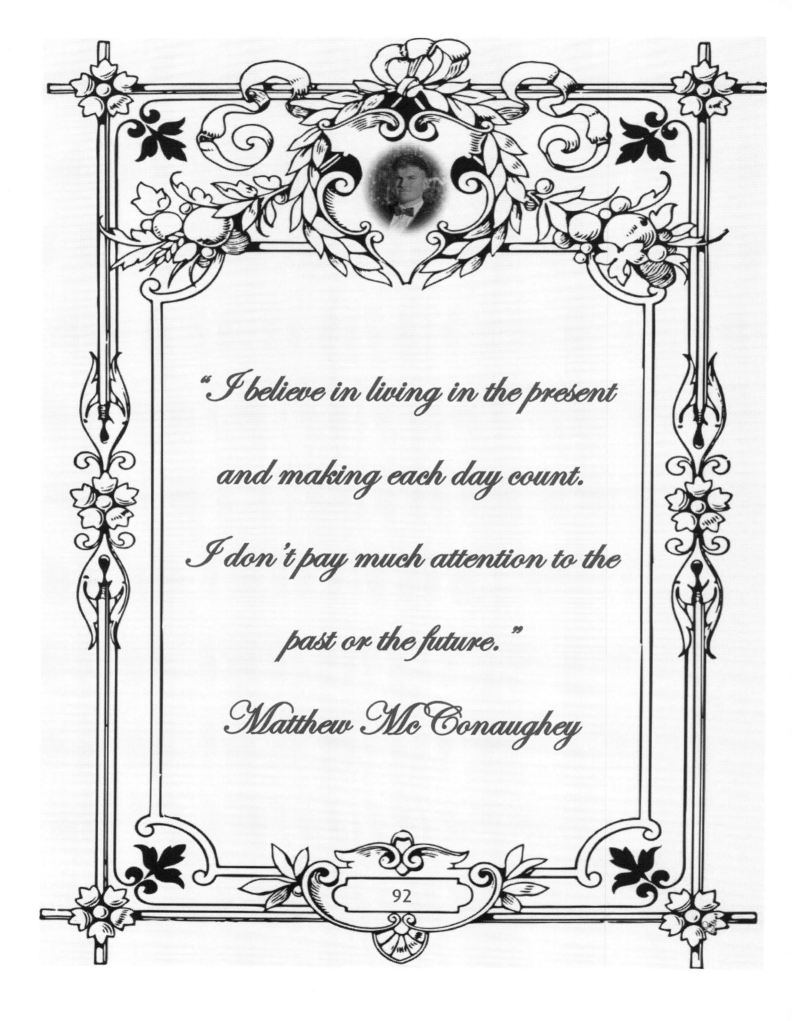

"*I believe in living in the present and making each day count. I don't pay much attention to the past or the future.*"

Matthew McConaughey

"I have become my own version of an optimist. If I can't make it through one door, I'll go through another door – or I'll make a door. Something terrific will come no matter how dark the present."

Rabindranath Tagore

93

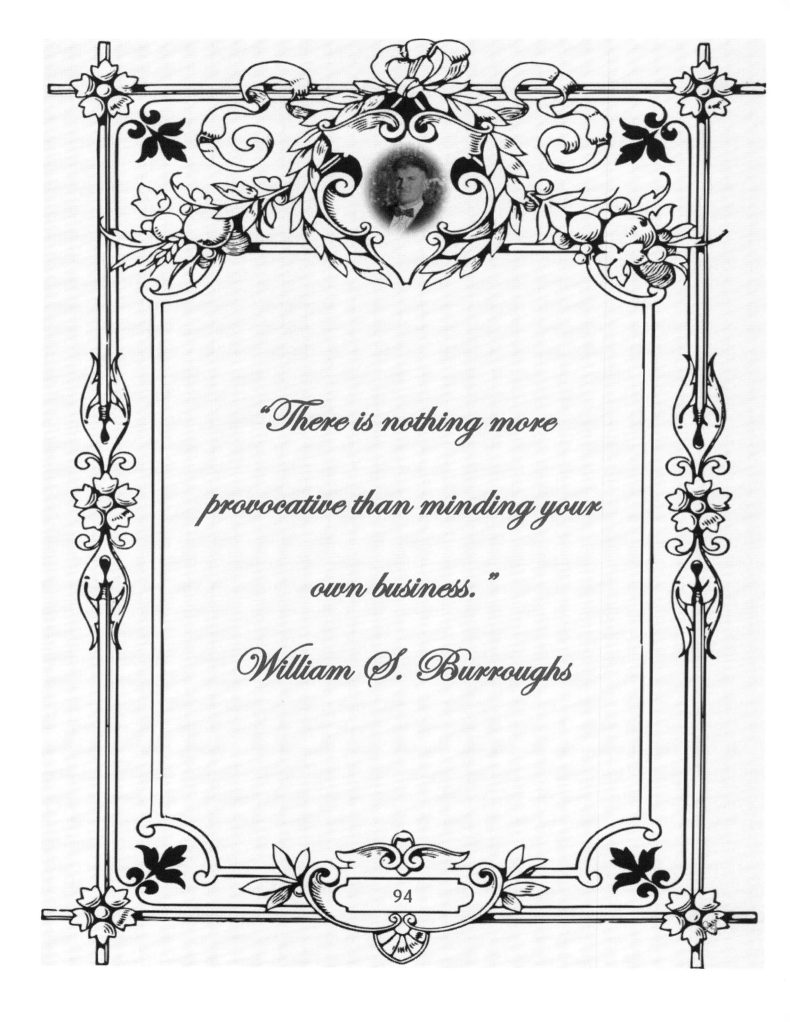

"There is nothing more

provocative than minding your

own business."

William S. Burroughs

94

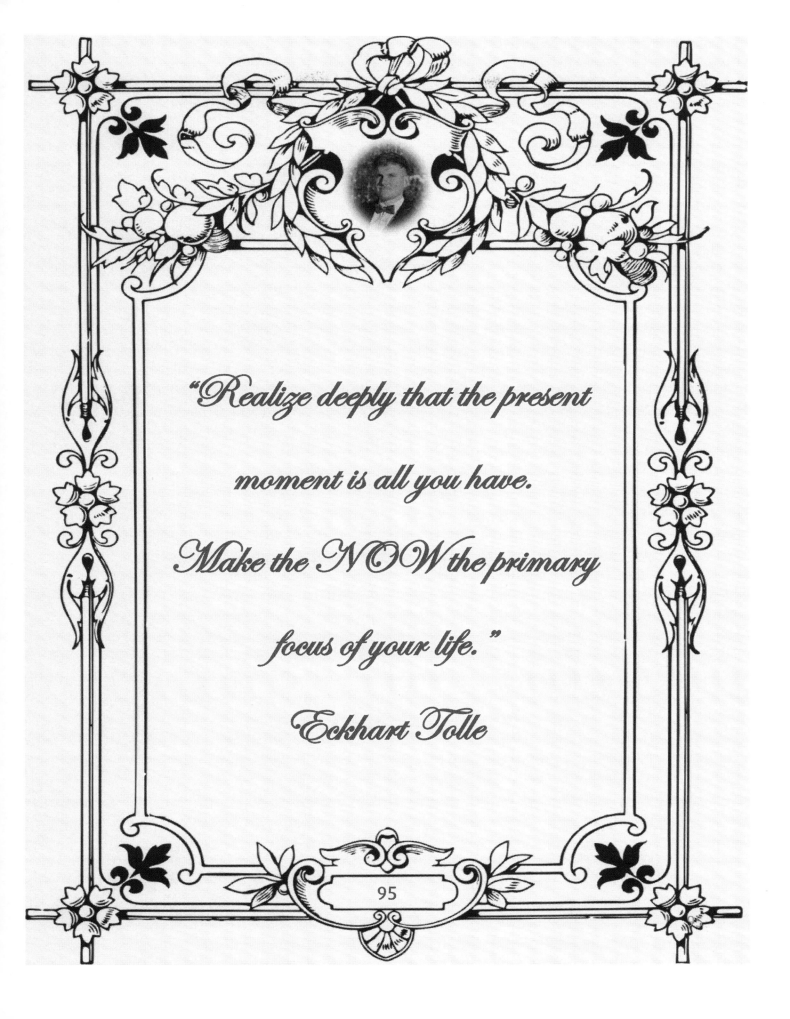

"Realize deeply that the present

moment is all you have.

Make the NOW the primary

focus of your life."

Eckhart Tolle

95

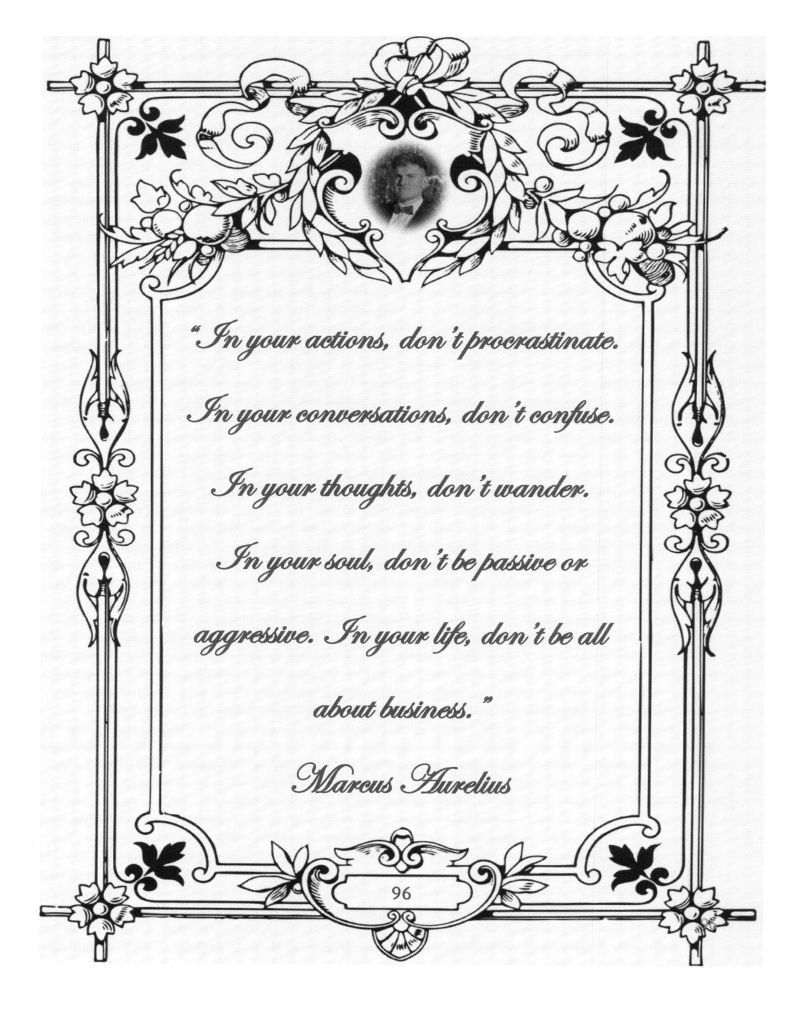

"In your actions, don't procrastinate.

In your conversations, don't confuse.

In your thoughts, don't wander.

In your soul, don't be passive or

aggressive. In your life, don't be all

about business."

Marcus Aurelius

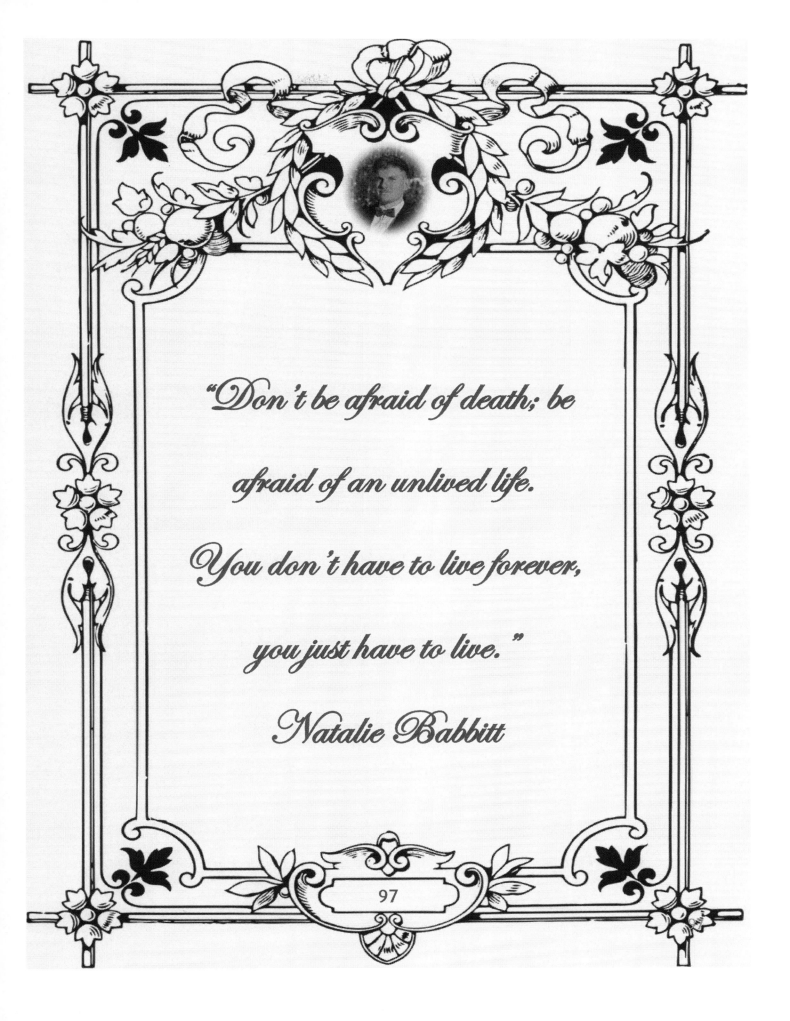

"Don't be afraid of death; be

afraid of an unlived life.

You don't have to live forever,

you just have to live."

Natalie Babbitt

97

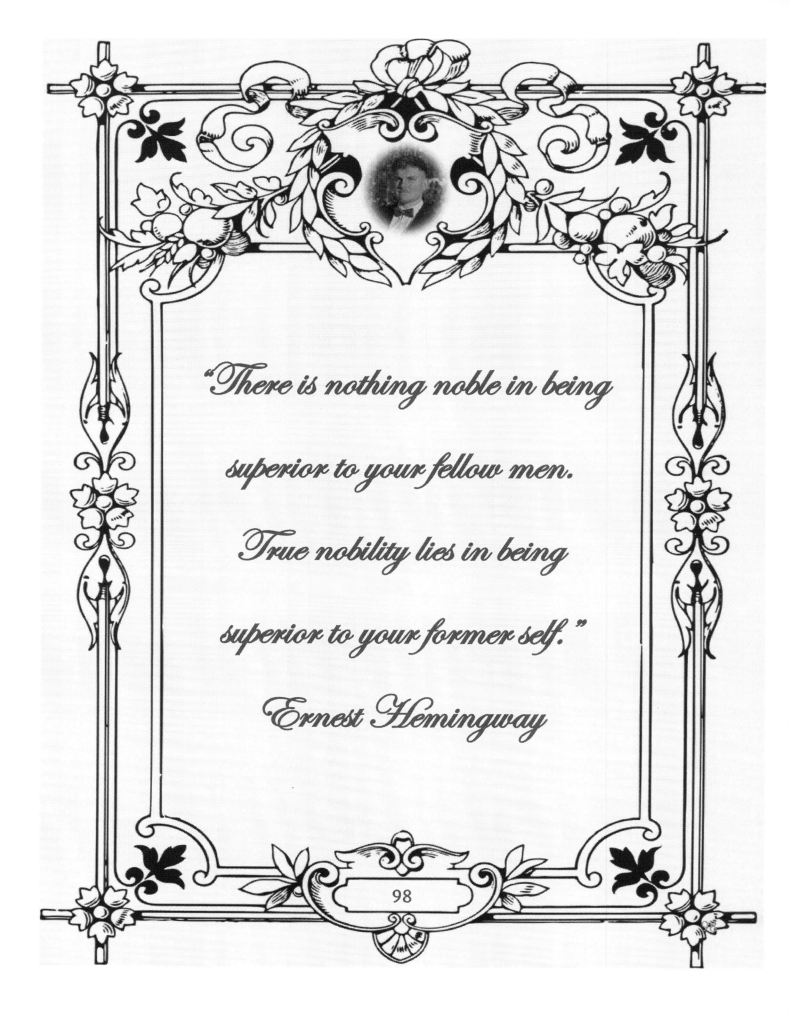

"There is nothing noble in being superior to your fellow men. True nobility lies in being superior to your former self."

Ernest Hemingway

98

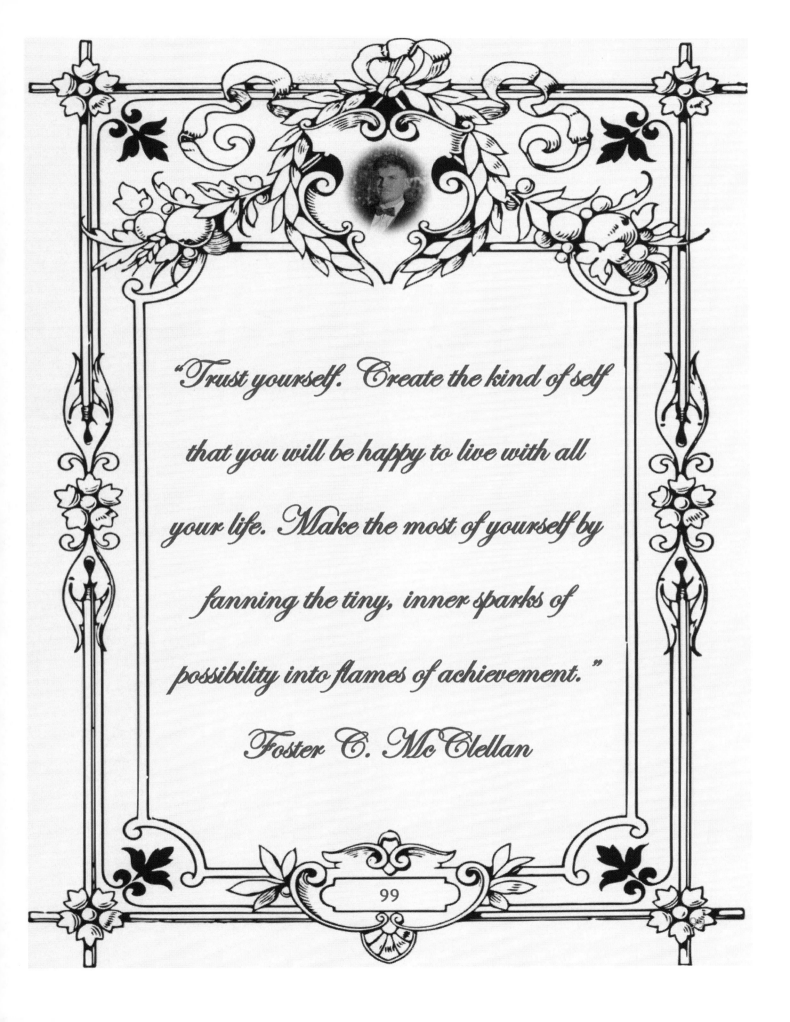

"Trust yourself. Create the kind of self that you will be happy to live with all your life. Make the most of yourself by fanning the tiny, inner sparks of possibility into flames of achievement."

Foster C. McClellan

"Live for each second

without hesitation."

Elton John

100

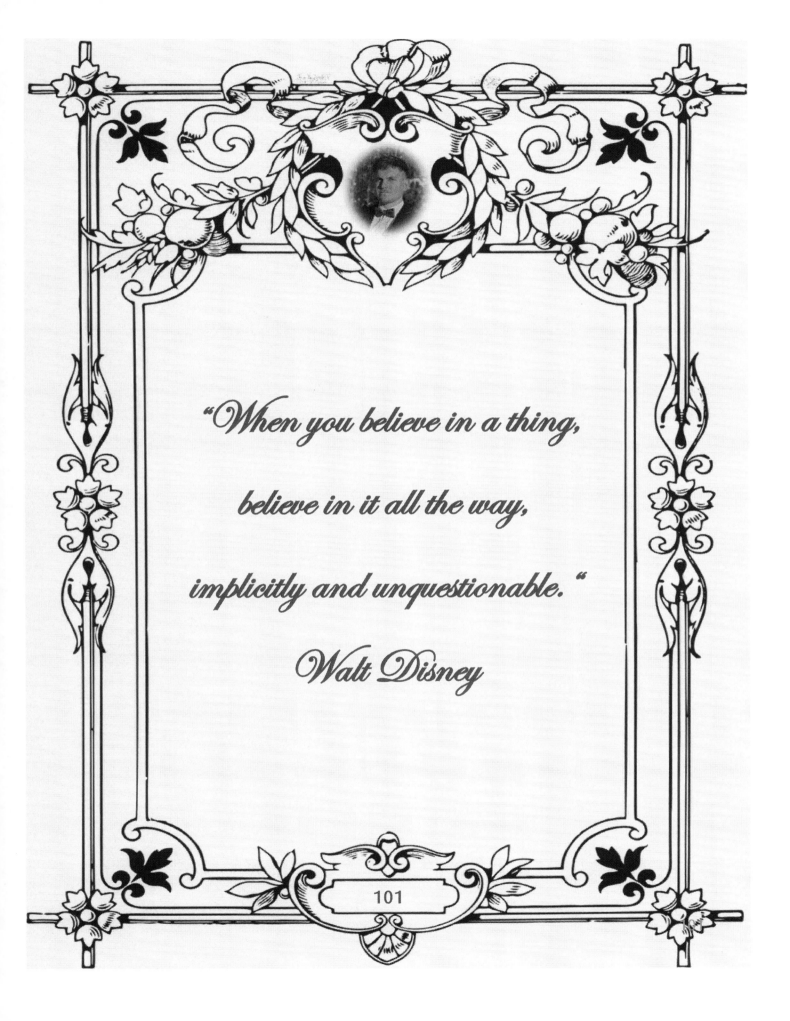

"When you believe in a thing,

believe in it all the way,

implicitly and unquestionable."

Walt Disney

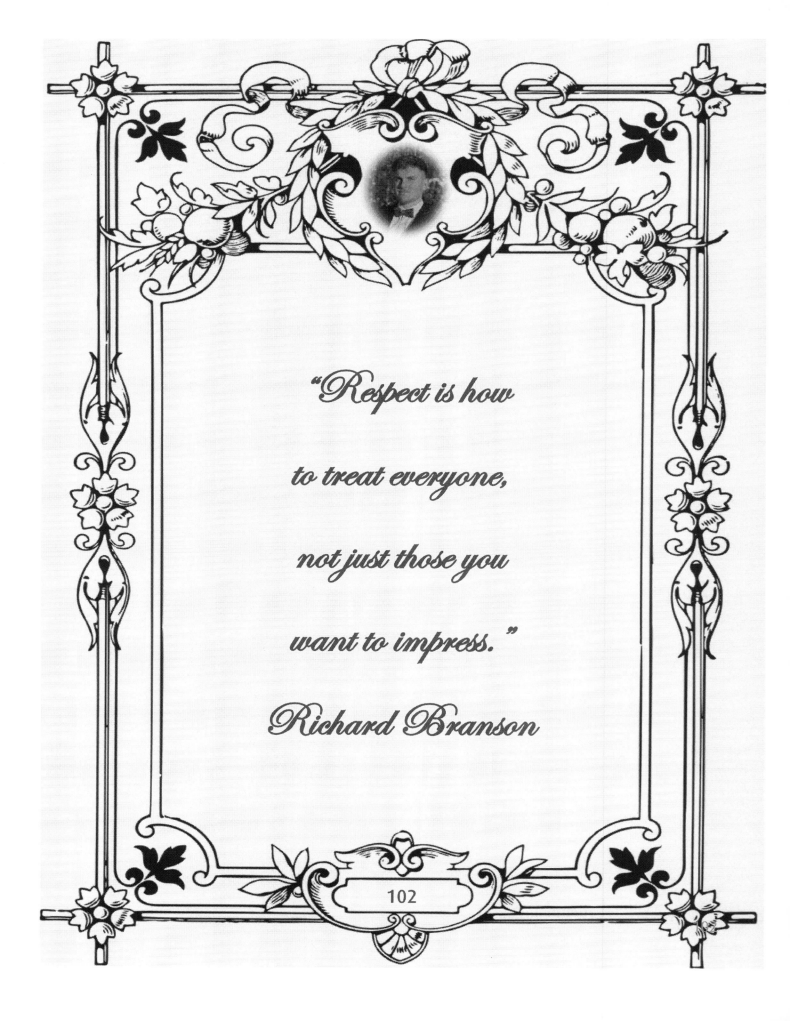

"*Respect is how*

to treat everyone,

not just those you

want to impress."

Richard Branson

"Be in love with your life,

every detail of it. "

Jack Kerouac

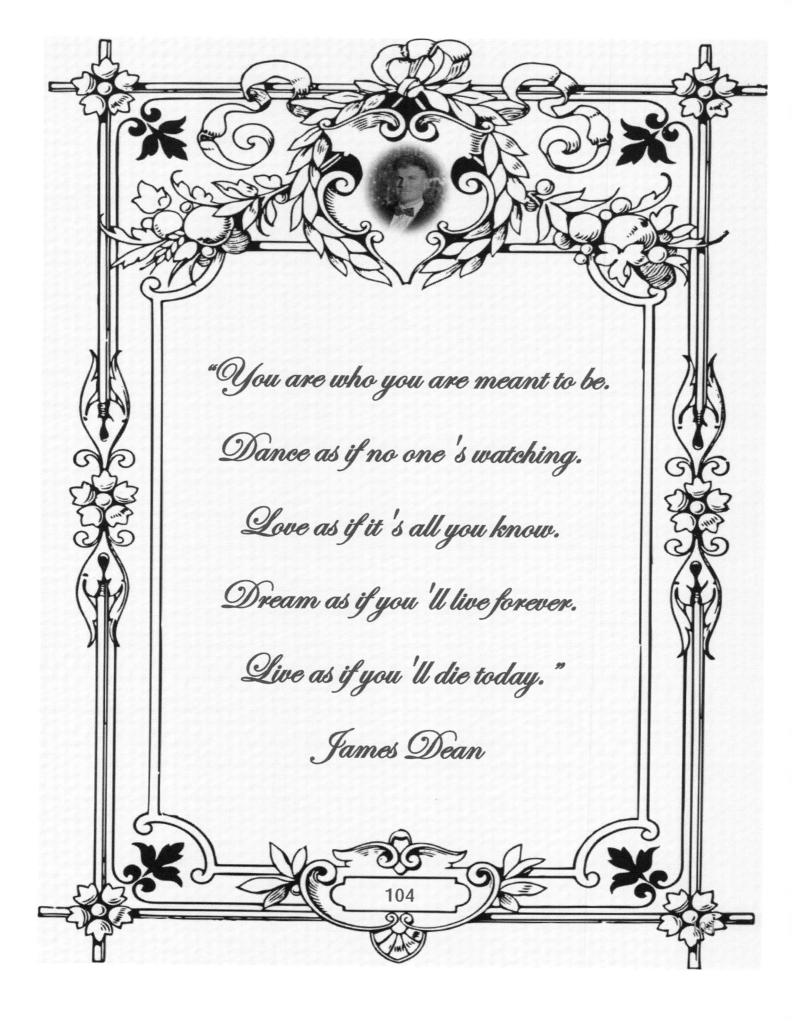

"You are who you are meant to be.

Dance as if no one's watching.

Love as if it's all you know.

Dream as if you'll live forever.

Live as if you'll die today."

James Dean

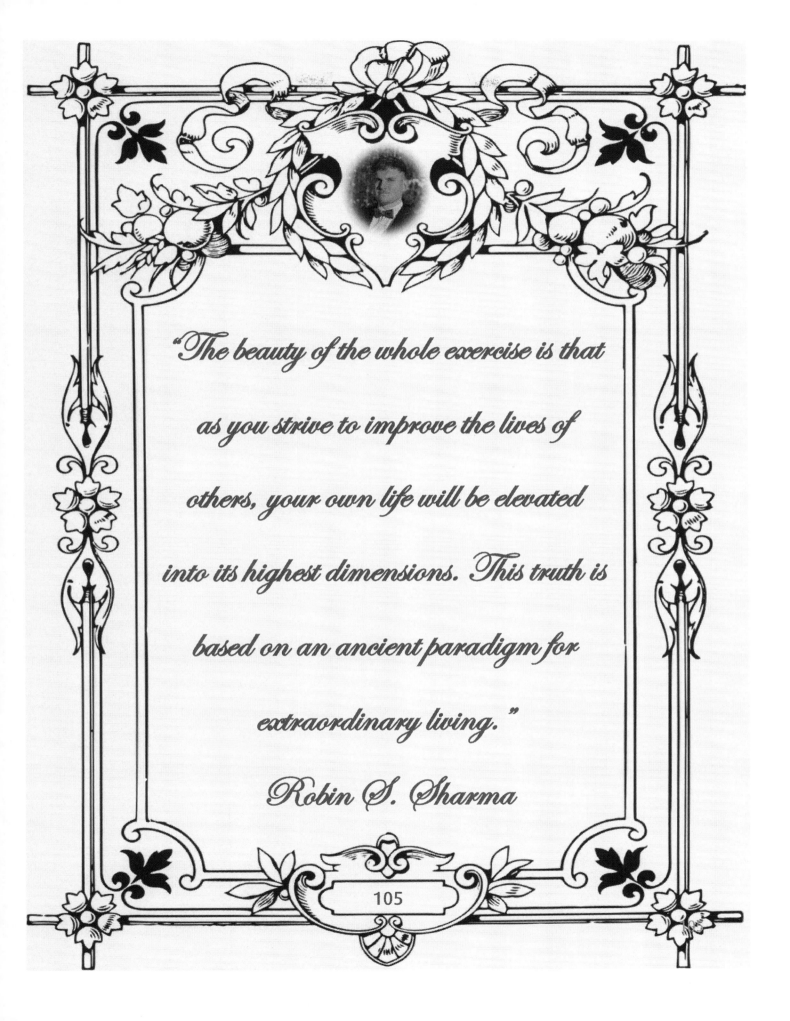

"The beauty of the whole exercise is that as you strive to improve the lives of others, your own life will be elevated into its highest dimensions. This truth is based on an ancient paradigm for extraordinary living."

Robin S. Sharma

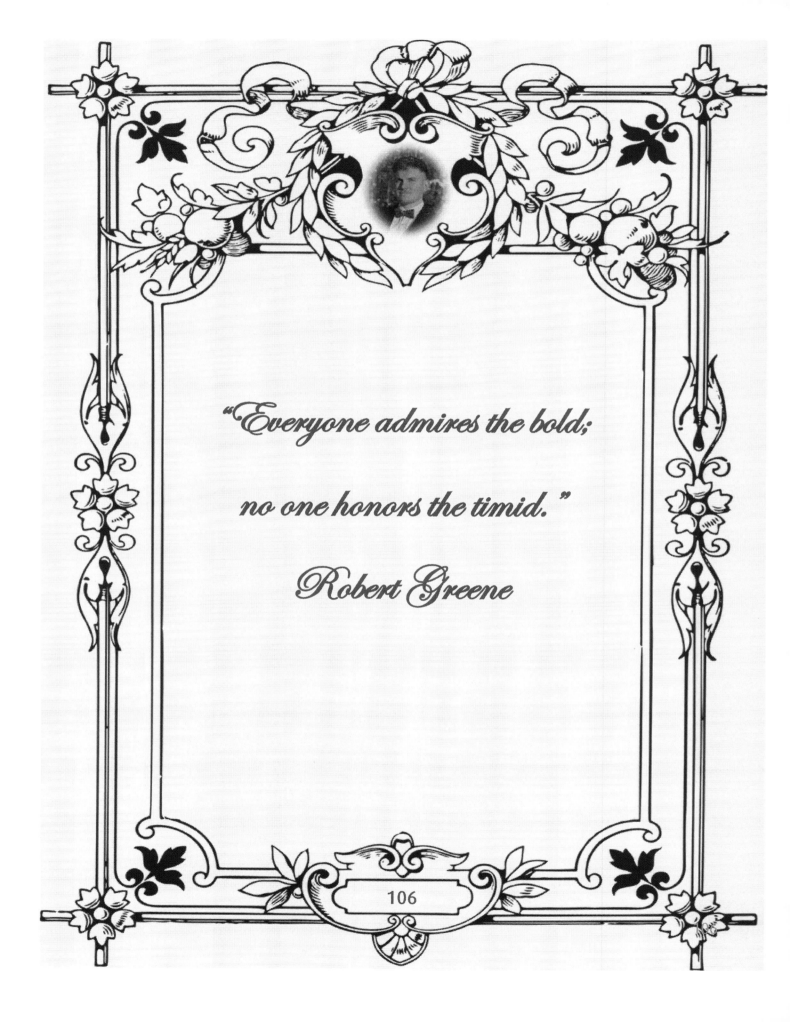

"Everyone admires the bold;

no one honors the timid."

Robert Greene

"Everything can be taken from a

man but one thing:

the last of the human freedoms –

to choose one's attitude in any

given set of circumstances,

to choose one's own way."

Viktor E. Frankl

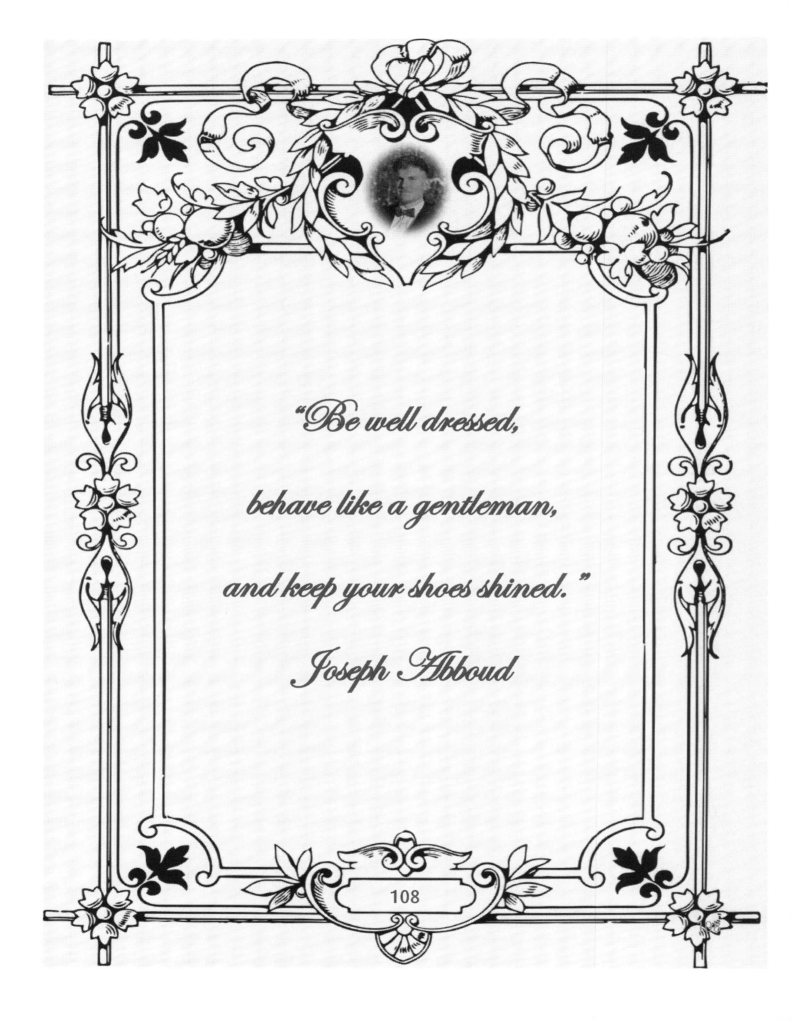

"Be well dressed,

behave like a gentleman,

and keep your shoes shined."

Joseph Abboud

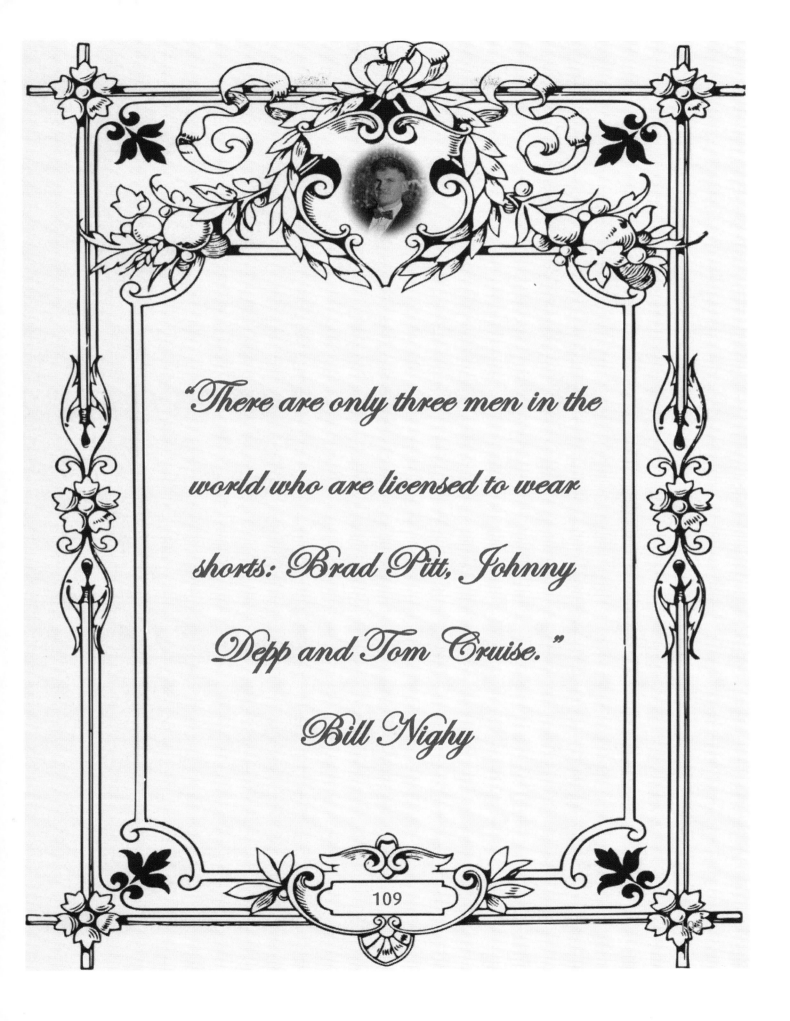

"There are only three men in the world who are licensed to wear shorts: Brad Pitt, Johnny Depp and Tom Cruise."

Bill Nighy

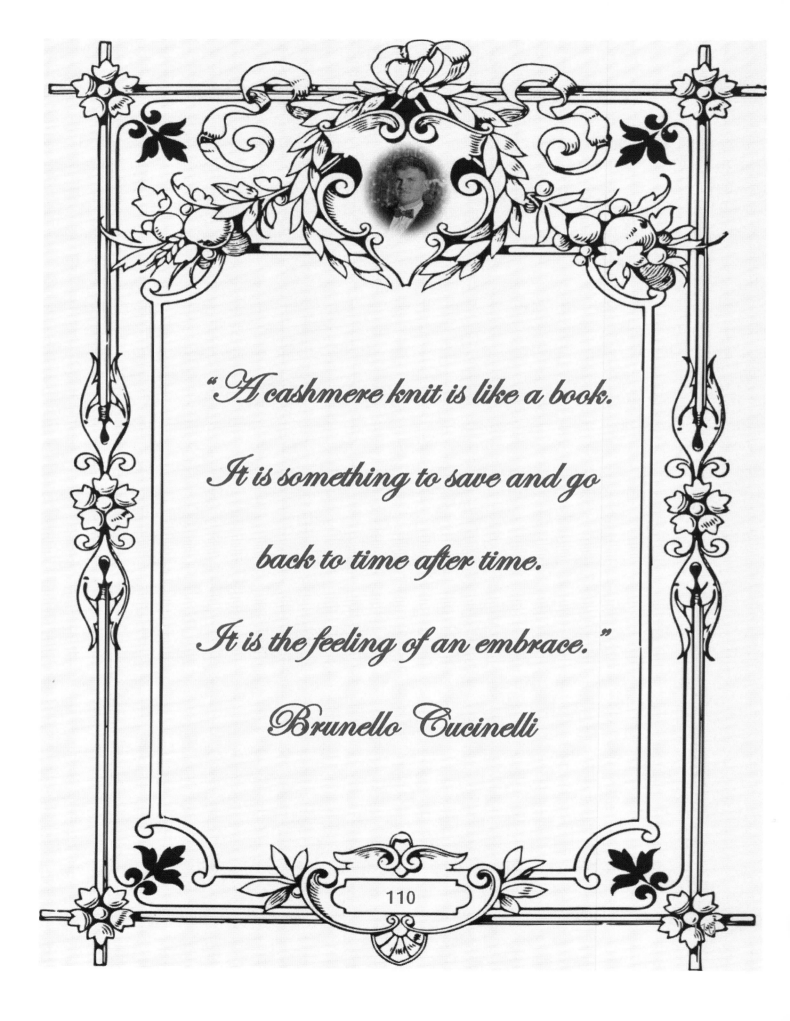

"A cashmere knit is like a book.

It is something to save and go

back to time after time.

It is the feeling of an embrace."

Brunello Cucinelli

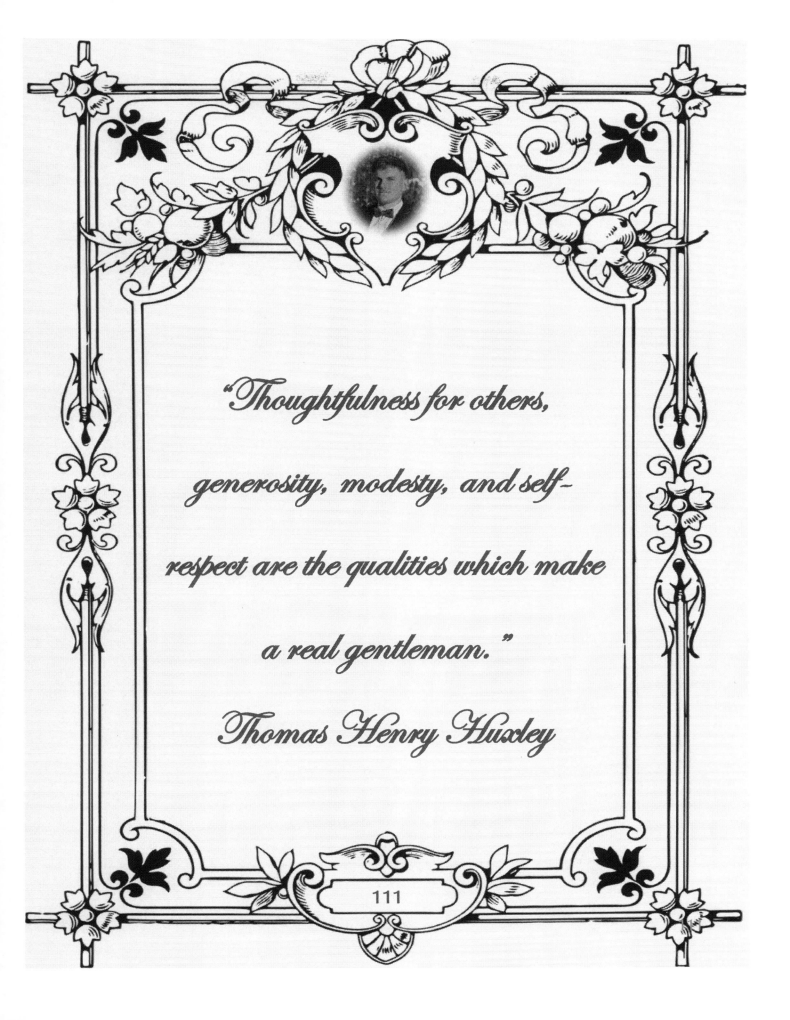

"Thoughtfulness for others, generosity, modesty, and self-respect are the qualities which make a real gentleman."

Thomas Henry Huxley

111

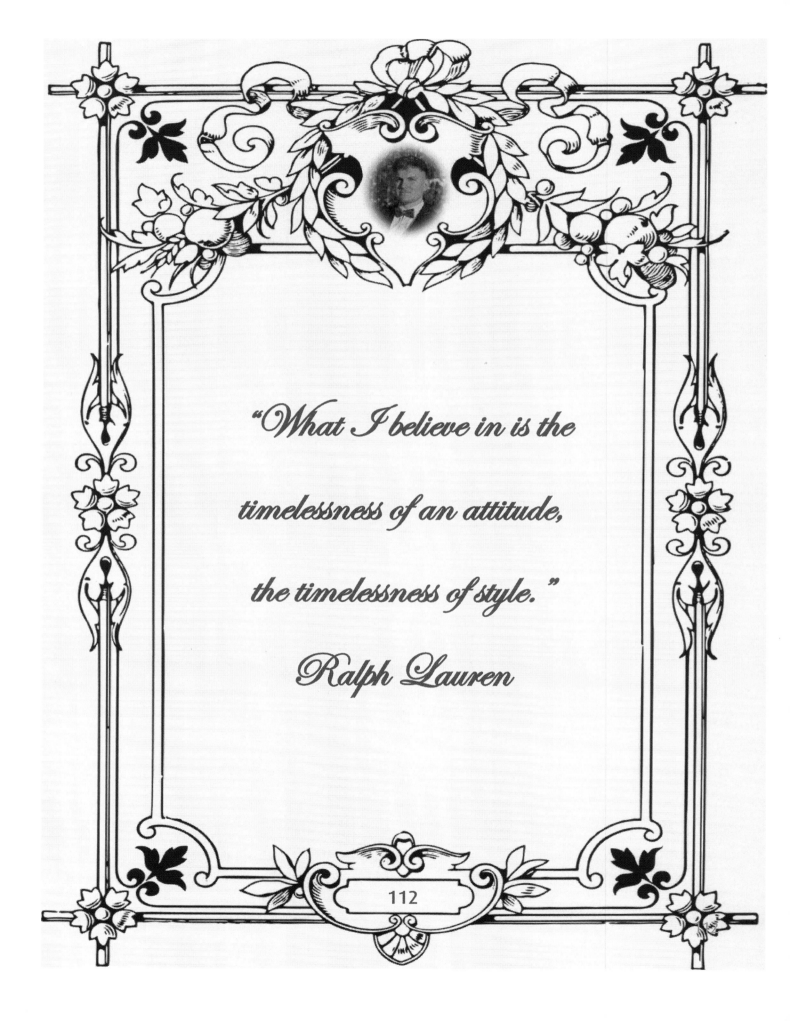

"What I believe in is the timelessness of an attitude, the timelessness of style."

Ralph Lauren

"*I don't think many people have a very good understanding of leisure and the importance it plays in our lives.*"

Jack Nicholson

113

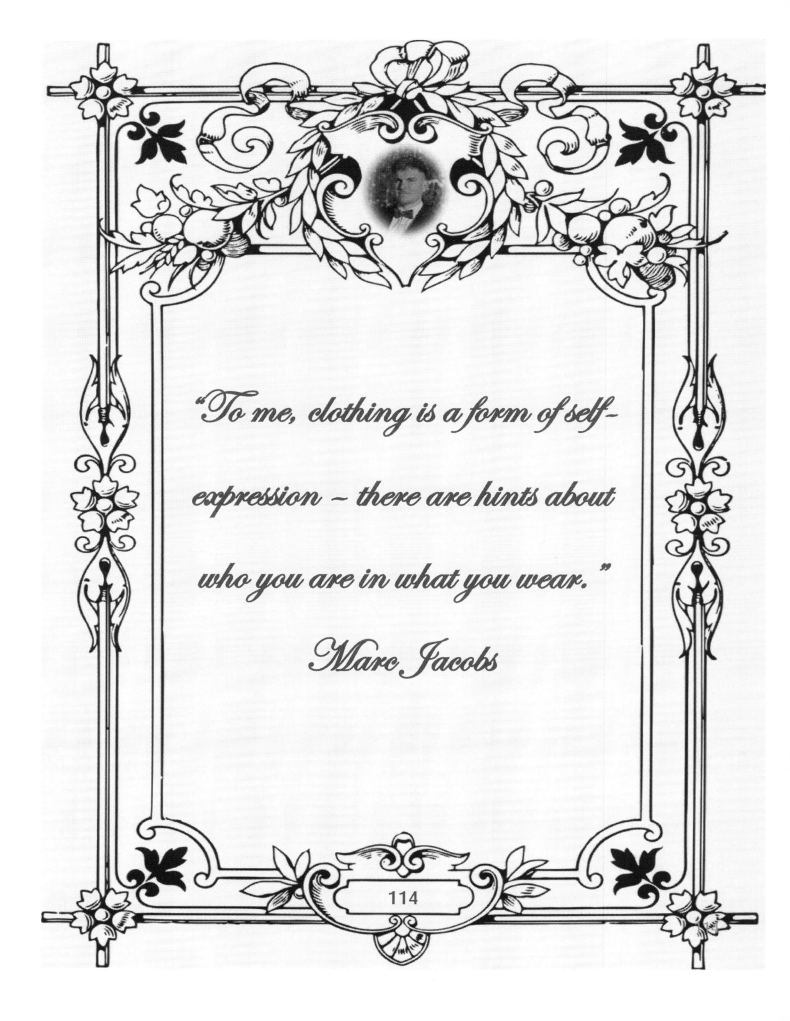

"To me, clothing is a form of self-expression – there are hints about who you are in what you wear."

Marc Jacobs

114

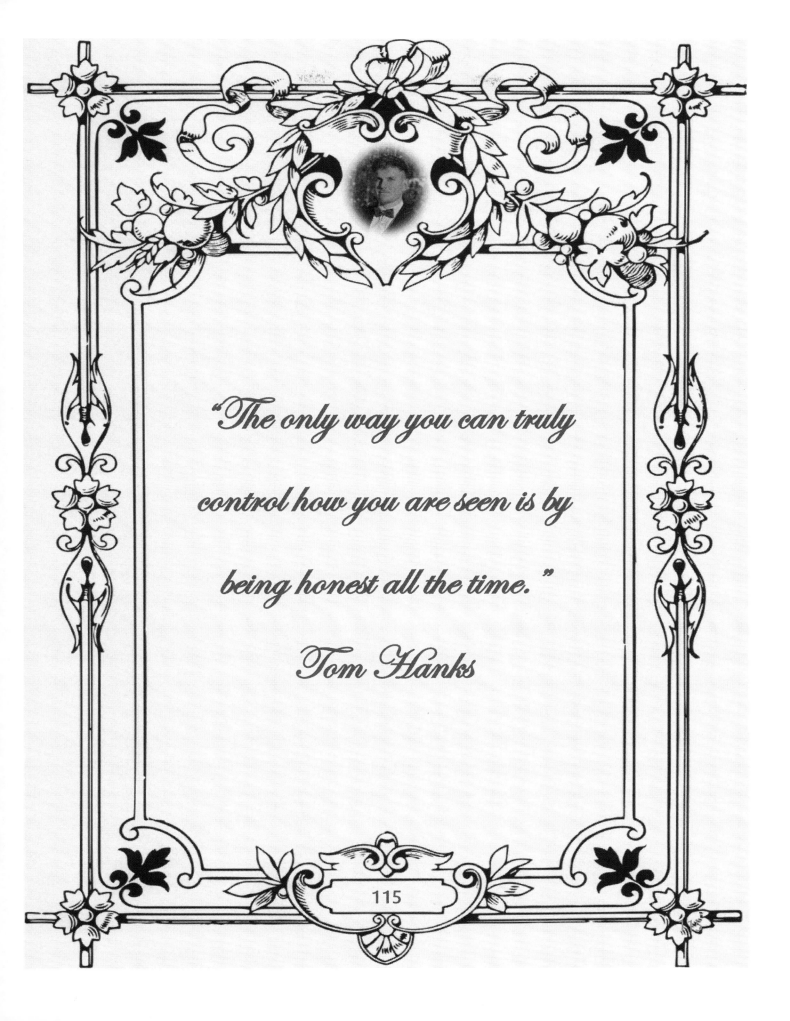

"The only way you can truly control how you are seen is by being honest all the time."

Tom Hanks

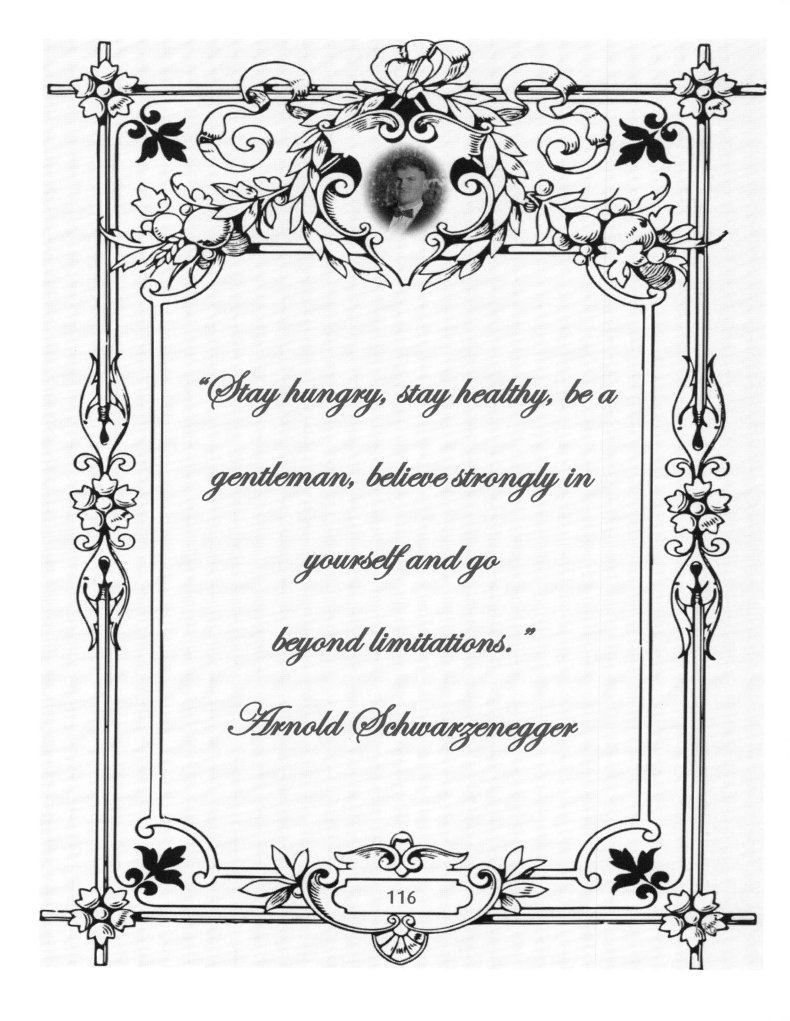

"Stay hungry, stay healthy, be a gentleman, believe strongly in yourself and go beyond limitations."

Arnold Schwarzenegger

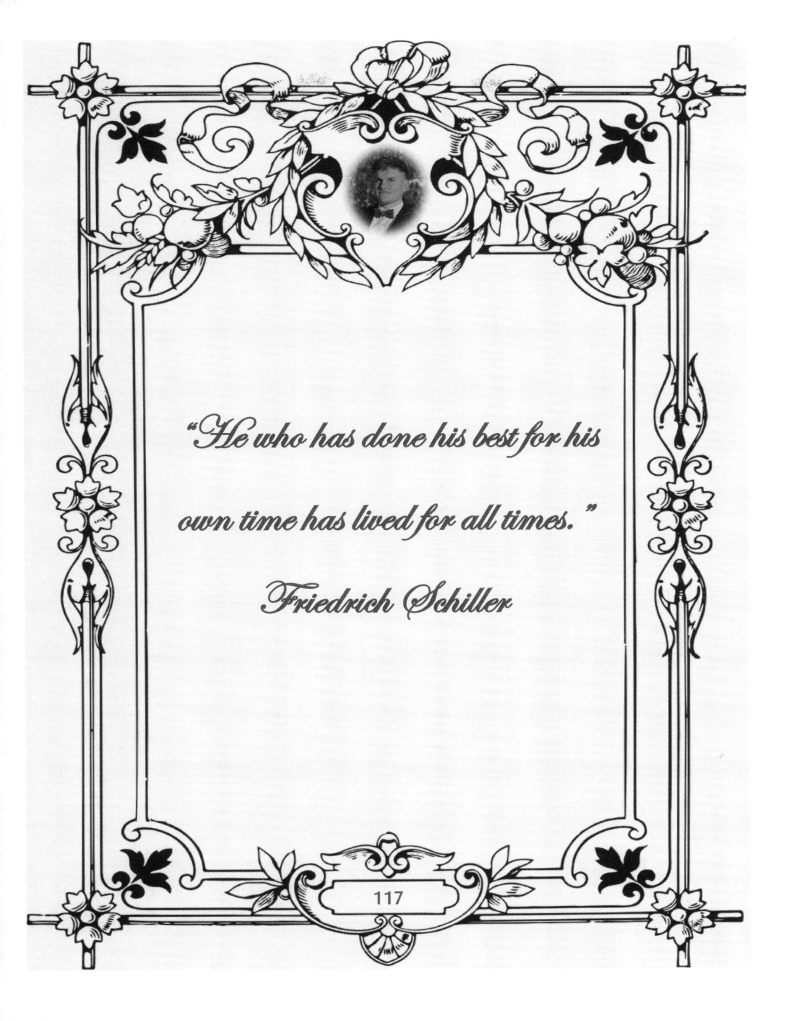

"He who has done his best for his own time has lived for all times."

Friedrich Schiller

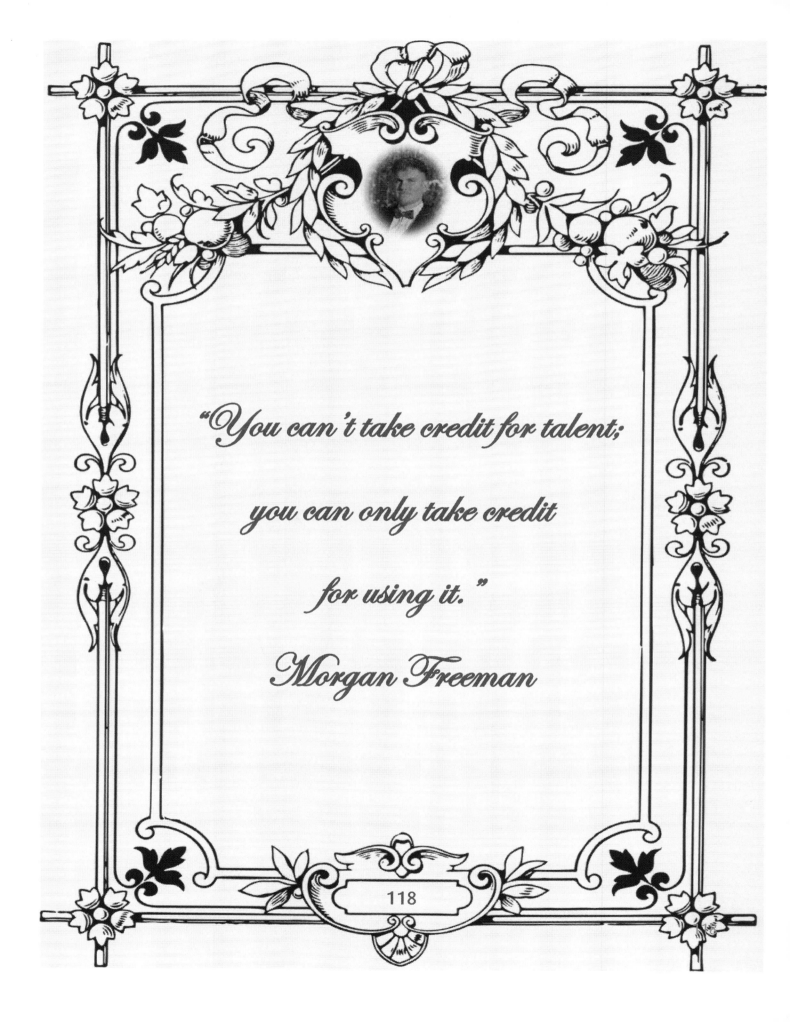

"You can't take credit for talent;

you can only take credit

for using it."

Morgan Freeman

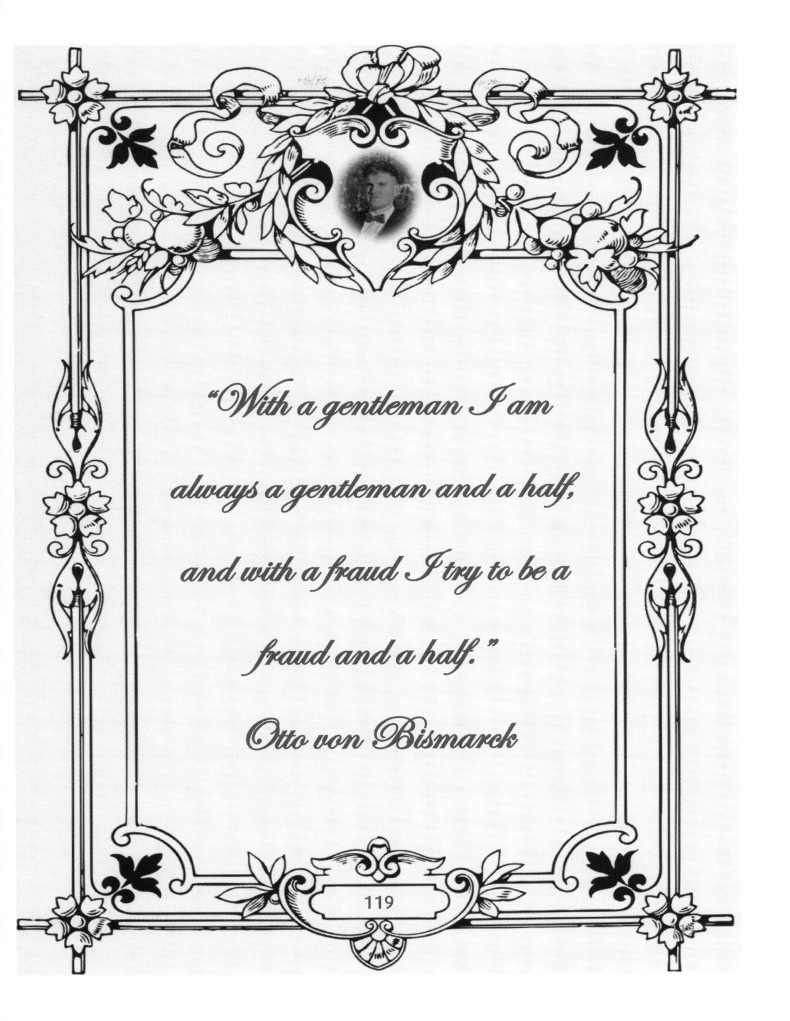

"With a gentleman I am always a gentleman and a half, and with a fraud I try to be a fraud and a half."

Otto von Bismarck

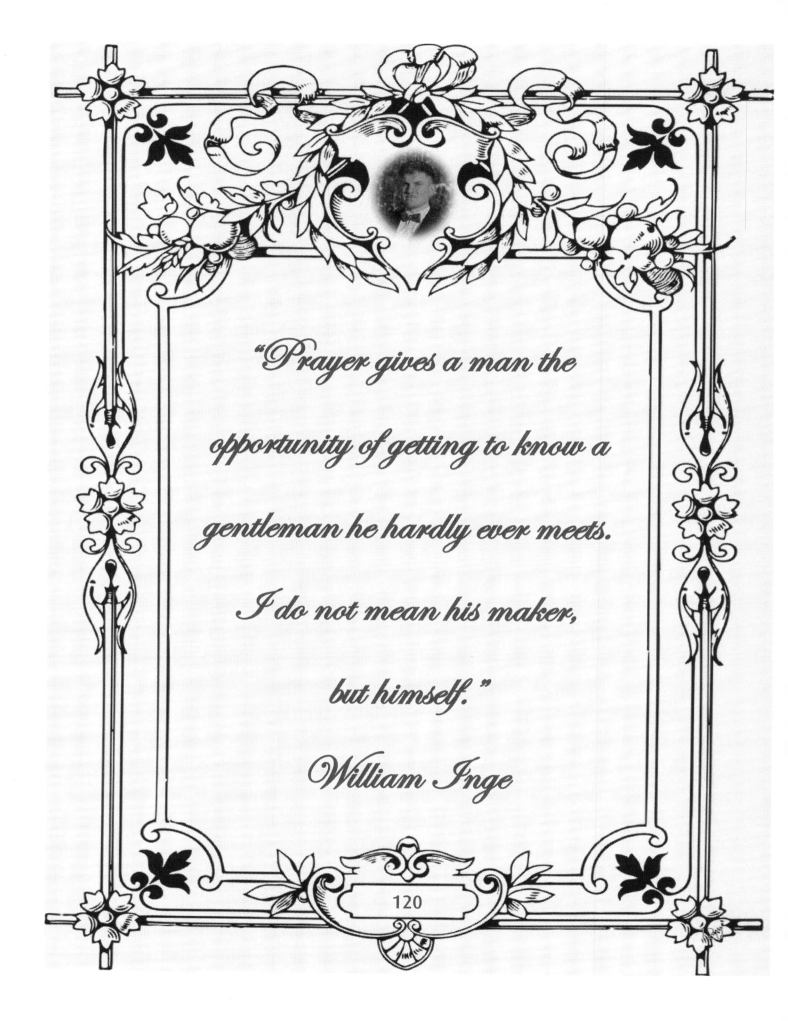

"Prayer gives a man the opportunity of getting to know a gentleman he hardly ever meets. I do not mean his maker, but himself."

William Inge

"*No gentleman ever*

discusses any relationship

with a lady."

Keith Miller

"In a tuxedo,

I'm a star.

In regular clothes,

I'm a nobody."

Dean Martin

122

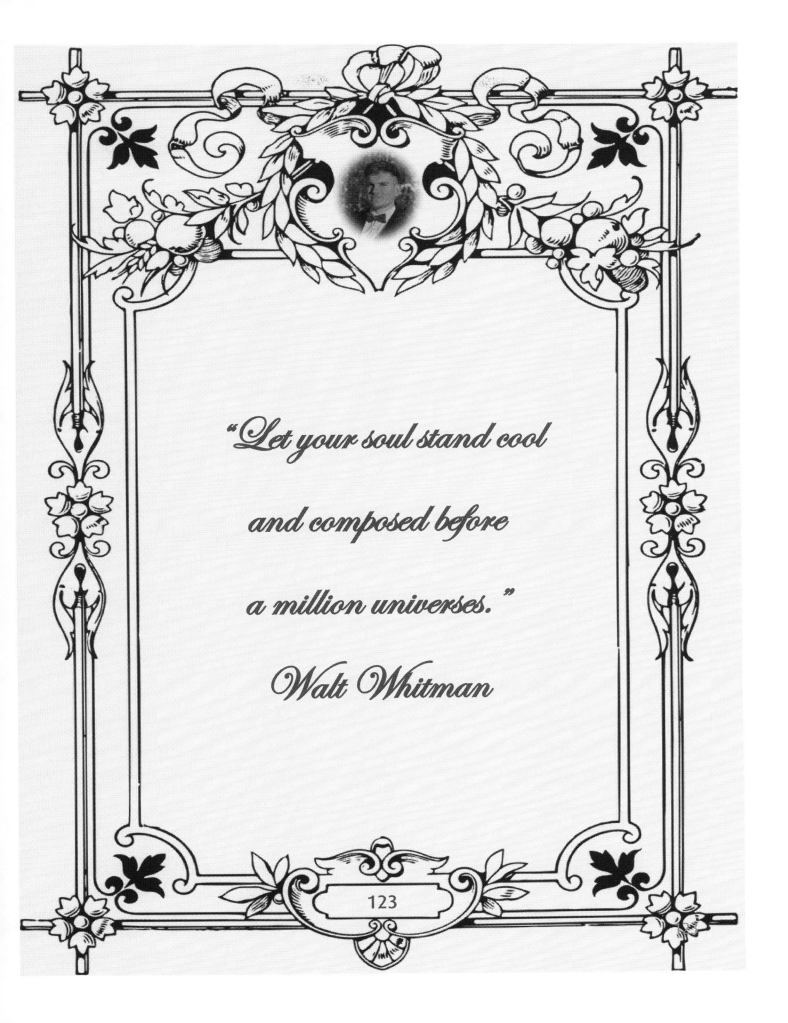

"Let your soul stand cool

and composed before

a million universes."

Walt Whitman

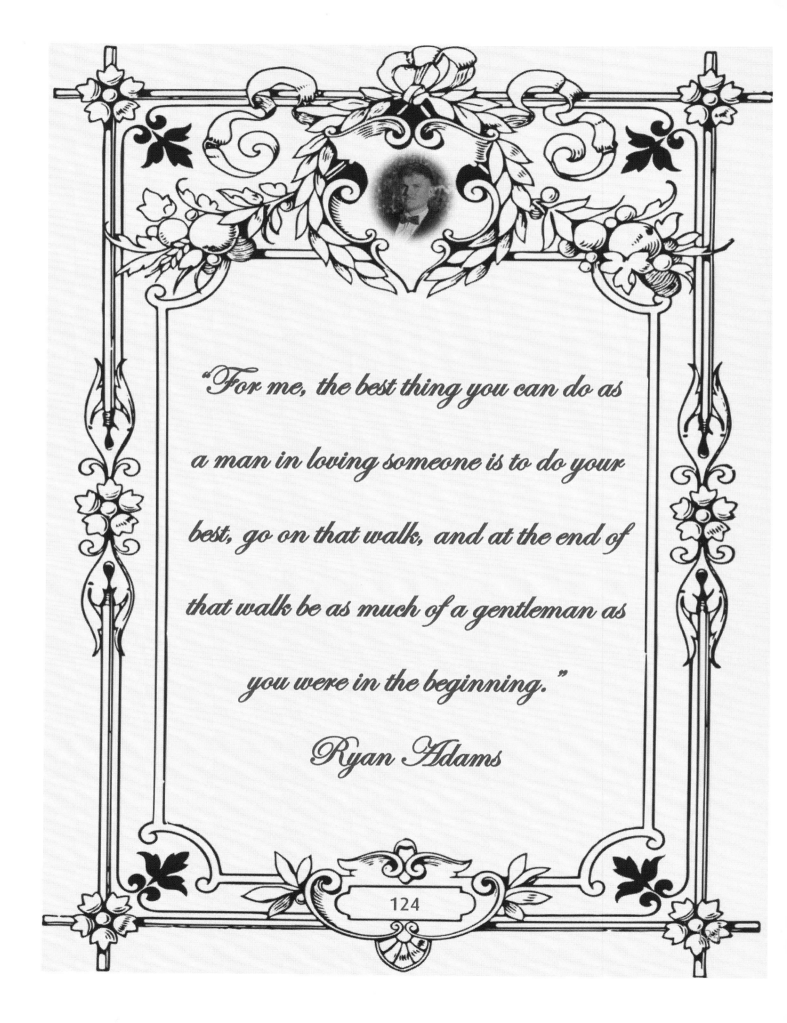

"For me, the best thing you can do as a man in loving someone is to do your best, go on that walk, and at the end of that walk be as much of a gentleman as you were in the beginning."

Ryan Adams

124

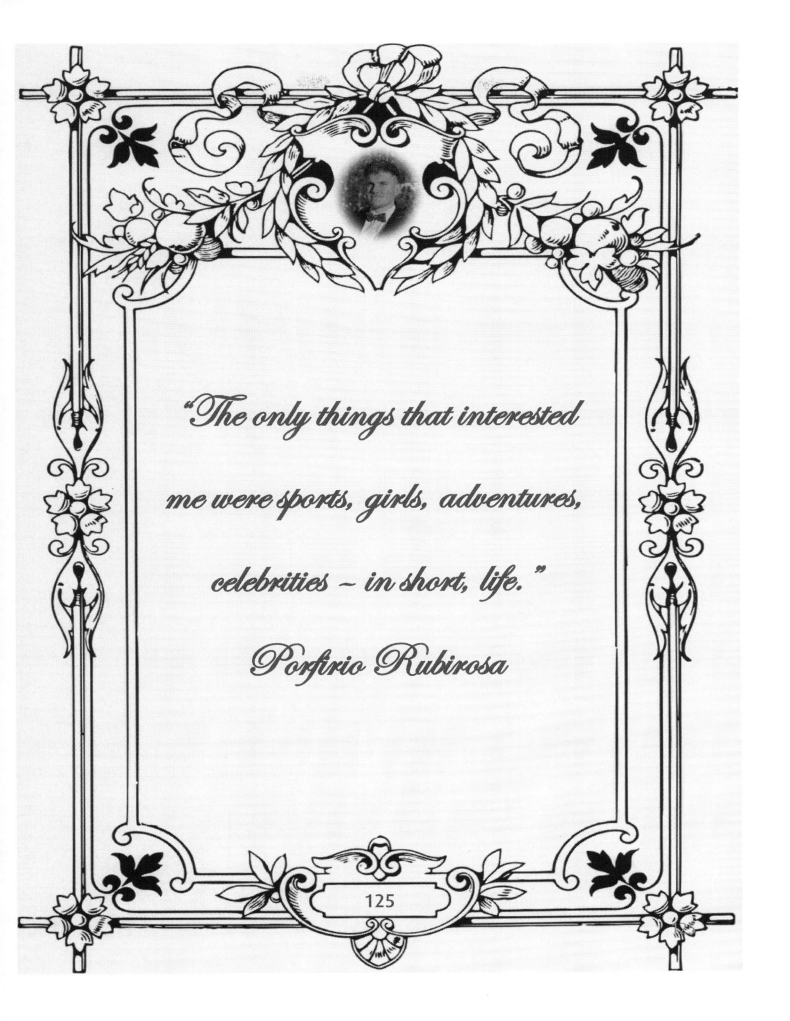

"The only things that interested me were sports, girls, adventures, celebrities – in short, life."

Porfirio Rubirosa

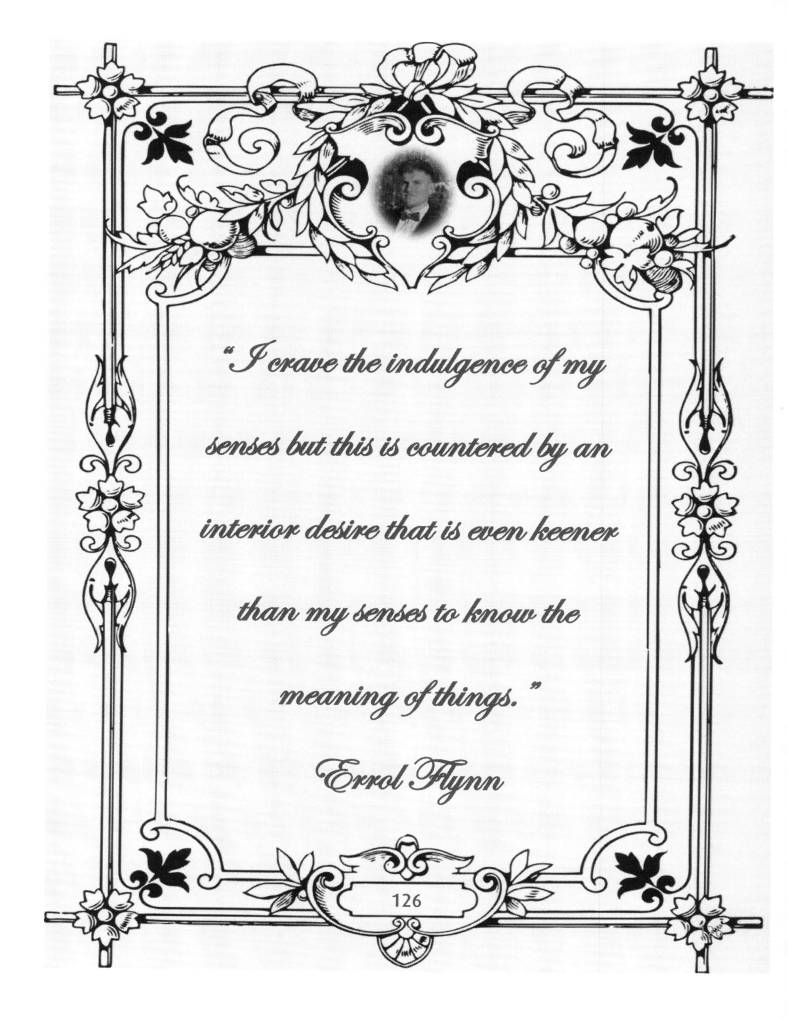

"*I crave the indulgence of my senses but this is countered by an interior desire that is even keener than my senses to know the meaning of things.*"

Errol Flynn

126

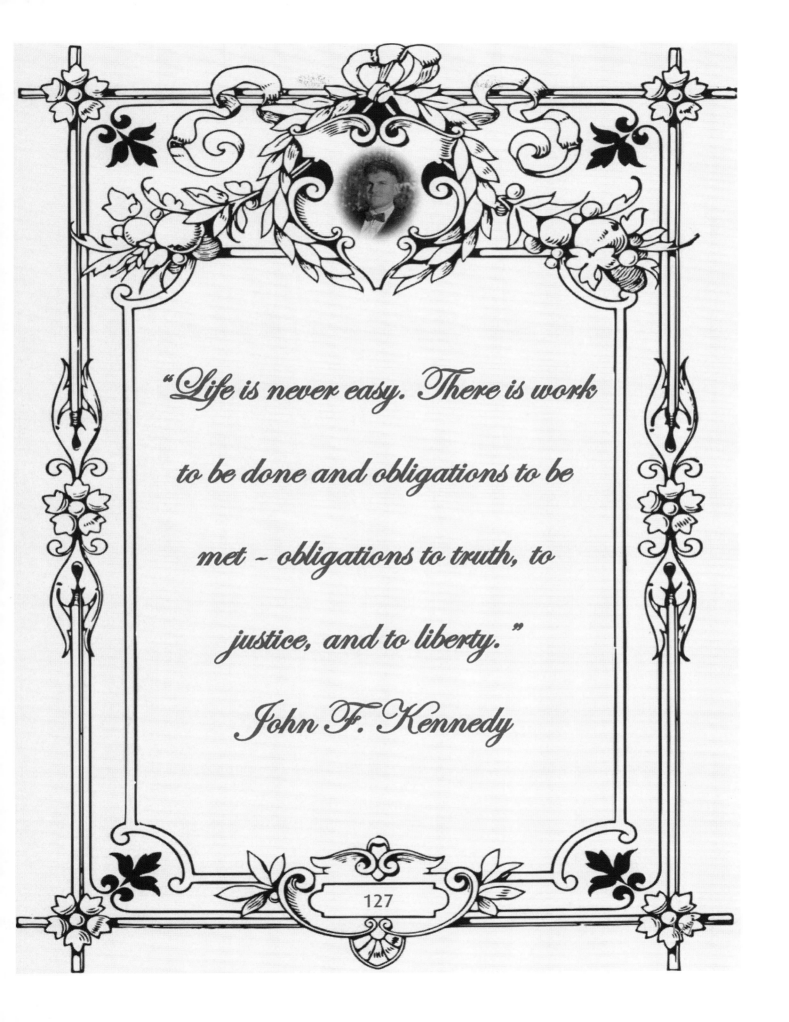

"*Life is never easy. There is work to be done and obligations to be met – obligations to truth, to justice, and to liberty.*"

John F. Kennedy

127

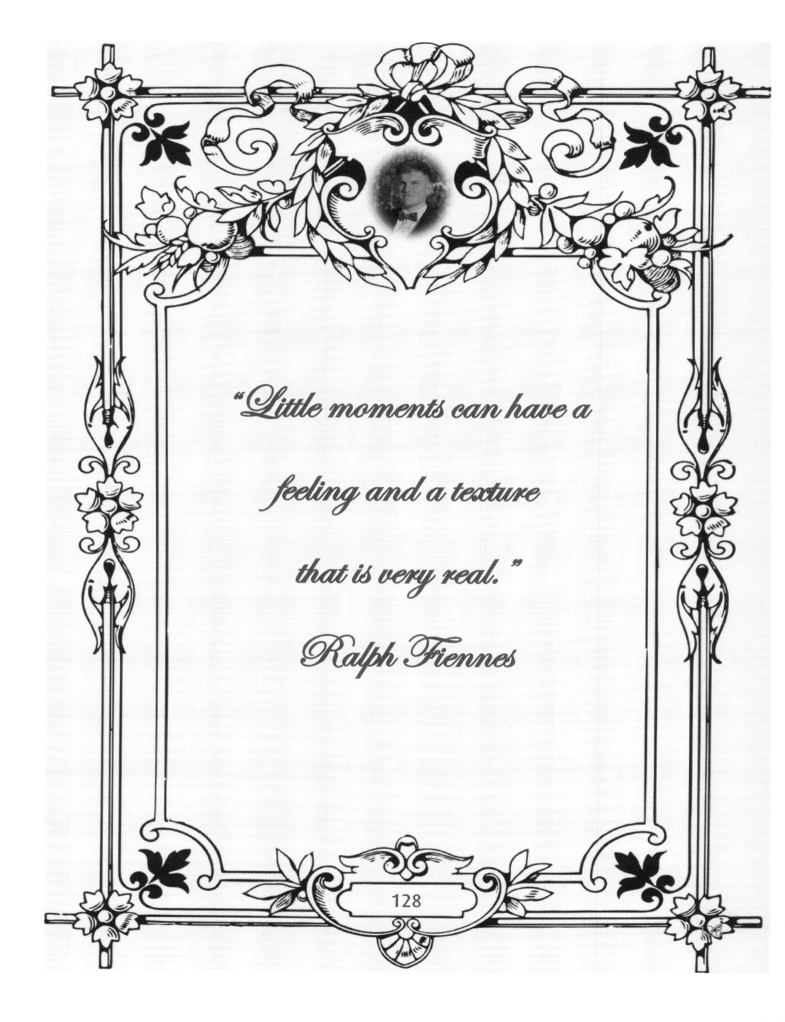

"Little moments can have a

feeling and a texture

that is very real."

Ralph Fiennes

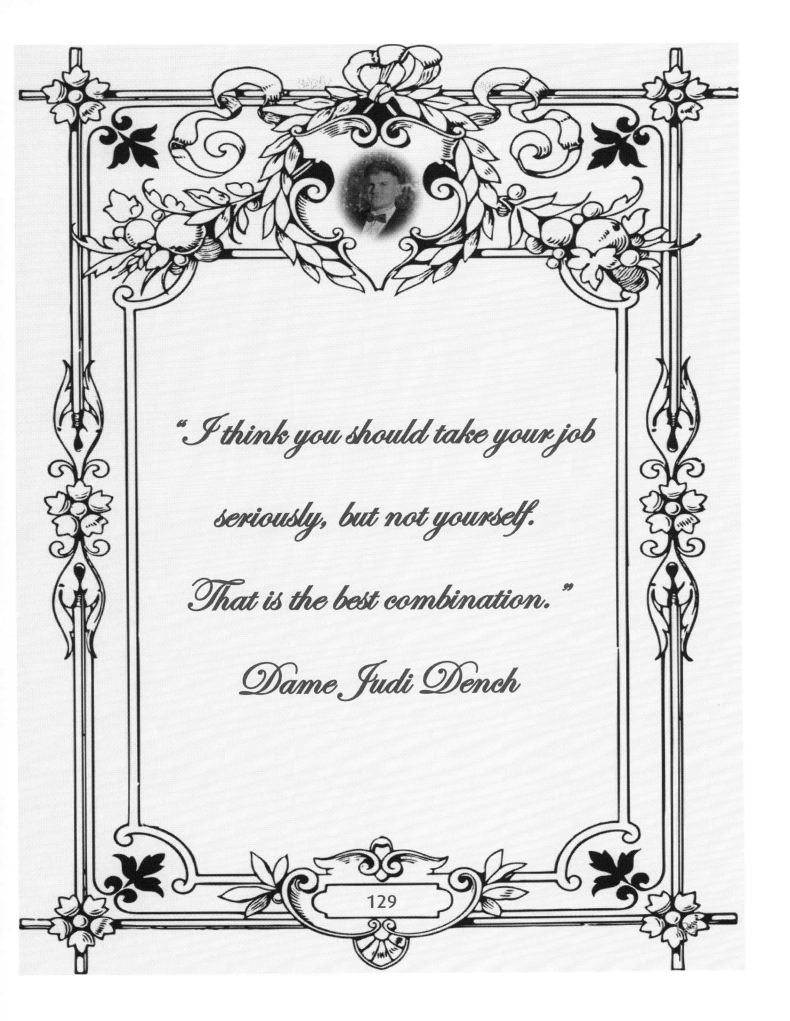

"I think you should take your job

seriously, but not yourself.

That is the best combination."

Dame Judi Dench

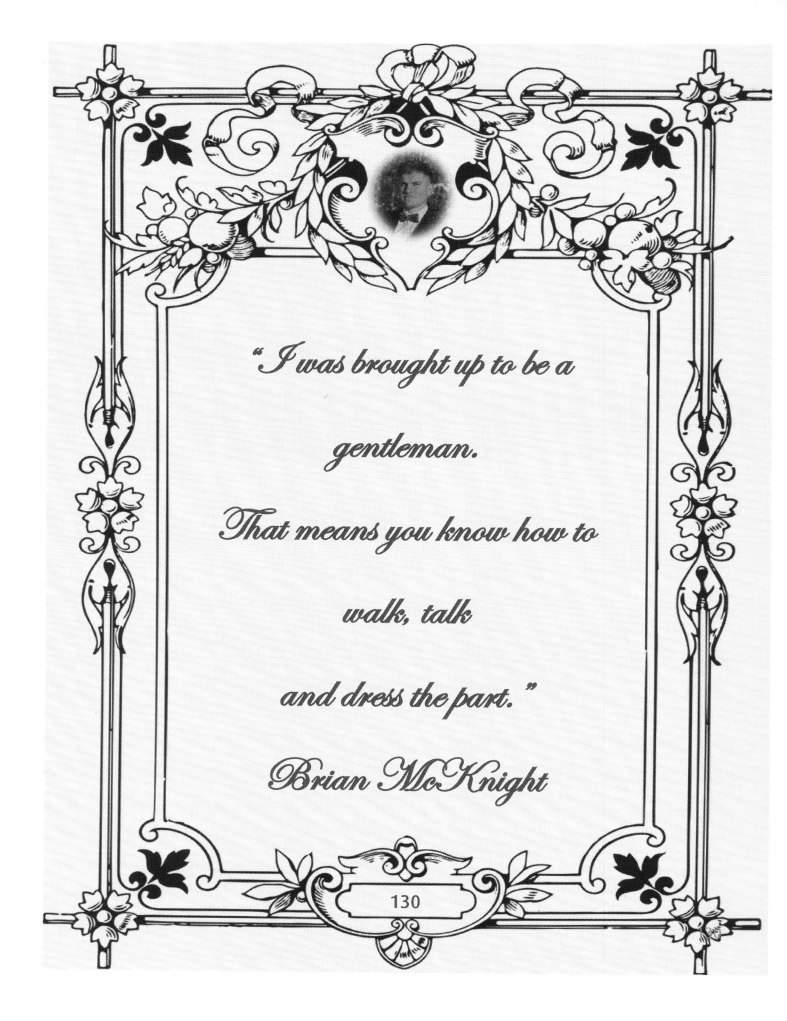

"I was brought up to be a

gentleman.

That means you know how to

walk, talk

and dress the part."

Brian McKnight

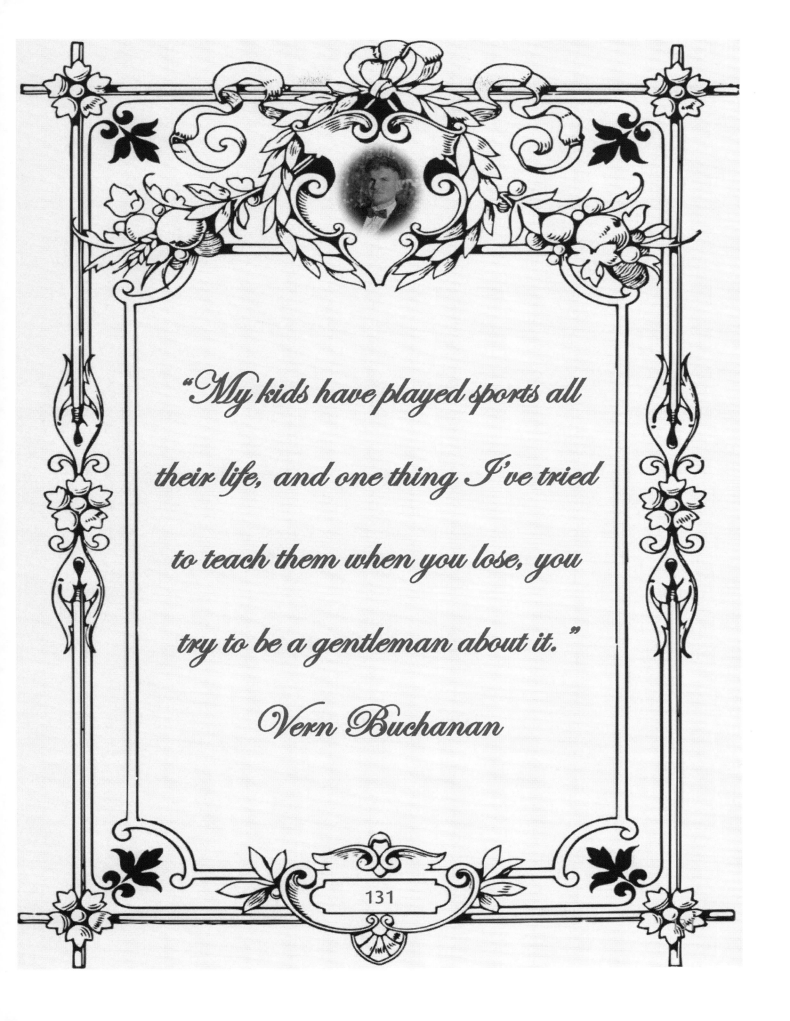

"My kids have played sports all their life, and one thing I've tried to teach them when you lose, you try to be a gentleman about it."

Vern Buchanan

131

"*Listening is an art that*

requires attention over talent,

spirit over ego,

others over self."

Dean Jackson

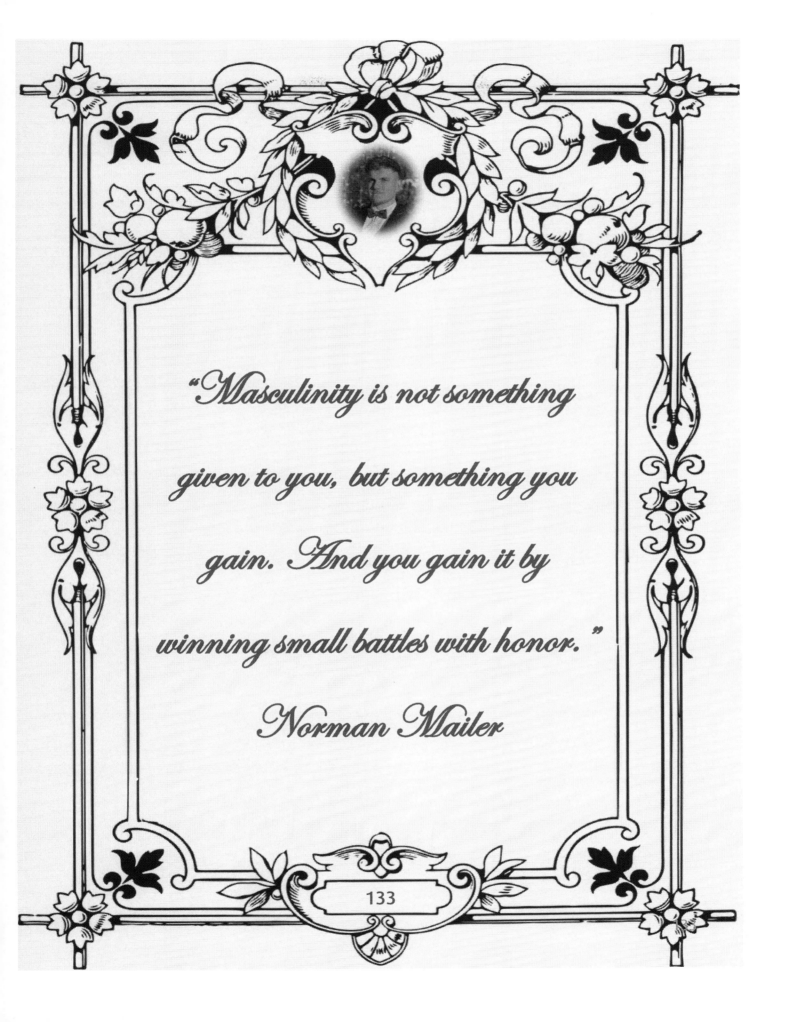

"Masculinity is not something given to you, but something you gain. And you gain it by winning small battles with honor."

Norman Mailer

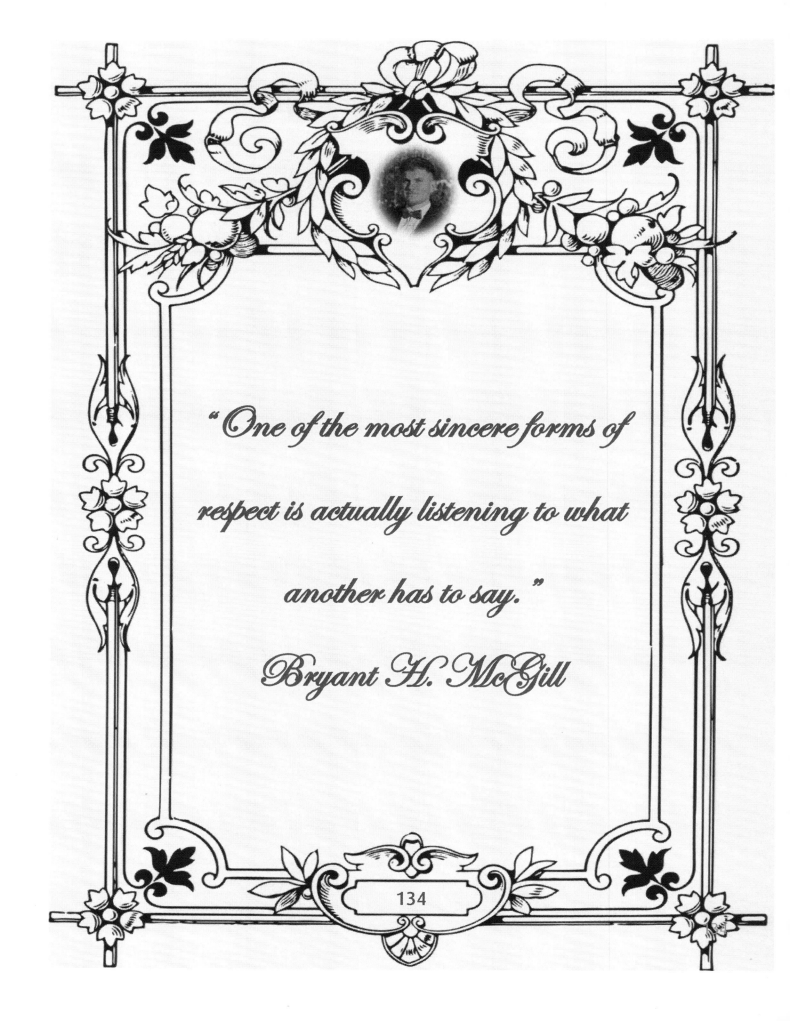

"One of the most sincere forms of

respect is actually listening to what

another has to say."

Bryant H. McGill

"Respect for ourselves guides our morals, respect for others guides our manners."

Laurence Sterne

"The very first thing you learn if

you're a gentleman is that you

never compare one

woman to another.

That's the way of all death."

Patrick Macnee

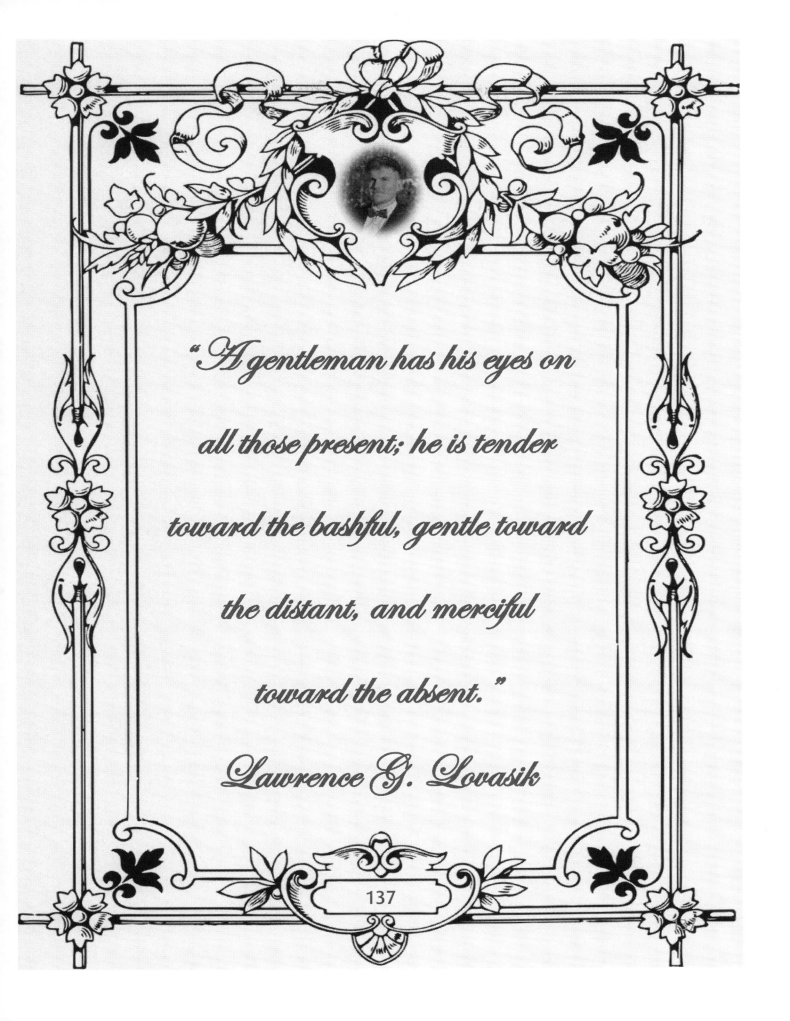

"A gentleman has his eyes on all those present; he is tender toward the bashful, gentle toward the distant, and merciful toward the absent."

Lawrence G. Lovasik

137

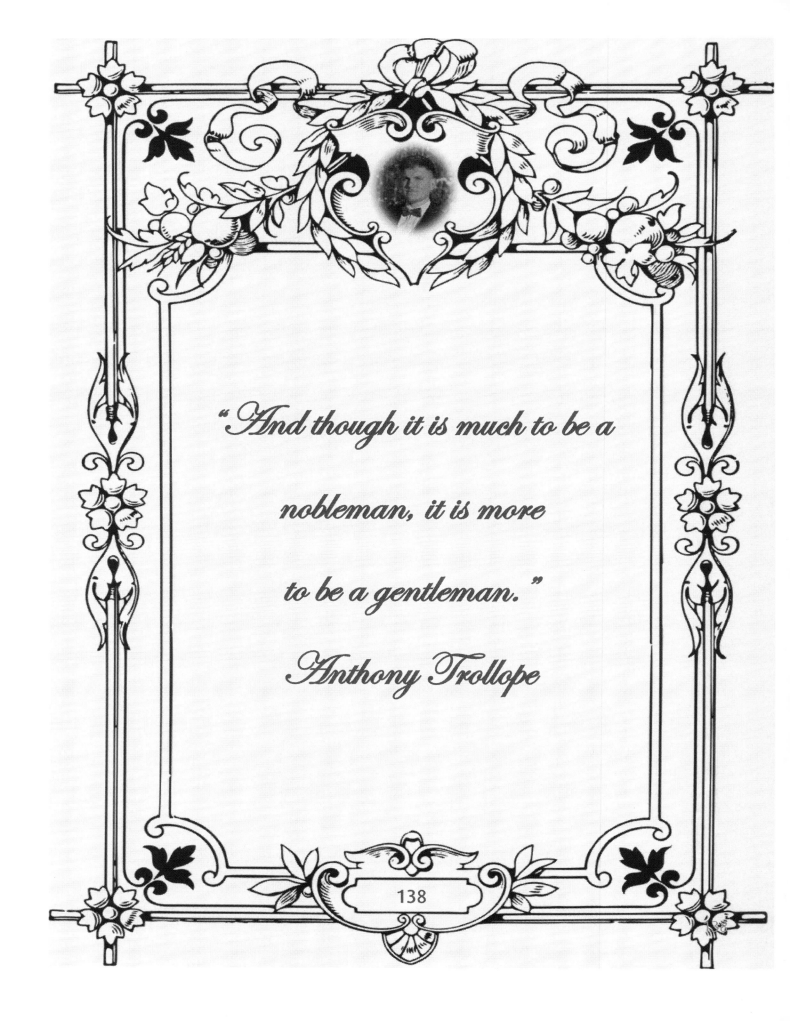

"And though it is much to be a

nobleman, it is more

to be a gentleman."

Anthony Trollope

"My formula for living is quite simple. I get up in the morning and I go to bed at night. In between, I occupy myself as best I can."

Cary Grant

"Well, I like to do some things

the old-fashioned way."

James Bond

140

"Do not pray for easy lives,

pray to be stronger men."

John F. Kennedy

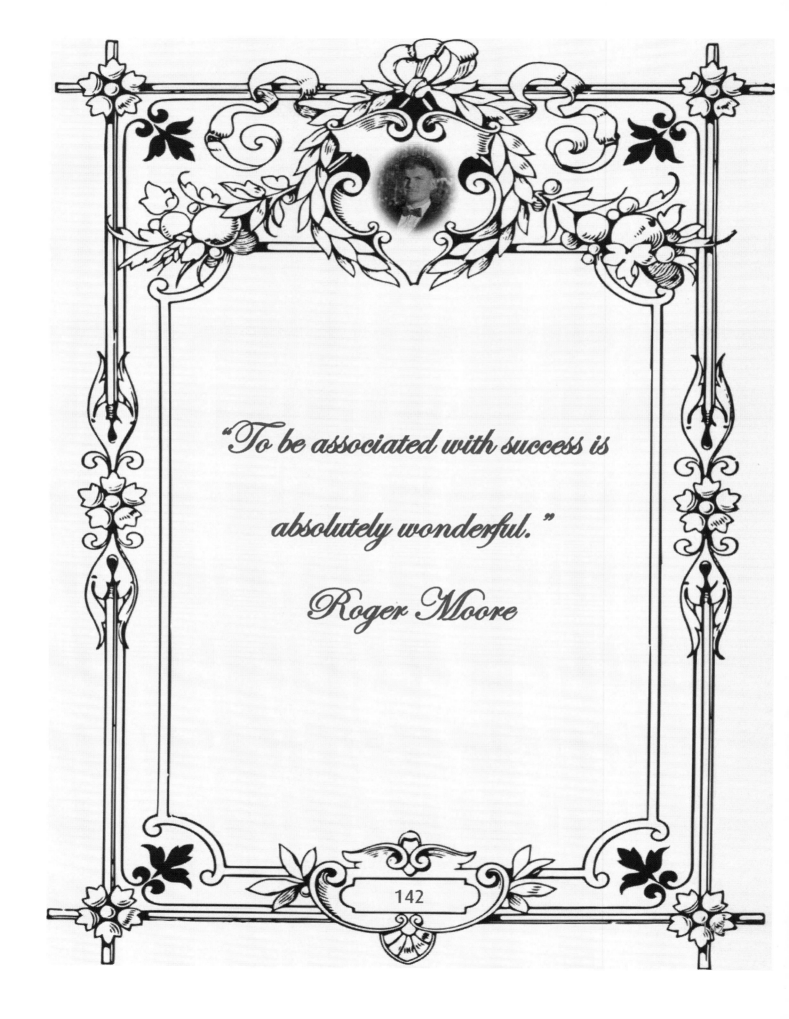

"To be associated with success is

absolutely wonderful."

Roger Moore

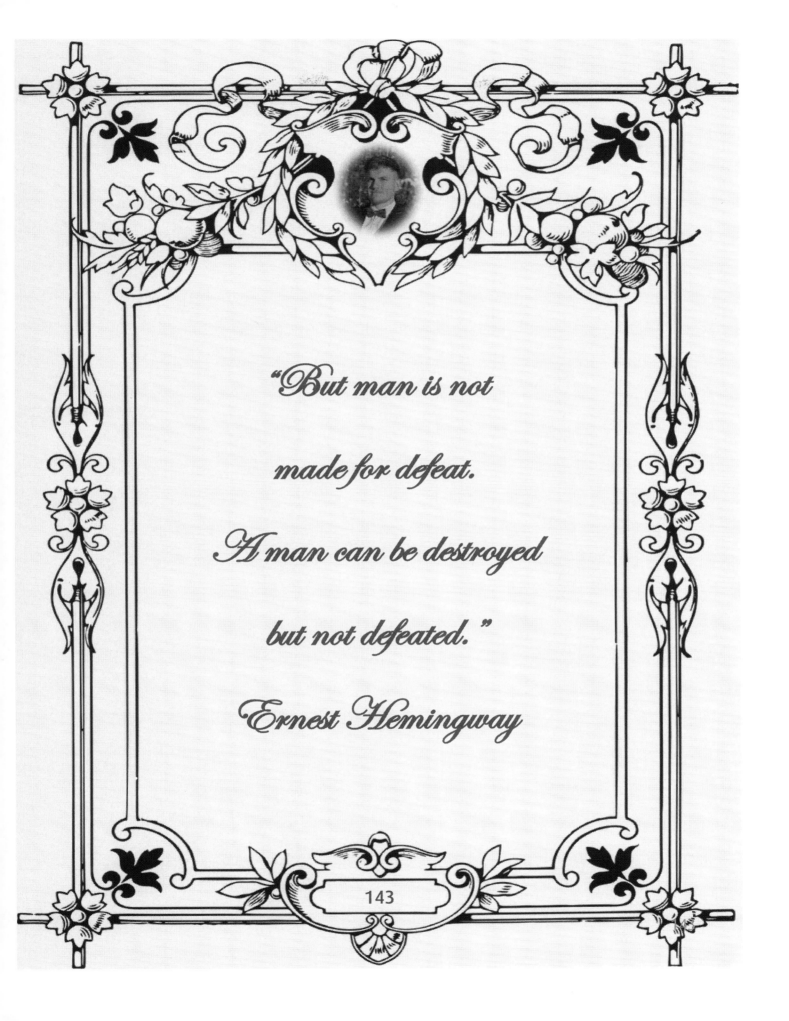

"But man is not

made for defeat.

A man can be destroyed

but not defeated."

Ernest Hemingway

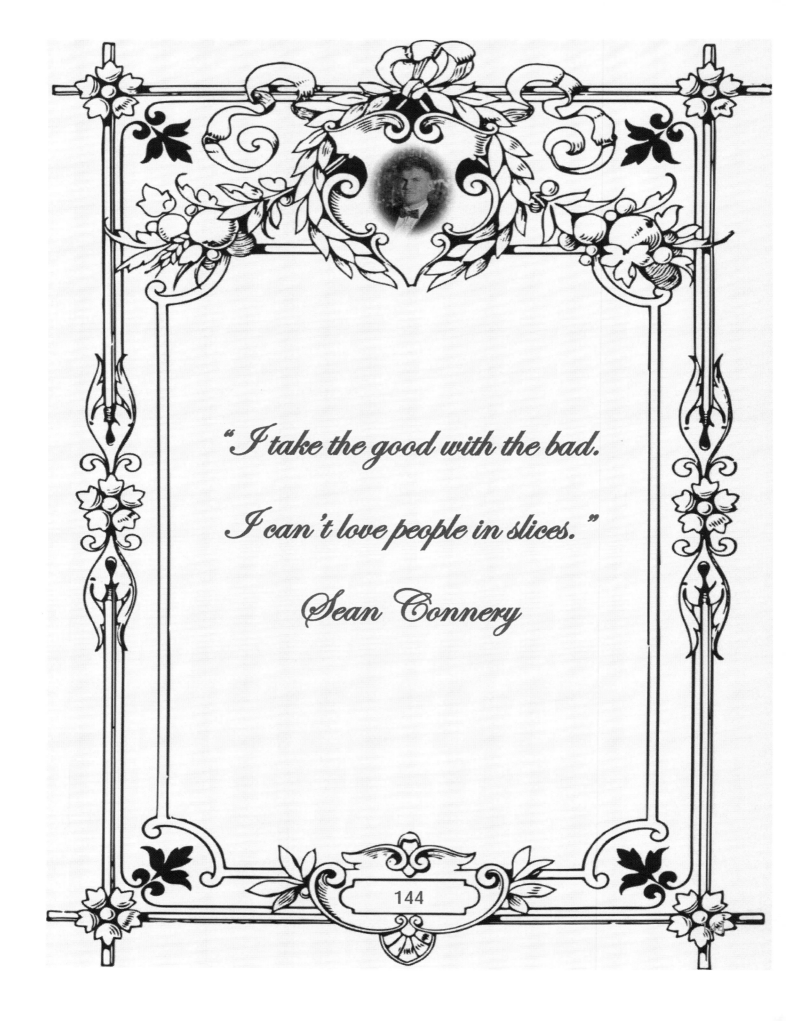

"I take the good with the bad.

I can't love people in slices."

Sean Connery

144

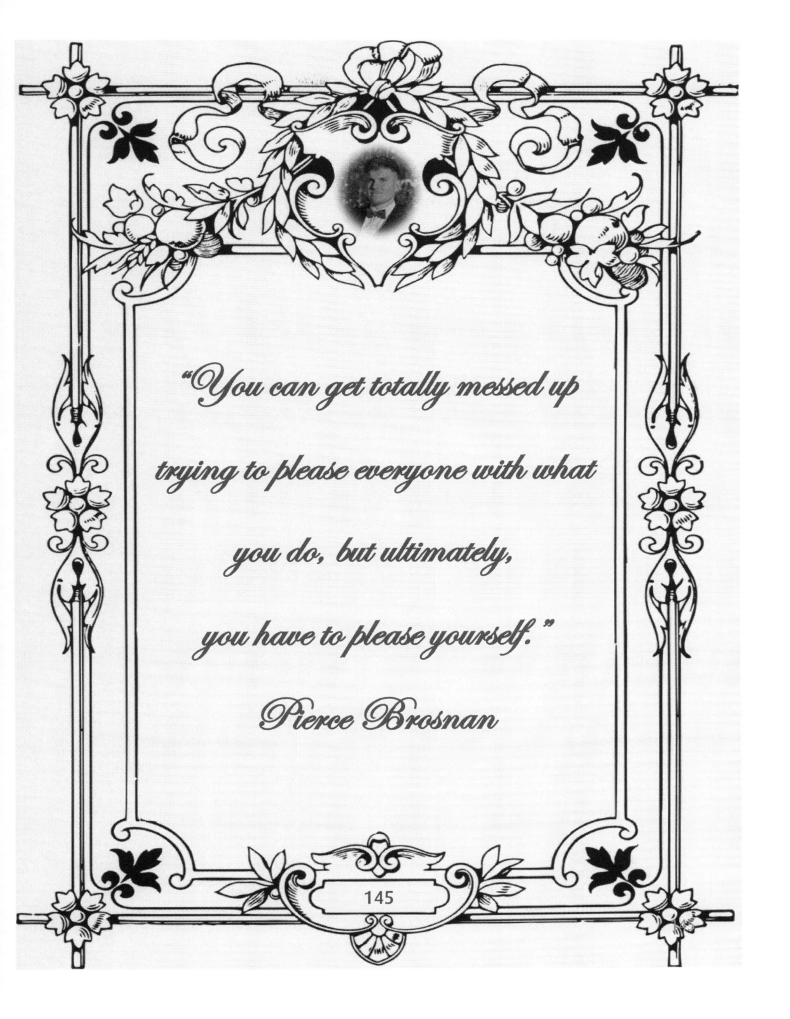

"You can get totally messed up

trying to please everyone with what

you do, but ultimately,

you have to please yourself."

Pierce Brosnan

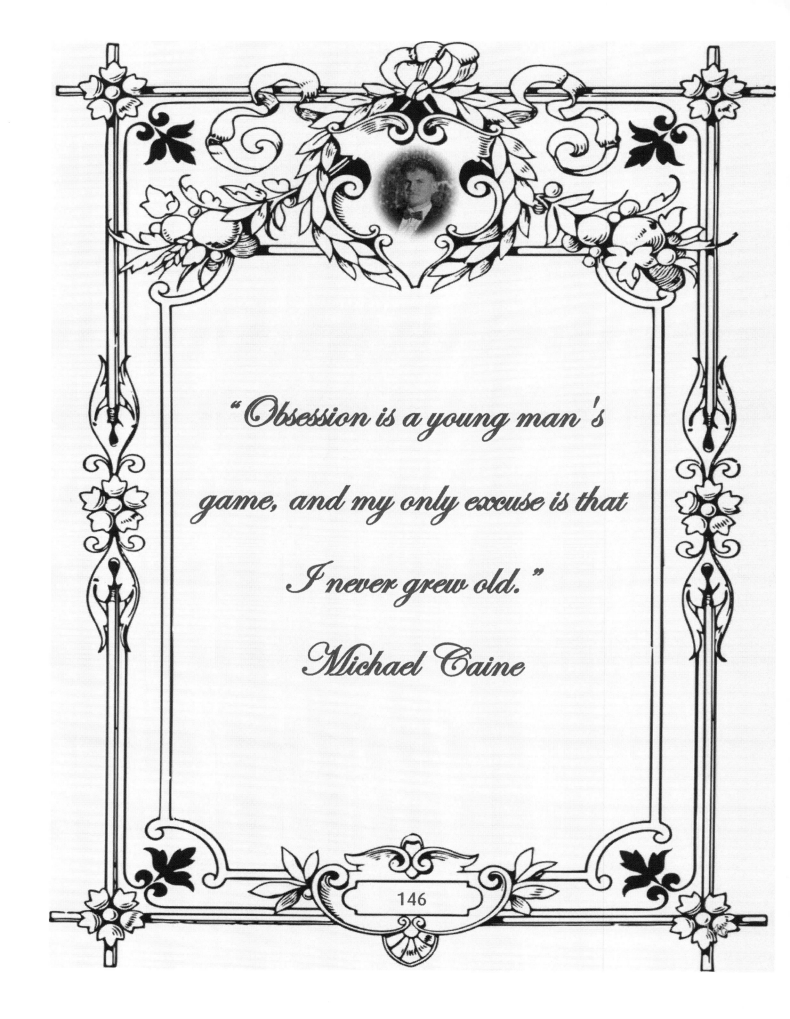

"*Obsession is a young man's game, and my only excuse is that I never grew old.*"

Michael Caine

"*It is necessary to relax your muscles when you can. Relaxing your brain is fatal.*"

Stirling Moss

"As human beings, we suffer from an innate tendency to jump to conclusions, to judge people too quickly, and to pronounce them failures or heroes without due consideration."

Charles, Prince of Wales

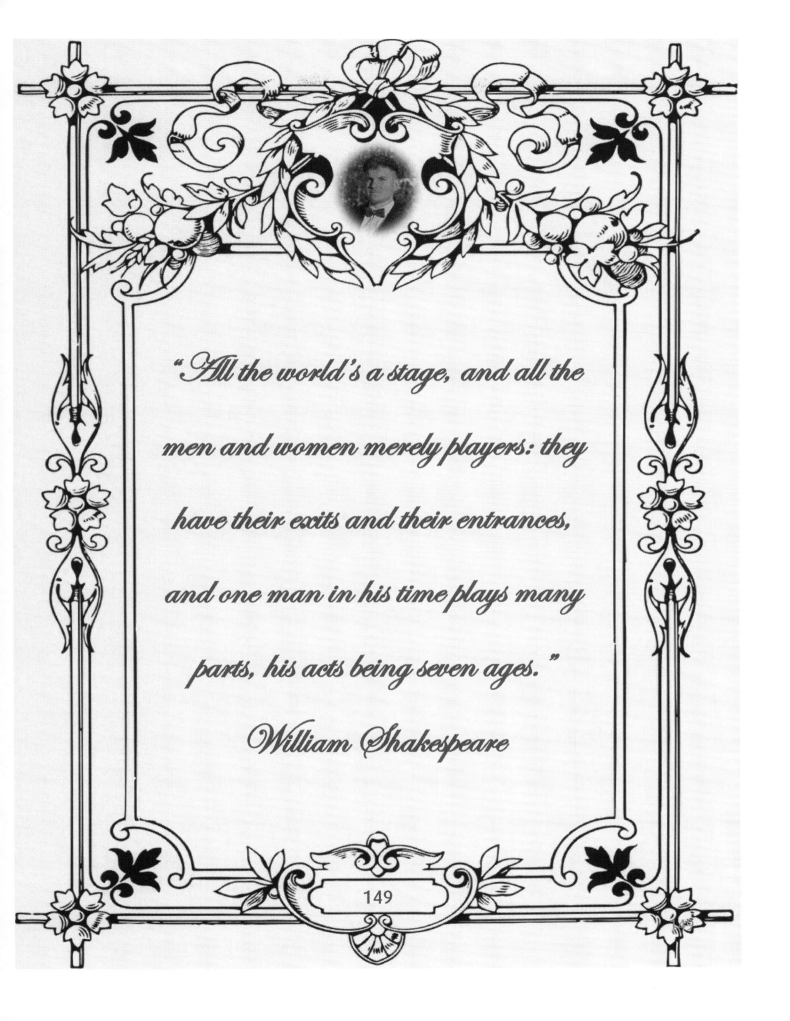

"All the world's a stage, and all the men and women merely players: they have their exits and their entrances, and one man in his time plays many parts, his acts being seven ages."

William Shakespeare

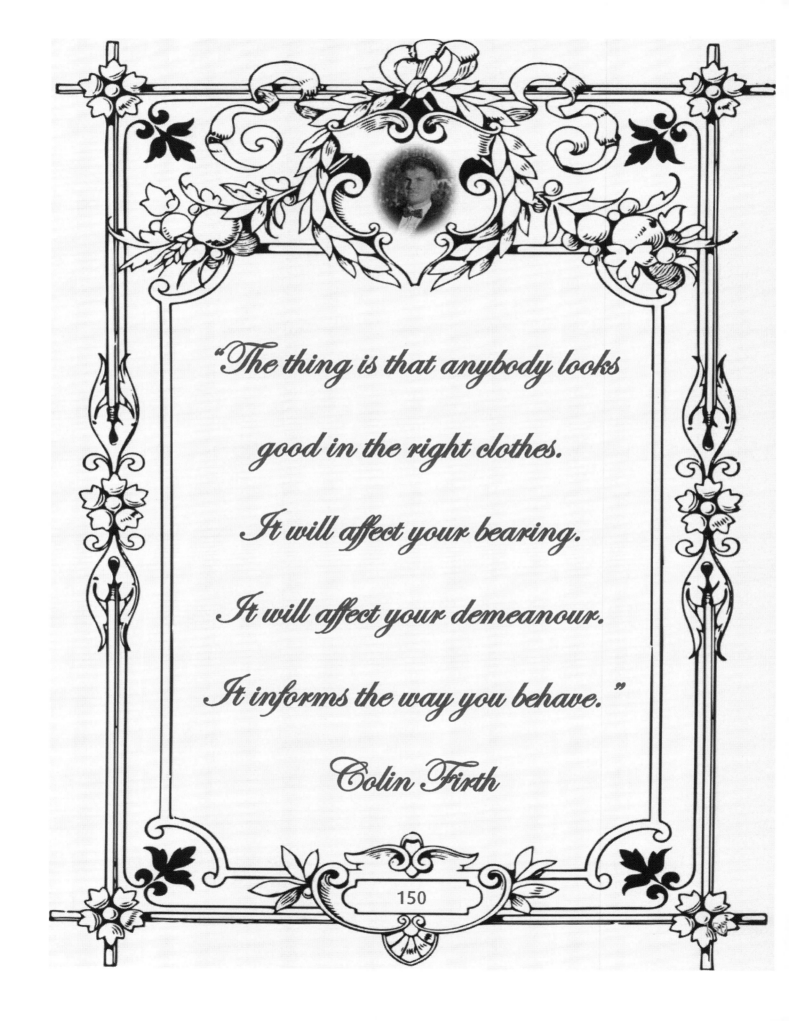

"The thing is that anybody looks

good in the right clothes.

It will affect your bearing.

It will affect your demeanour.

It informs the way you behave."

Colin Firth

"There's no way around hard work. Embrace it. You have to put in the hours because there's always something which you can improve."

Roger Federer

151

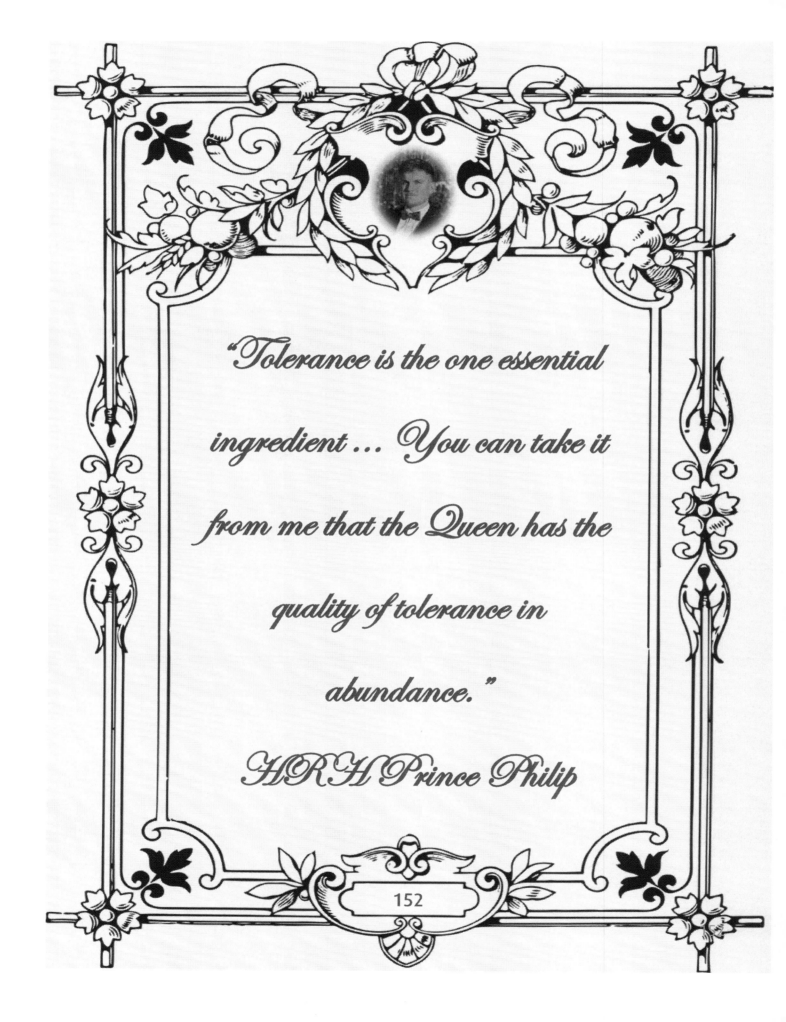

"Tolerance is the one essential ingredient ... You can take it from me that the Queen has the quality of tolerance in abundance."

HRH Prince Philip

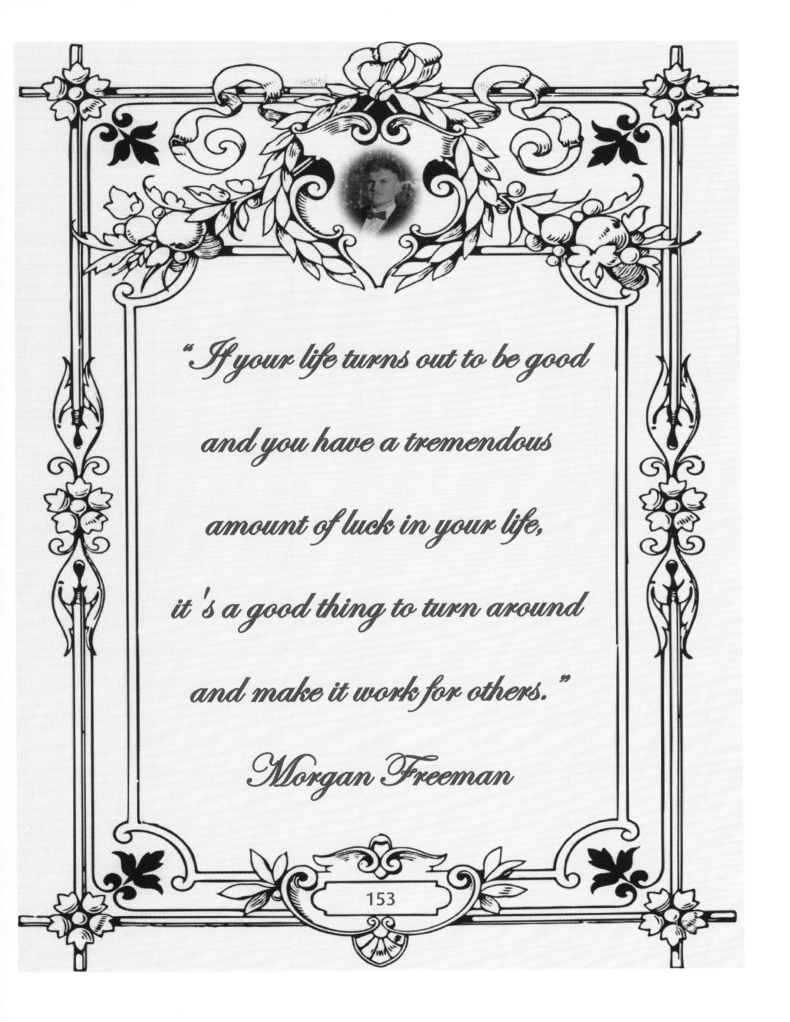

"If your life turns out to be good

and you have a tremendous

amount of luck in your life,

it's a good thing to turn around

and make it work for others."

Morgan Freeman

153

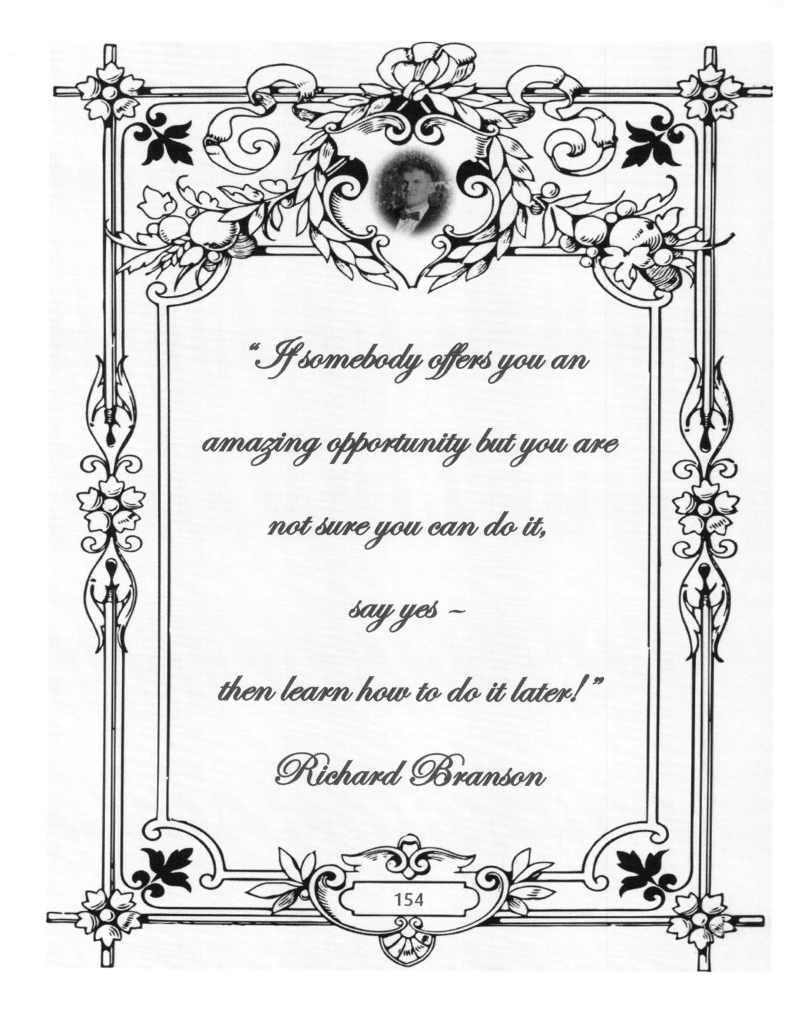

"If somebody offers you an

amazing opportunity but you are

not sure you can do it,

say yes –

then learn how to do it later!"

Richard Branson

154

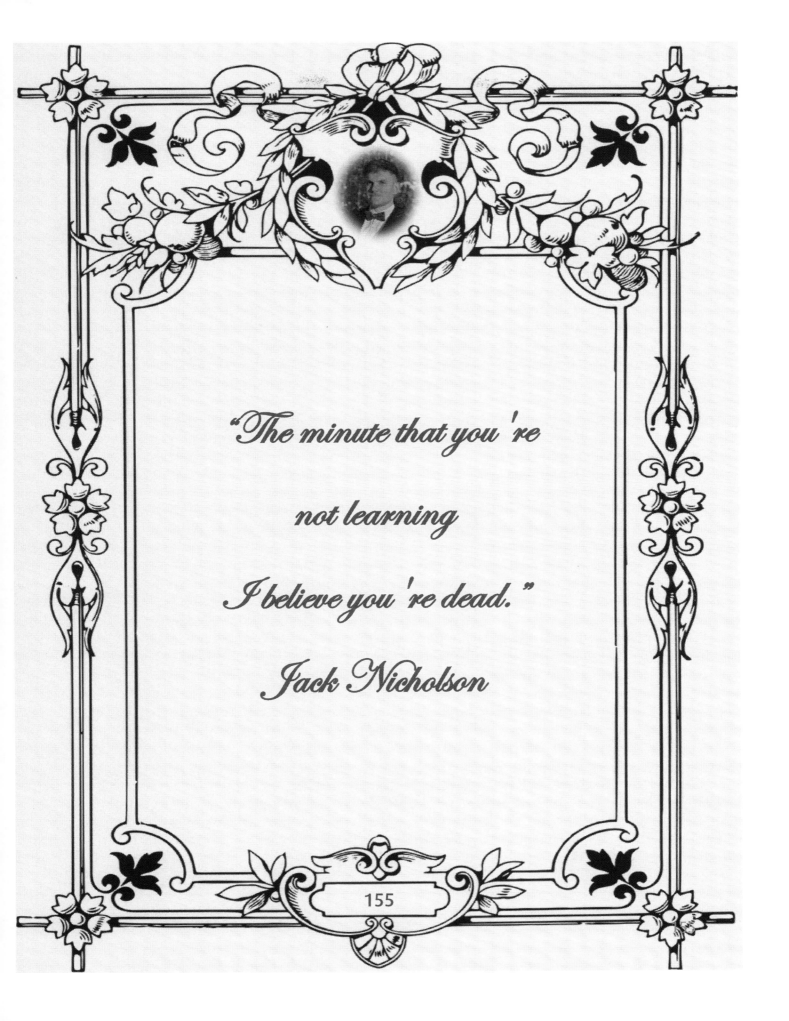

"The minute that you're

not learning

I believe you're dead."

Jack Nicholson

155

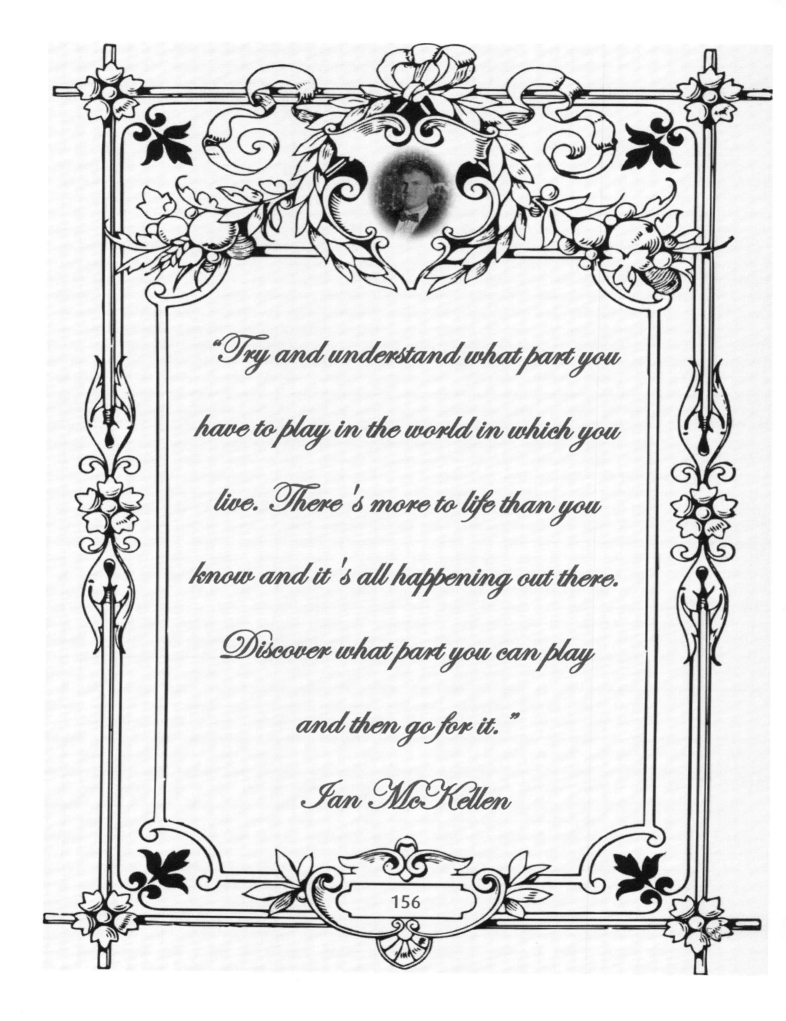

"Try and understand what part you have to play in the world in which you live. There's more to life than you know and it's all happening out there. Discover what part you can play and then go for it."

Ian McKellen

156

"*If I stopped having passion,*

I'd be done."

Tom Hanks

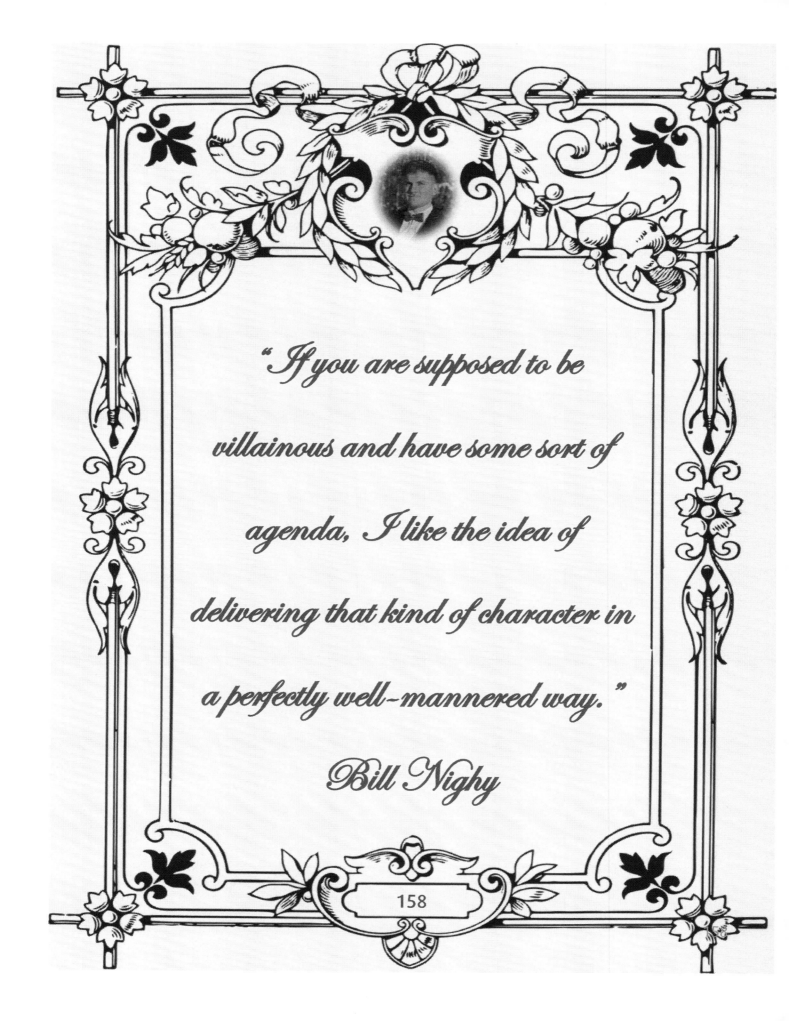

"If you are supposed to be villainous and have some sort of agenda, I like the idea of delivering that kind of character in a perfectly well-mannered way."

Bill Nighy

"My only obligation

is to keep myself and

other people guessing."

Jude Law

"Built in 1928, designed by the Baglietto yard, Varazze, Italy. Nothing like it in the world. Rarer than rare.

It's not for sale."

Giancarlo Giannini

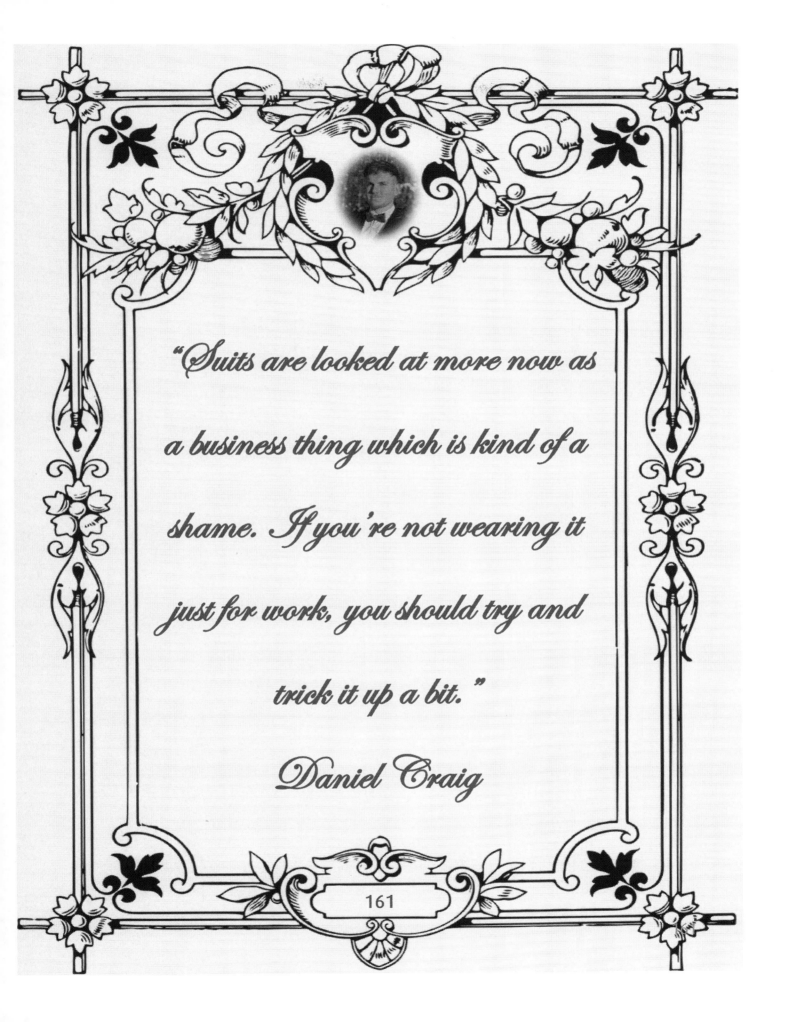

"Suits are looked at more now as a business thing which is kind of a shame. If you're not wearing it just for work, you should try and trick it up a bit."

Daniel Craig

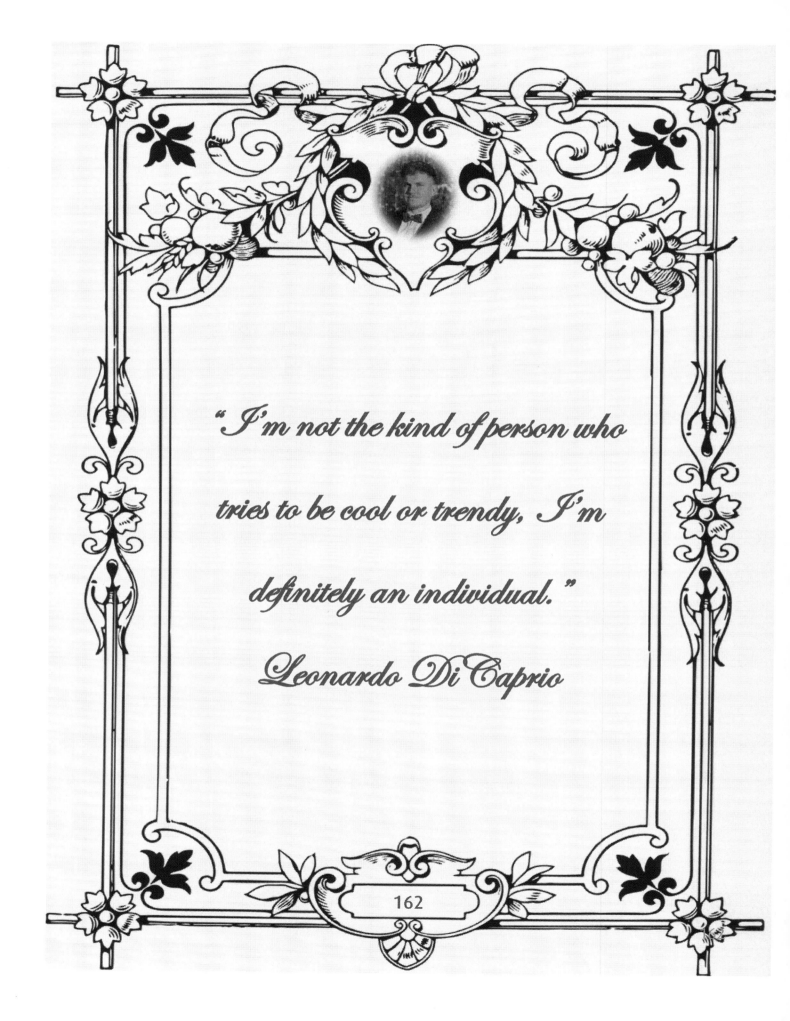

"*I'm not the kind of person who tries to be cool or trendy, I'm definitely an individual.*"

Leonardo Di Caprio

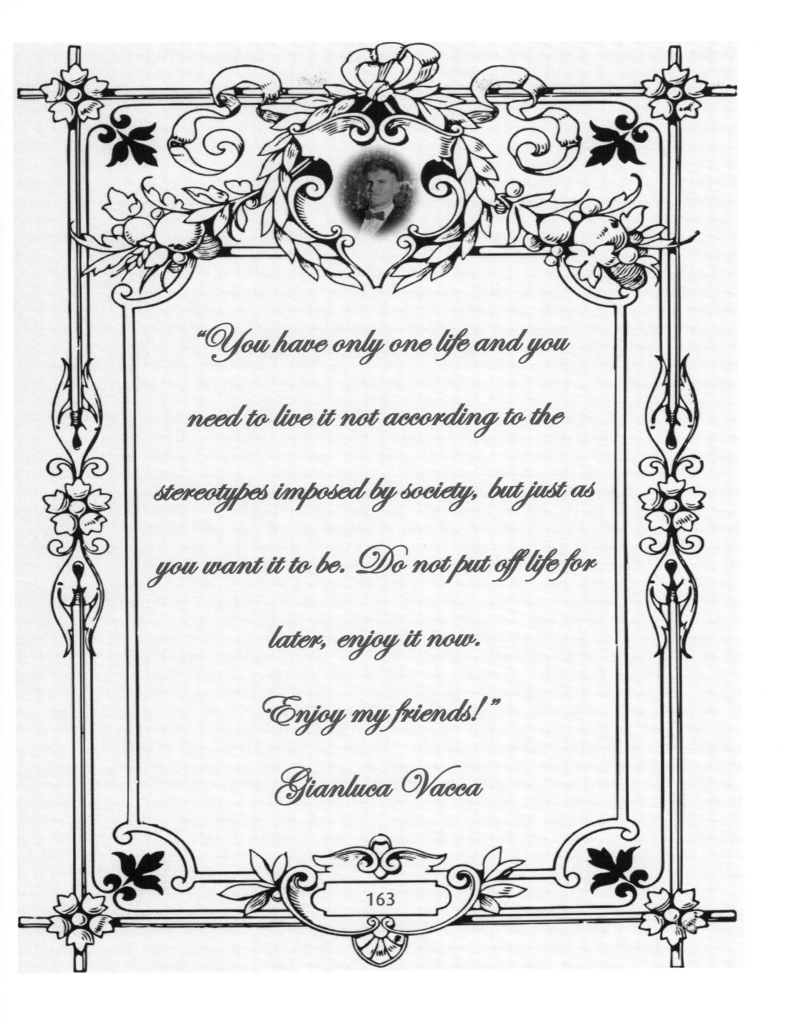

"You have only one life and you need to live it not according to the stereotypes imposed by society, but just as you want it to be. Do not put off life for later, enjoy it now. Enjoy my friends!"

Gianluca Vacca

163

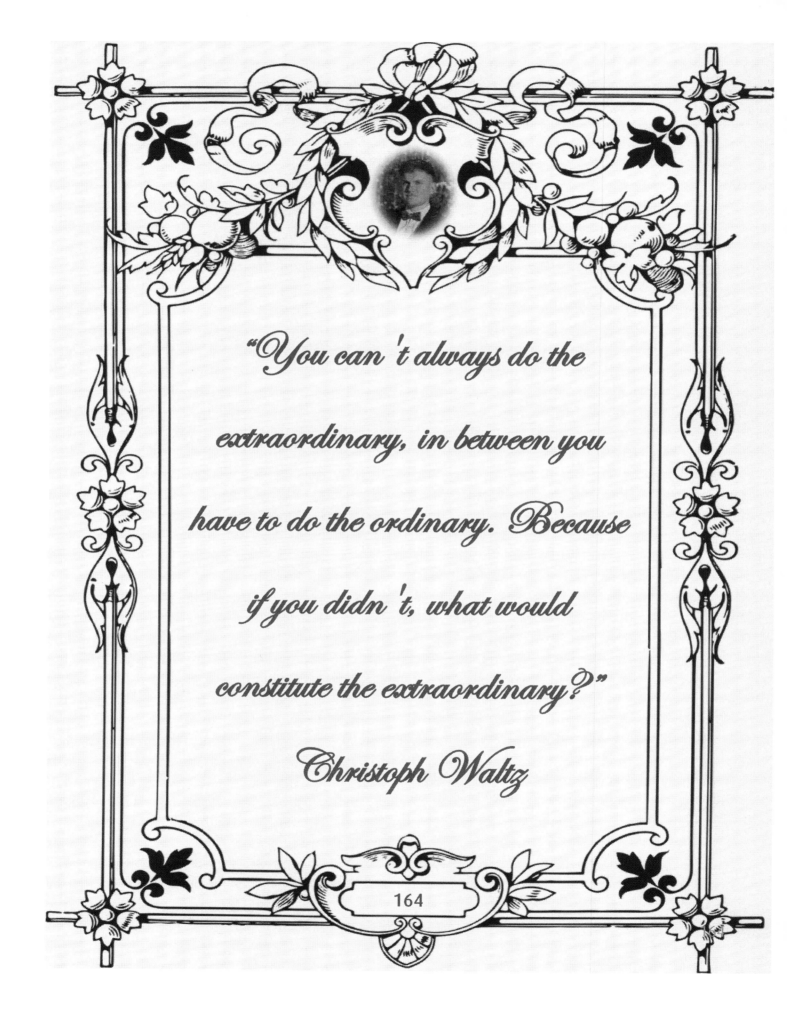

"You can't always do the extraordinary, in between you have to do the ordinary. Because if you didn't, what would constitute the extraordinary?"

Christoph Waltz

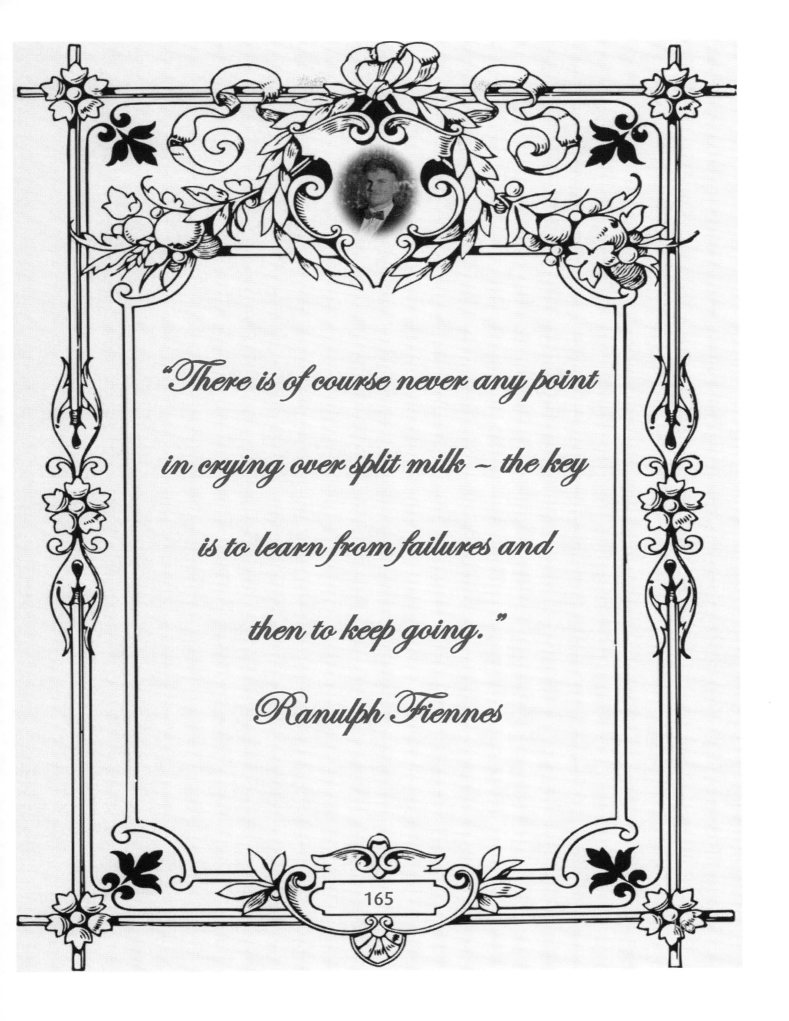

"There is of course never any point in crying over split milk ~ the key is to learn from failures and then to keep going."

Ranulph Fiennes

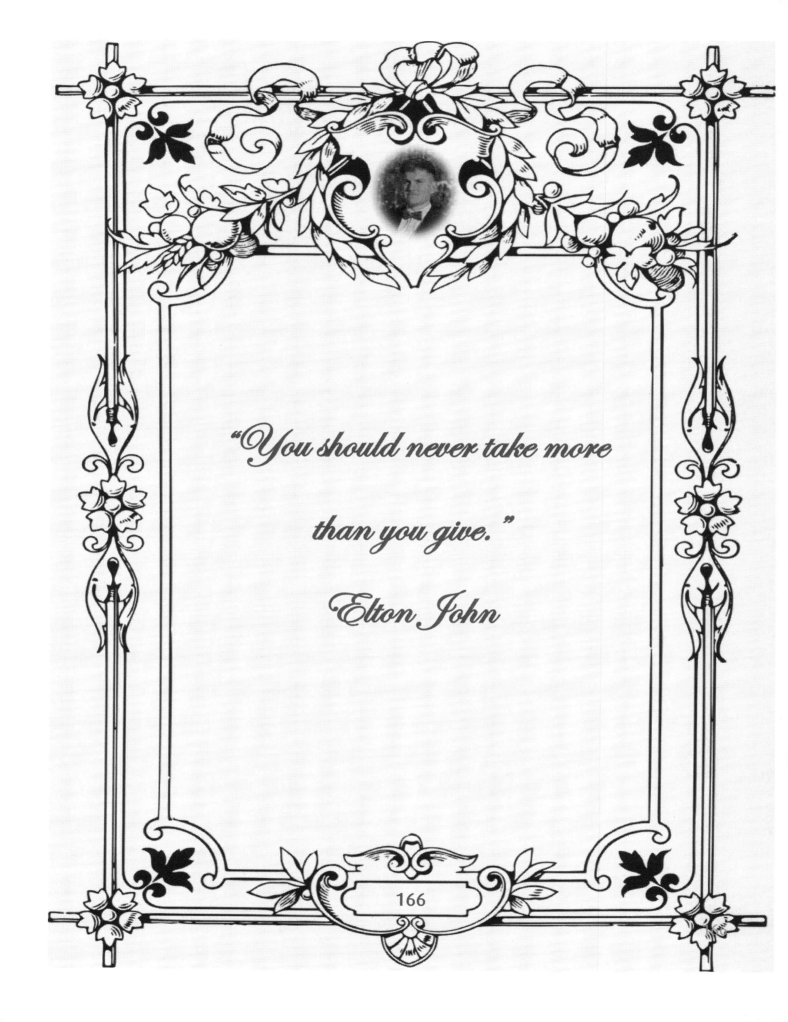

"You should never take more

than you give."

Elton John

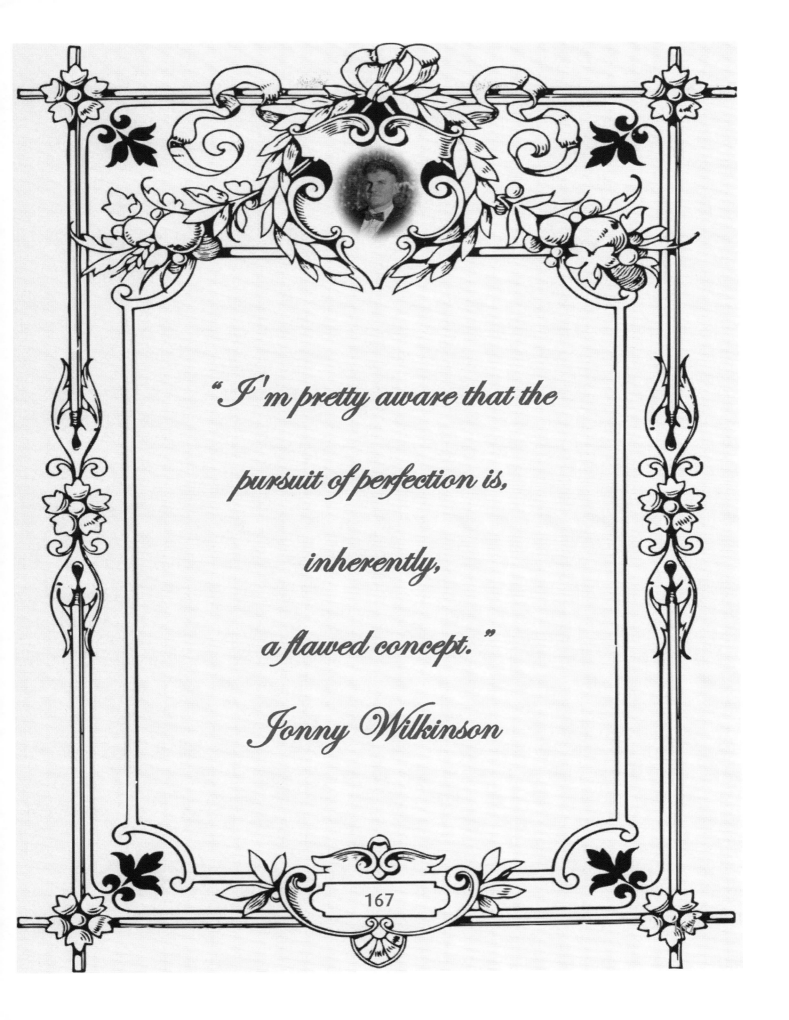

"I'm pretty aware that the

pursuit of perfection is,

inherently,

a flawed concept."

Jonny Wilkinson

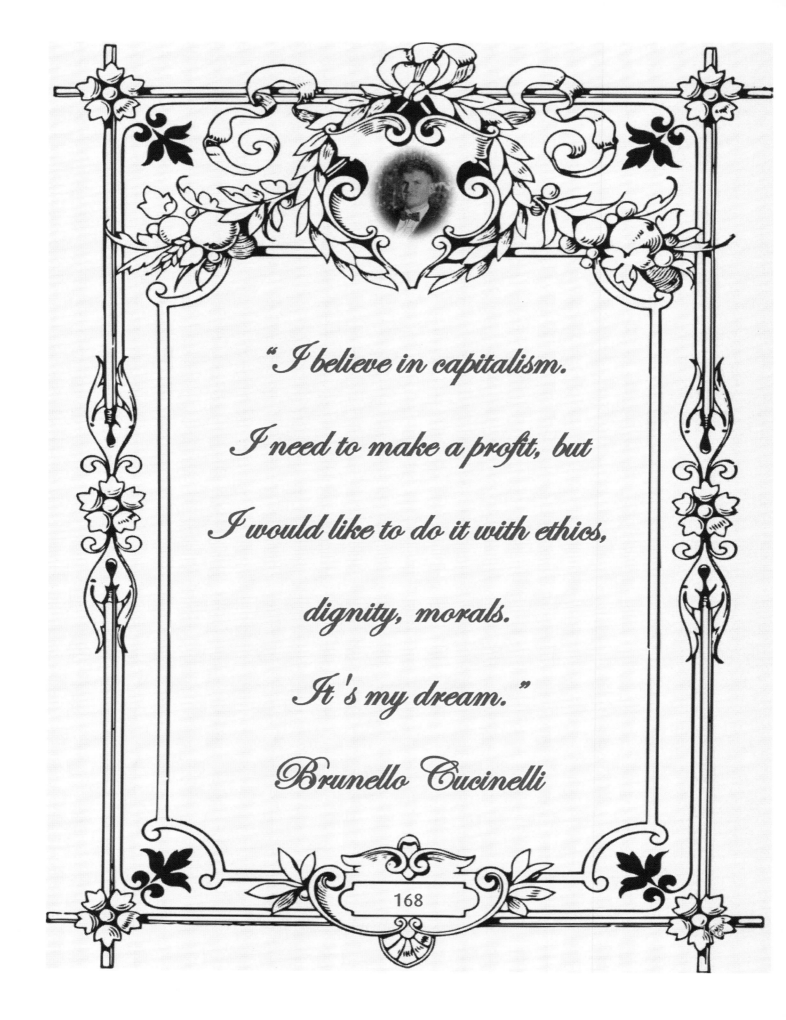

"I believe in capitalism.

I need to make a profit, but

I would like to do it with ethics,

dignity, morals.

It's my dream."

Brunello Cucinelli

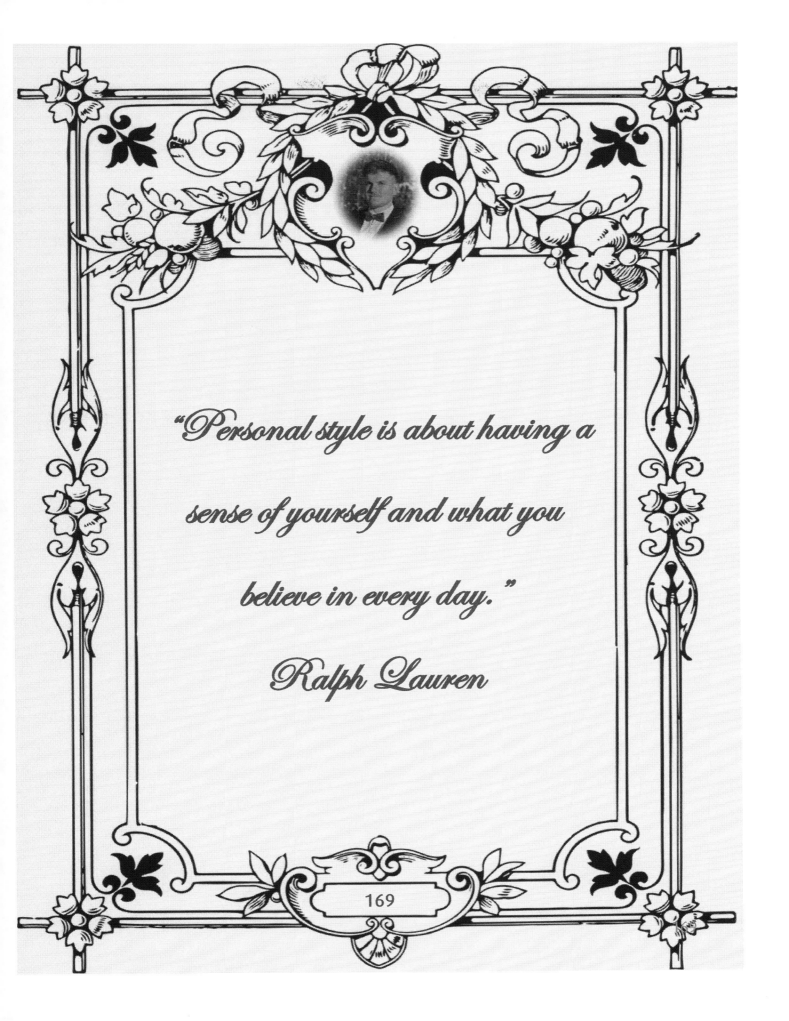

"Personal style is about having a

sense of yourself and what you

believe in every day."

Ralph Lauren

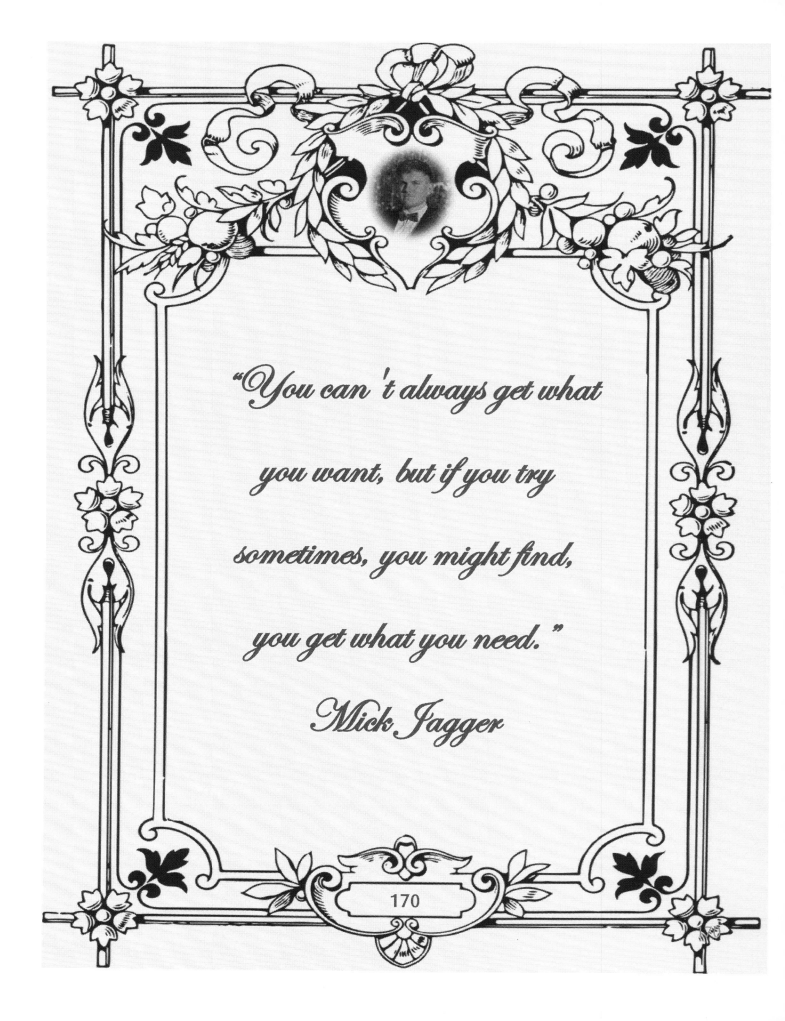

"You can't always get what

you want, but if you try

sometimes, you might find,

you get what you need."

Mick Jagger

"*If a man can bridge the gap*

between life and death,

if he can live on after he's dead,

then maybe he was a great man."

James Dean

171

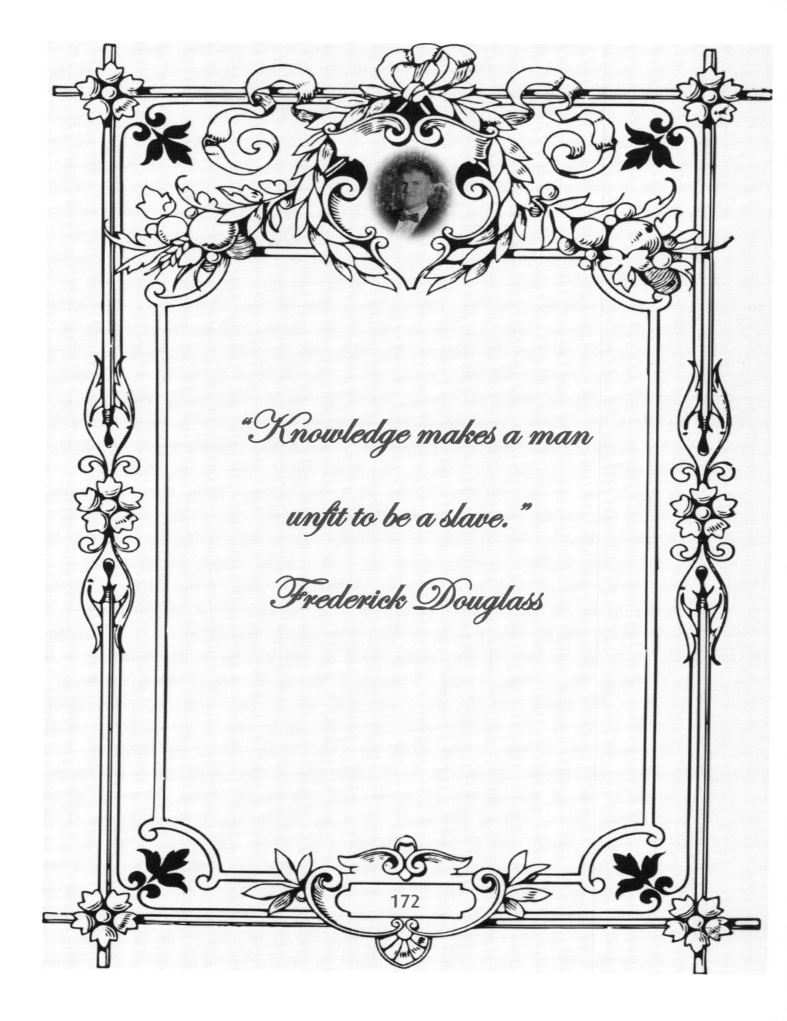

"*Knowledge makes a man unfit to be a slave.*"

Frederick Douglass

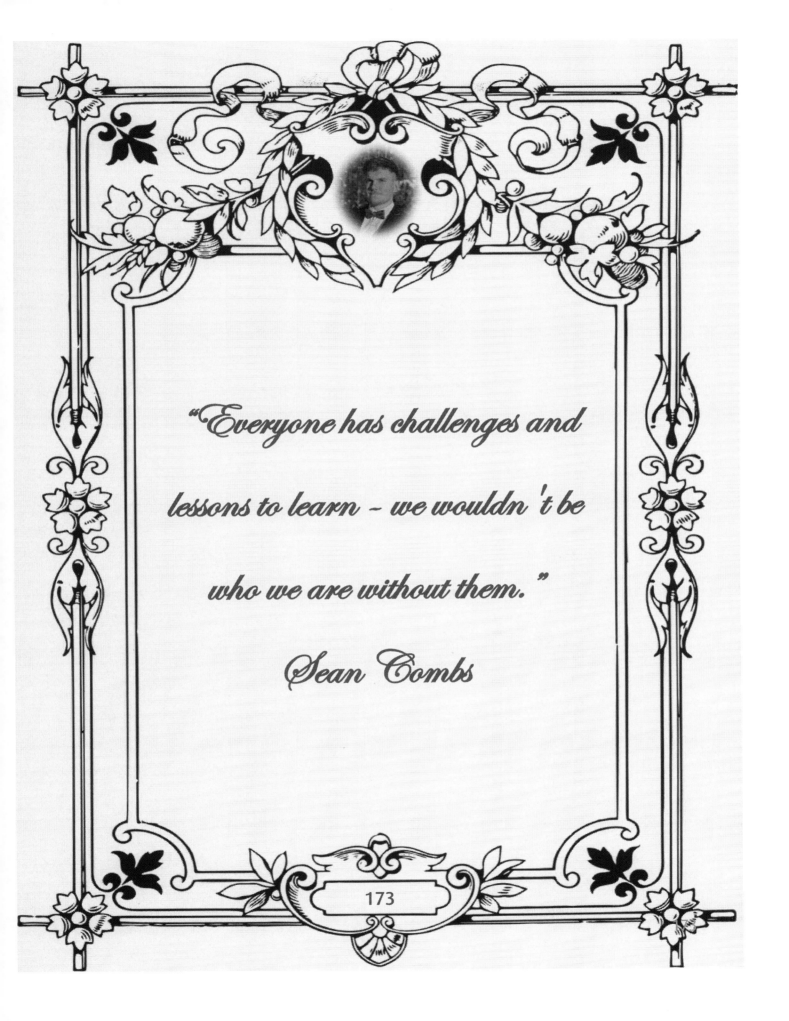

"Everyone has challenges and lessons to learn – we wouldn't be who we are without them."

Sean Combs

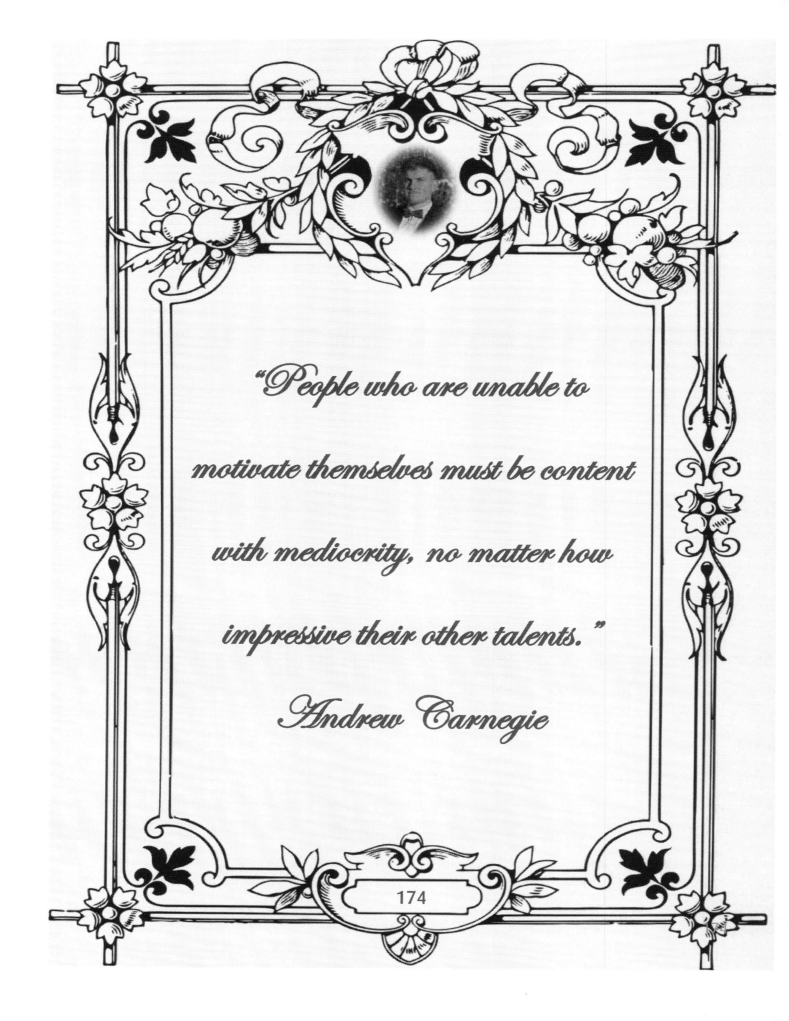

"People who are unable to motivate themselves must be content with mediocrity, no matter how impressive their other talents."

Andrew Carnegie

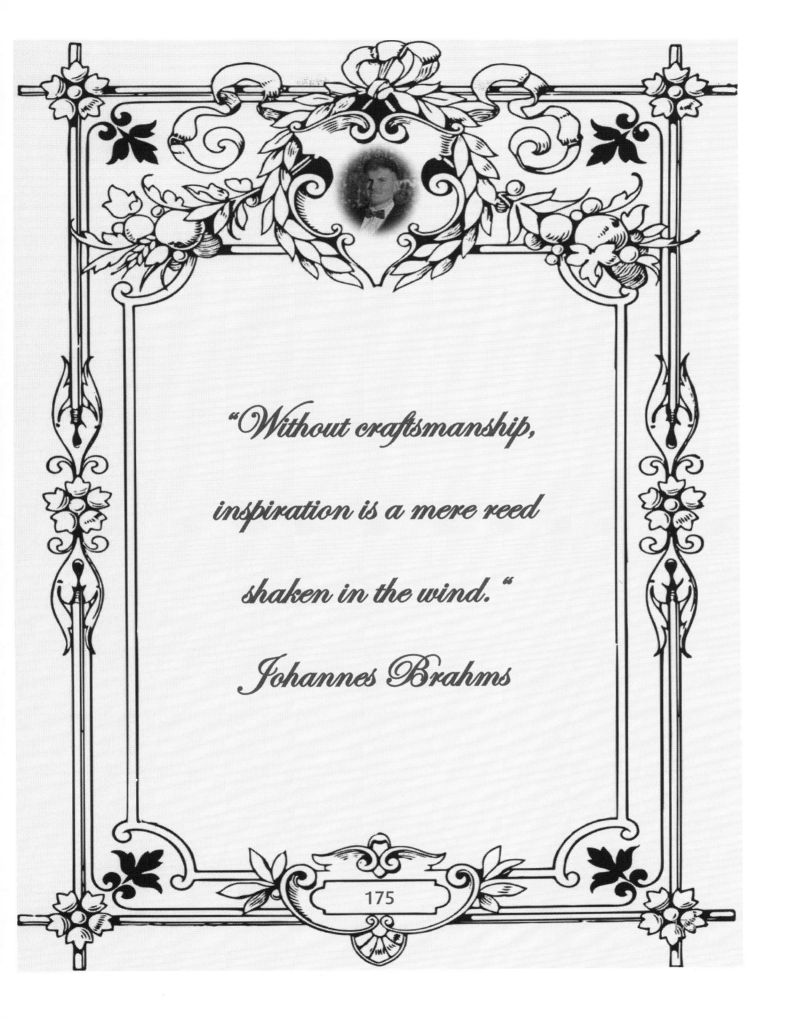

"Without craftsmanship,

inspiration is a mere reed

shaken in the wind."

Johannes Brahms

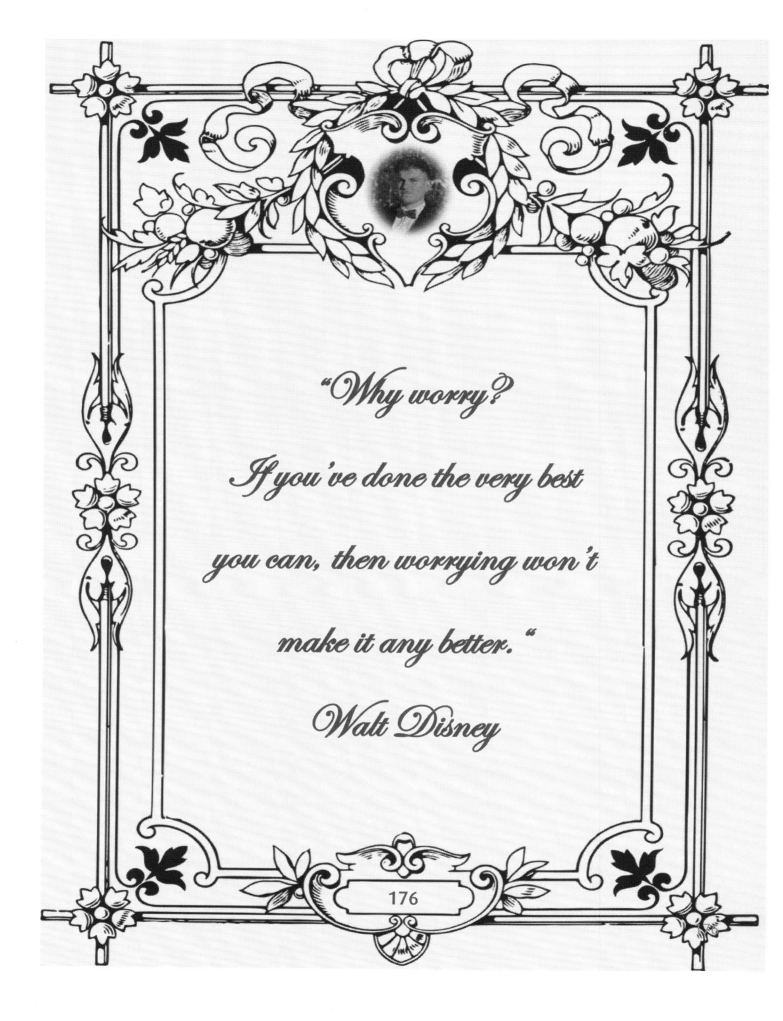

"Why worry?

If you've done the very best

you can, then worrying won't

make it any better."

Walt Disney

176

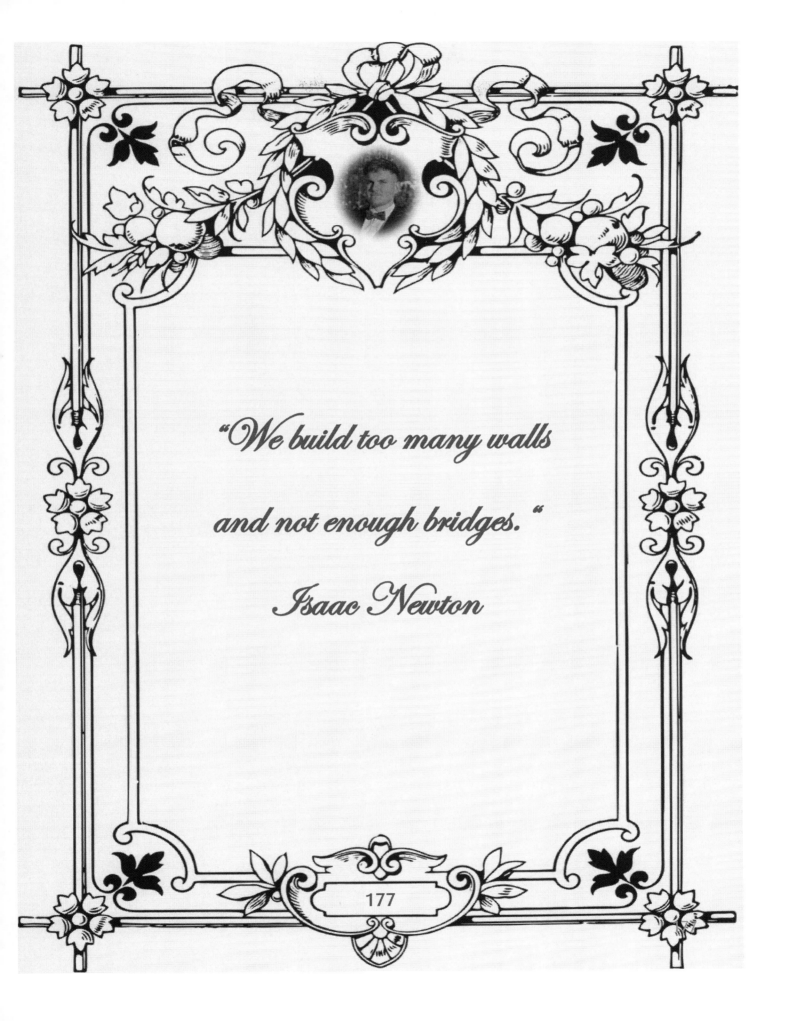

"We build too many walls

and not enough bridges."

Isaac Newton

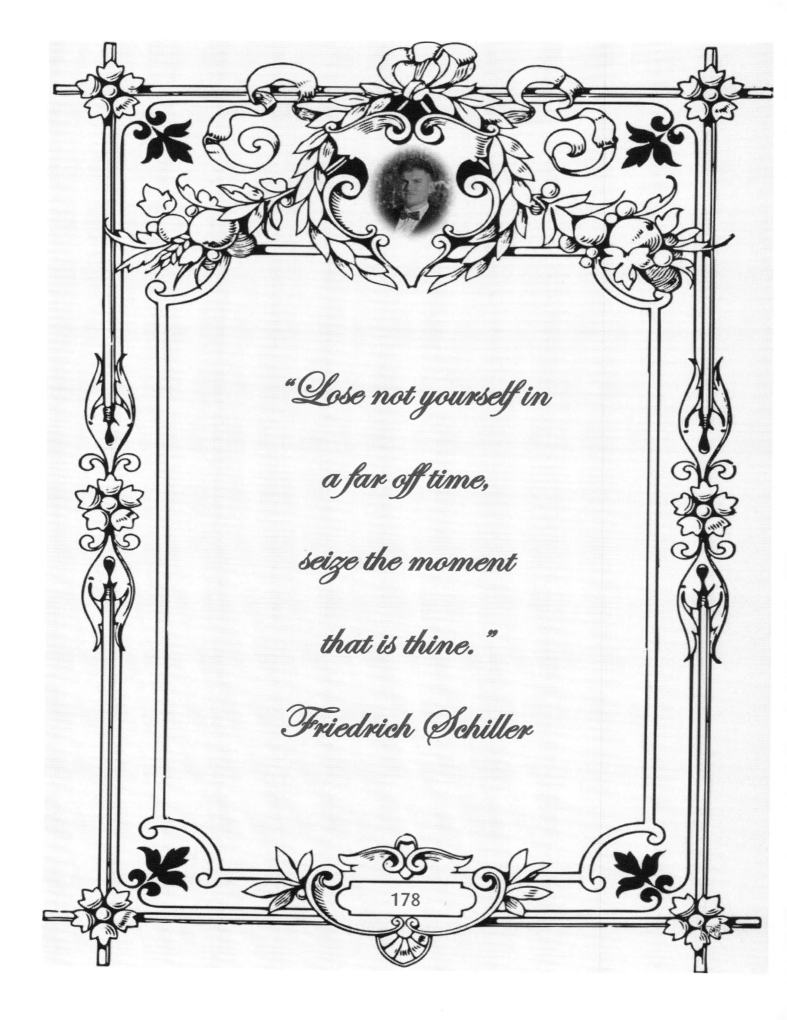

"Lose not yourself in

a far off time,

seize the moment

that is thine."

Friedrich Schiller

178

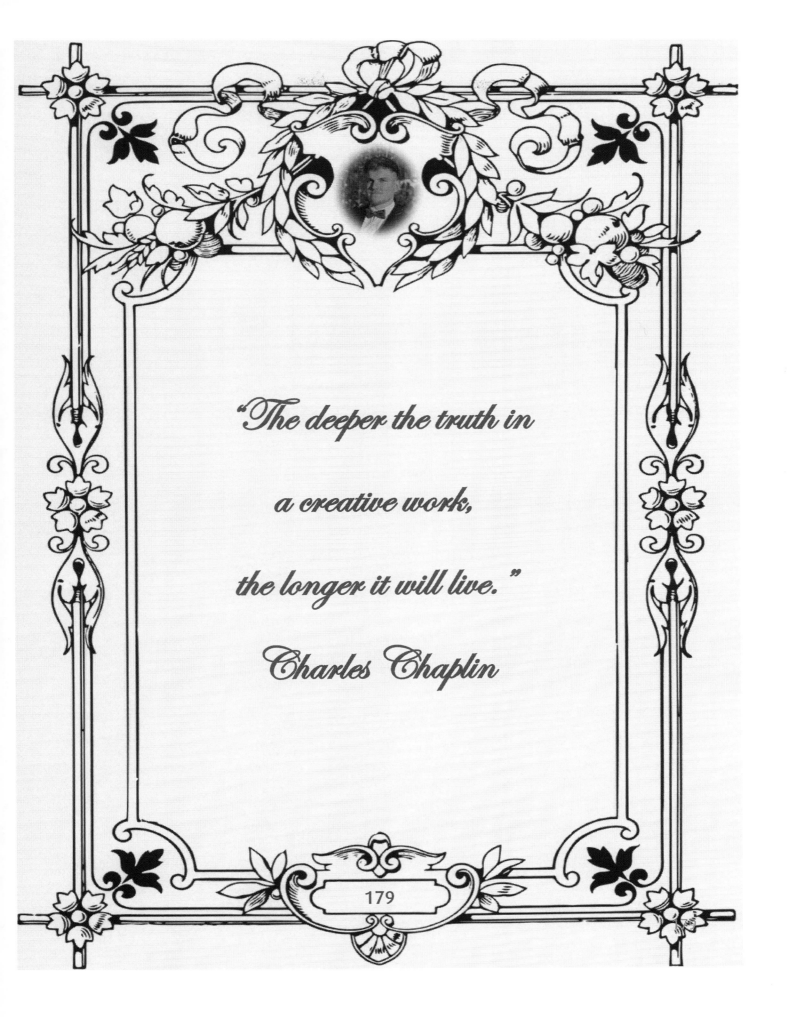

"The deeper the truth in

a creative work,

the longer it will live."

Charles Chaplin

"Cities,

like cats,

will reveal themselves

at night."

Rupert Brooke

180

"Maybe that's what life is…

a wink of the eye

and winking stars."

Jack Kerouac

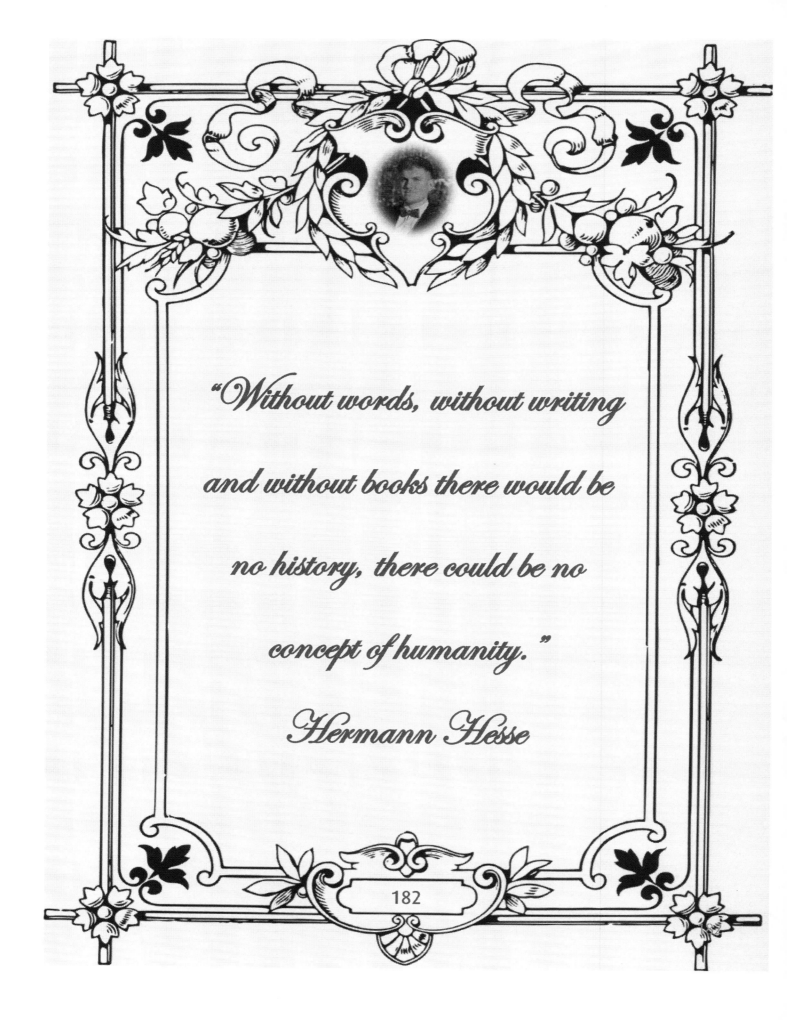

"Without words, without writing and without books there would be no history, there could be no concept of humanity."

Hermann Hesse

"Because it's there."

George Leigh Mallory

183

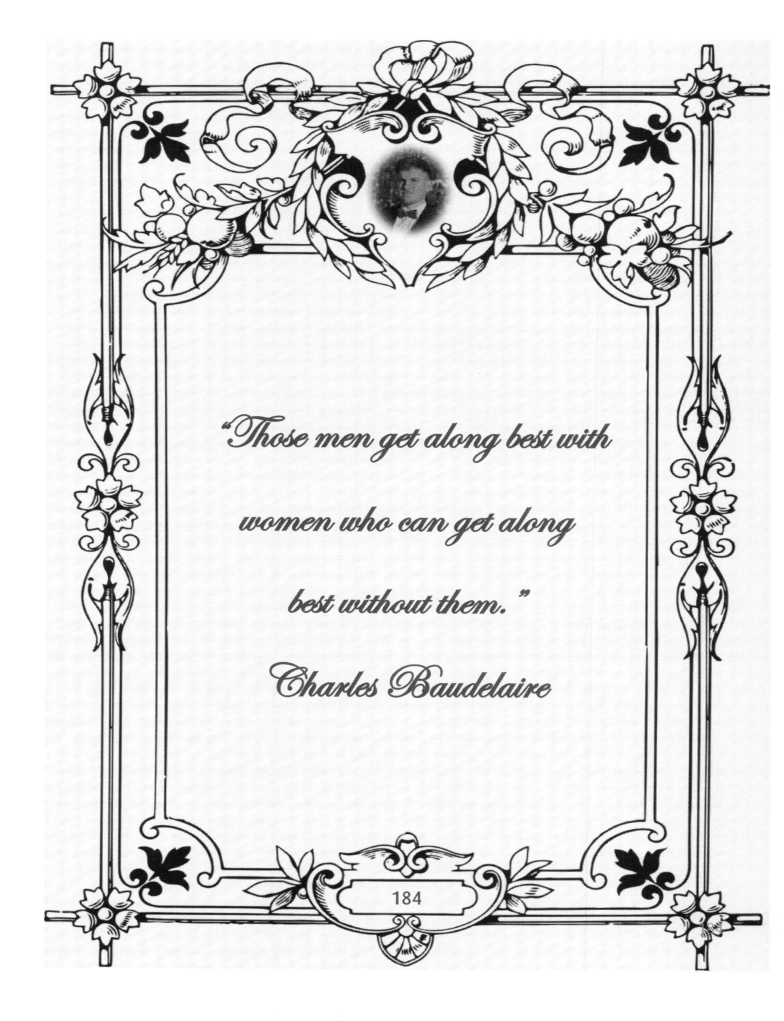

"Those men get along best with
women who can get along
best without them."

Charles Baudelaire

"The greatest deception men suffer

is from their own opinions."

Leonardo da Vinci

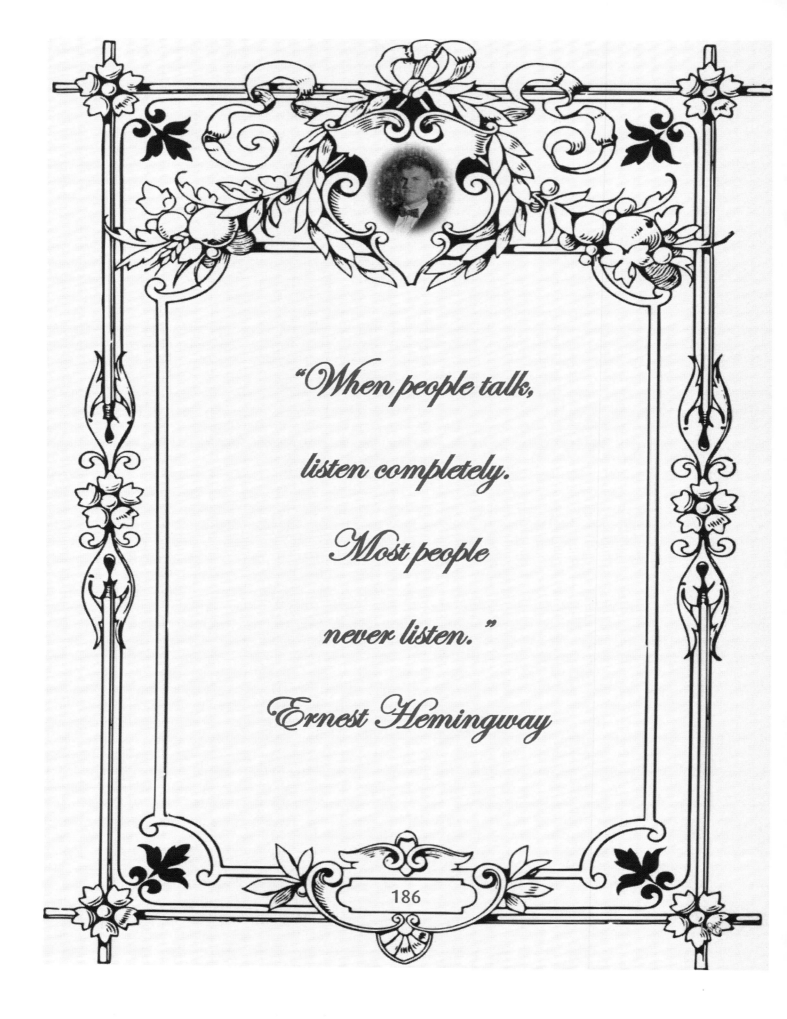

"When people talk,

listen completely.

Most people

never listen."

Ernest Hemingway

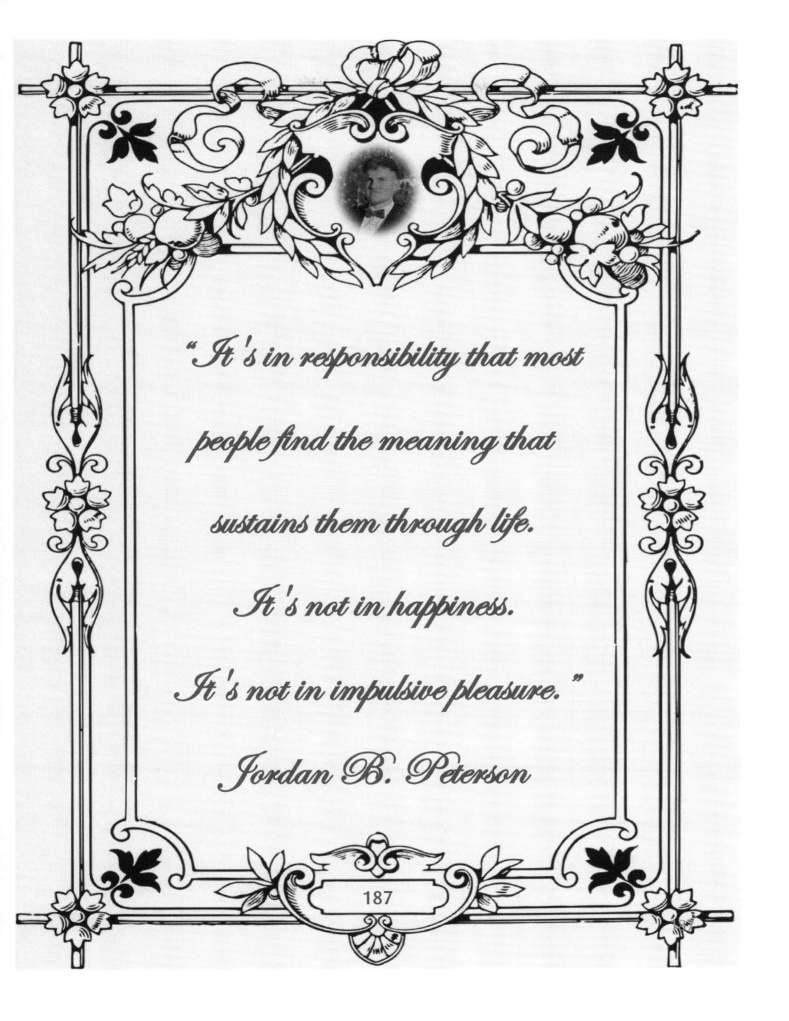

"It's in responsibility that most people find the meaning that sustains them through life.

It's not in happiness.

It's not in impulsive pleasure."

Jordan B. Peterson

187

"Man only likes to

count his troubles;

he doesn't calculate

his happiness."

Fyodor Dostoevsky

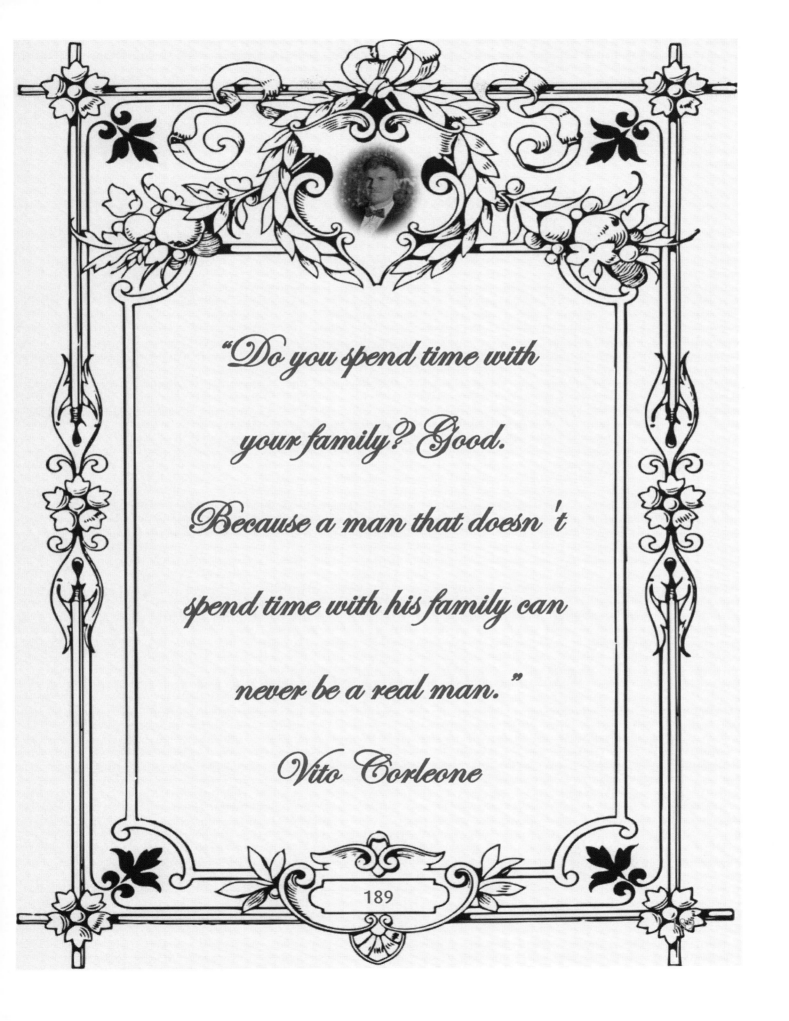

"Do you spend time with your family? Good.

Because a man that doesn't spend time with his family can never be a real man."

Vito Corleone

189

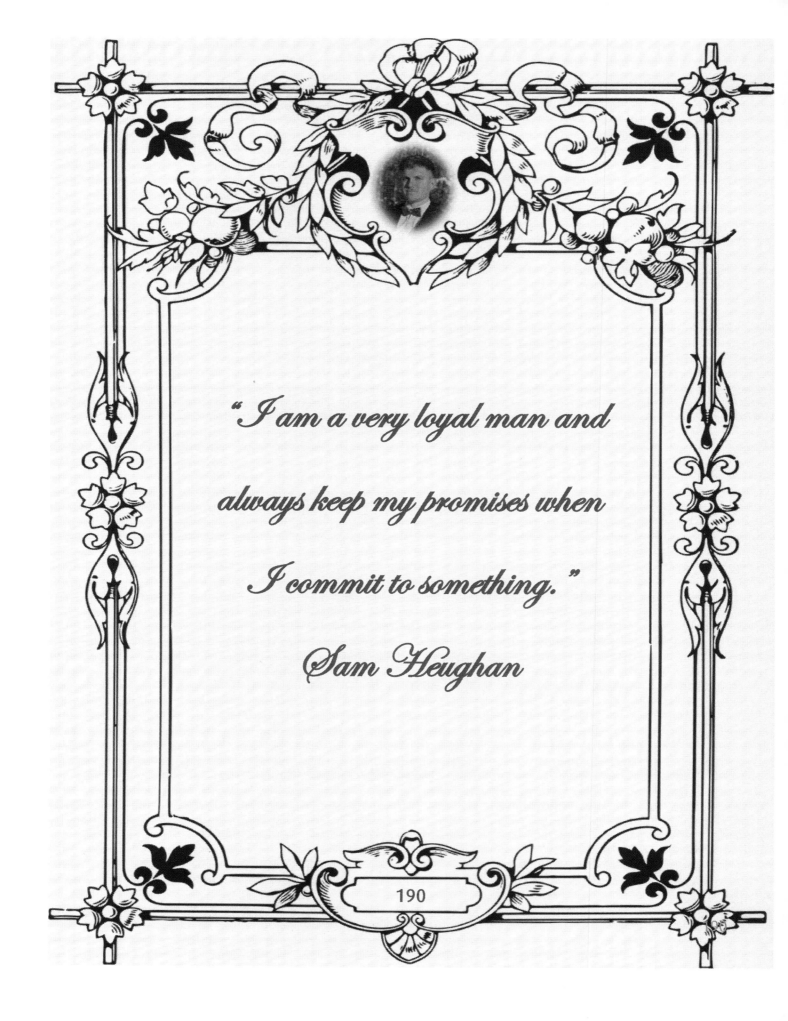

"*I am a very loyal man and always keep my promises when I commit to something.*"

Sam Heughan

190

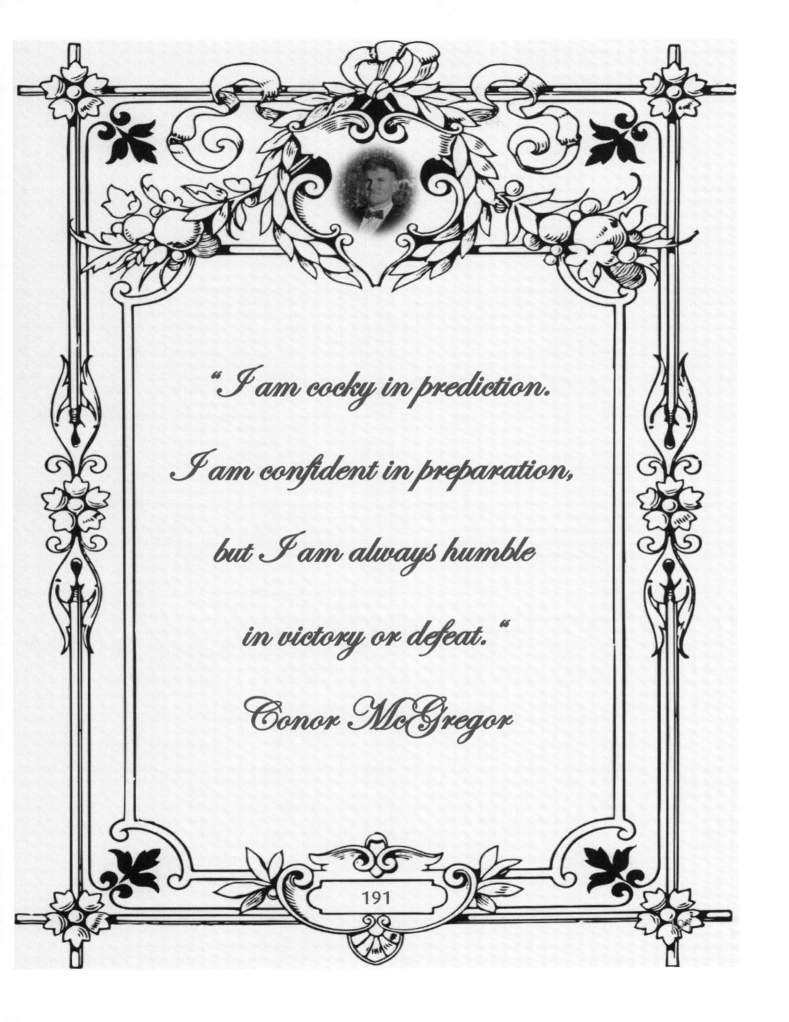

"I am cocky in prediction.

I am confident in preparation,

but I am always humble

in victory or defeat."

Conor McGregor

"*I've always had a*

weakness for lost causes,

once they're really lost."

Rhett Butler

"*It may be normal,*

darling;

but I'd rather be natural."

Truman Capote

"Take everything

you like seriously,

except yourselves."

Rudyard Kipling

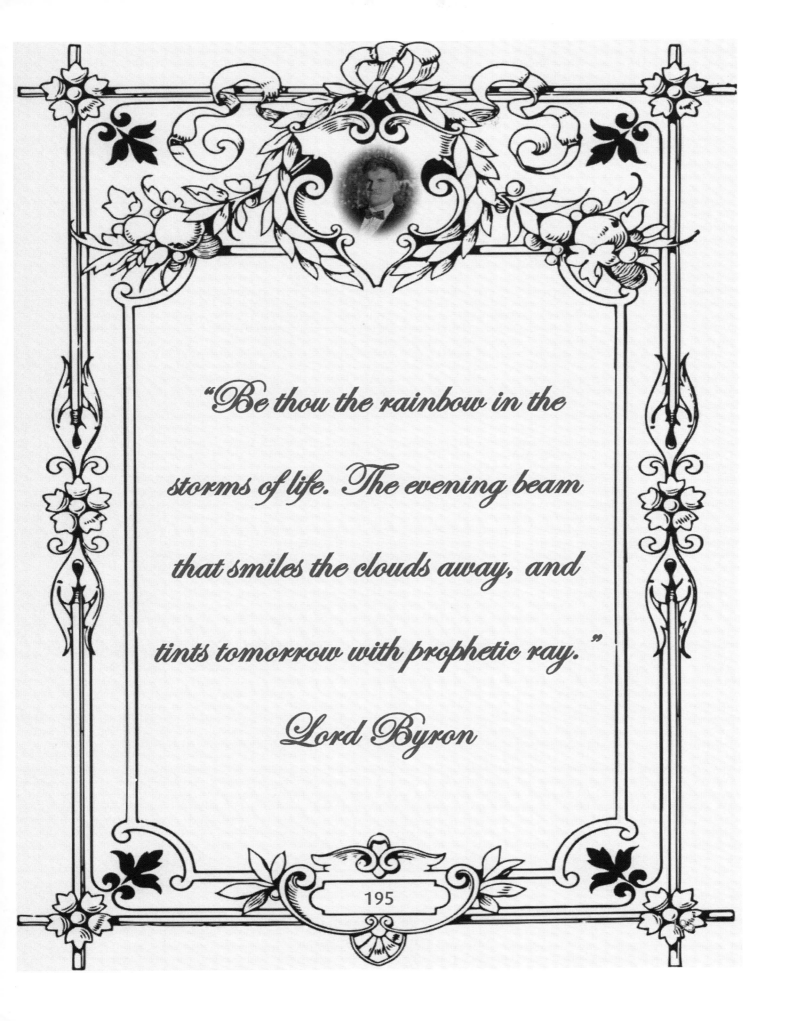

"Be thou the rainbow in the storms of life. The evening beam that smiles the clouds away, and tints tomorrow with prophetic ray."

Lord Byron

195

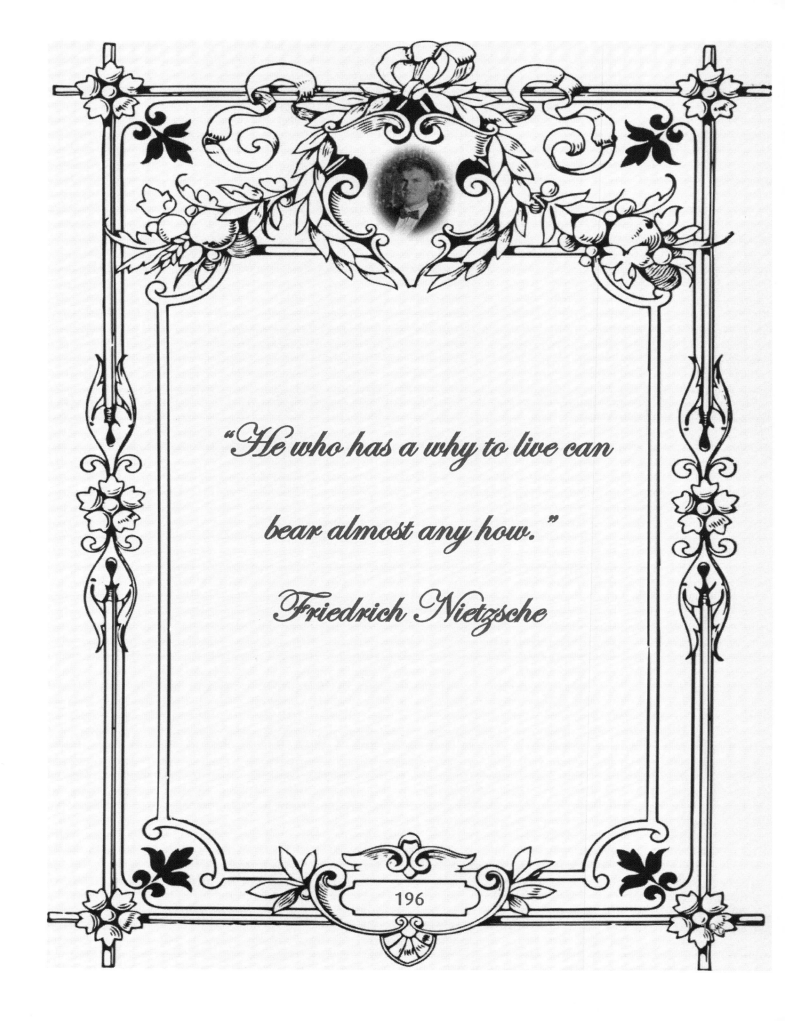

"He who has a why to live can

bear almost any how."

Friedrich Nietzsche

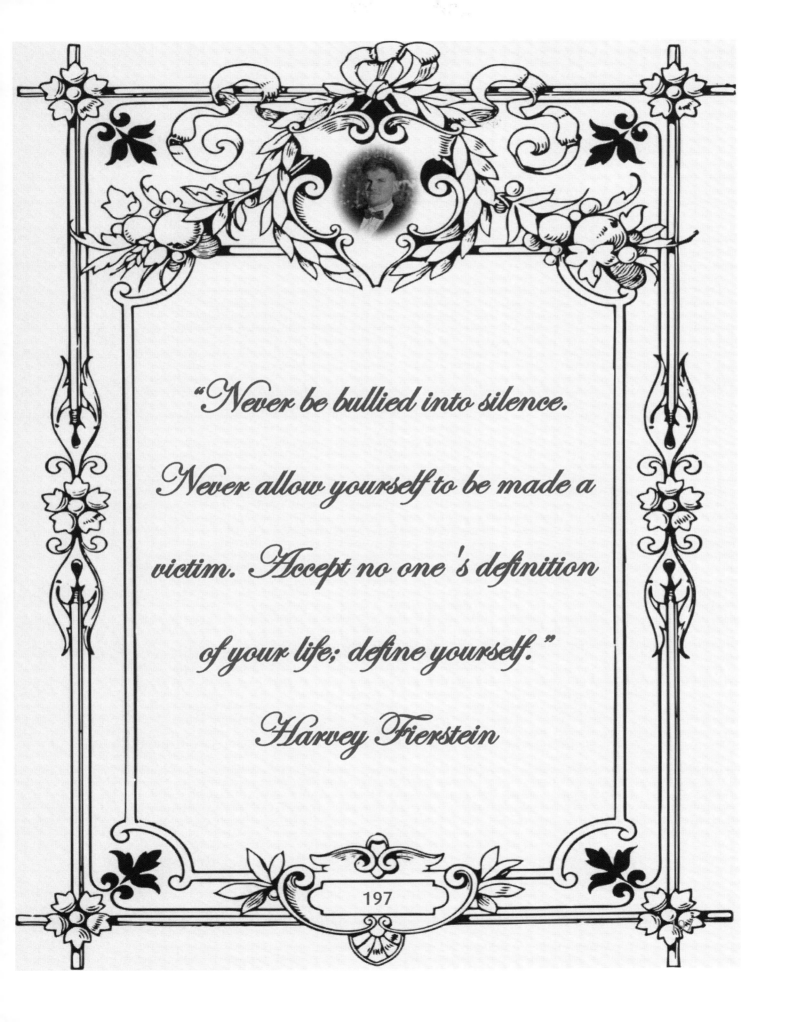

"Never be bullied into silence.

Never allow yourself to be made a

victim. Accept no one's definition

of your life; define yourself."

Harvey Fierstein

"*Every man dies.*

Not every man really lives."

William Wallace

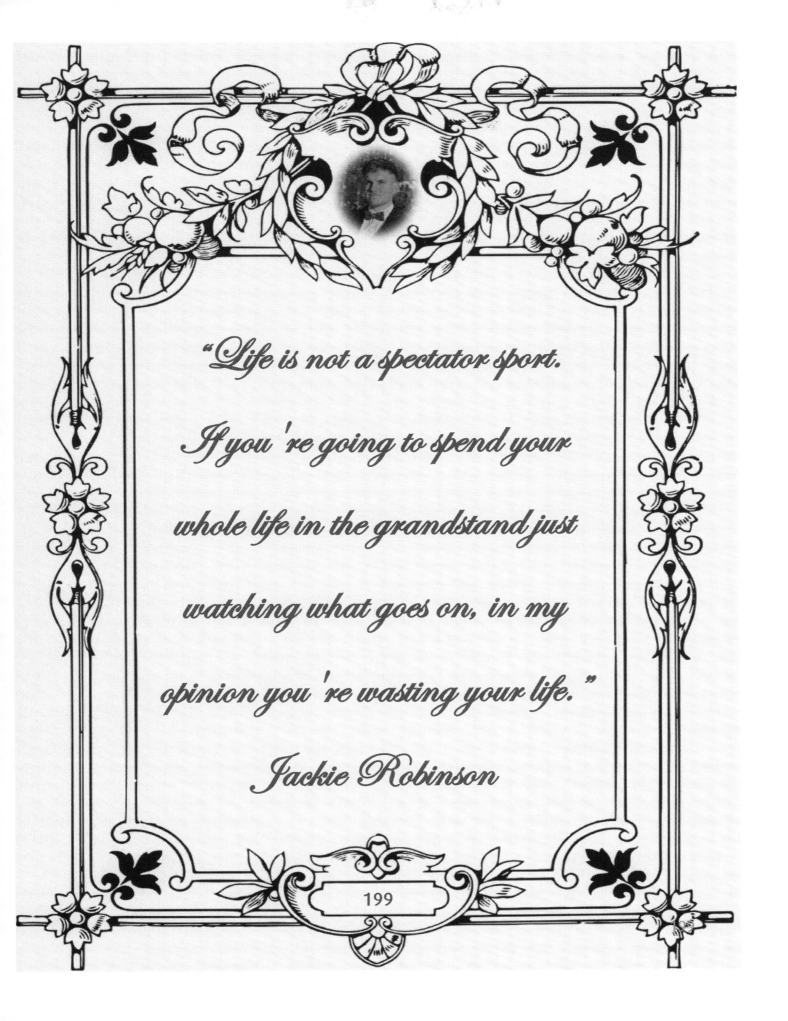

"Life is not a spectator sport.

If you're going to spend your

whole life in the grandstand just

watching what goes on, in my

opinion you're wasting your life."

Jackie Robinson

199

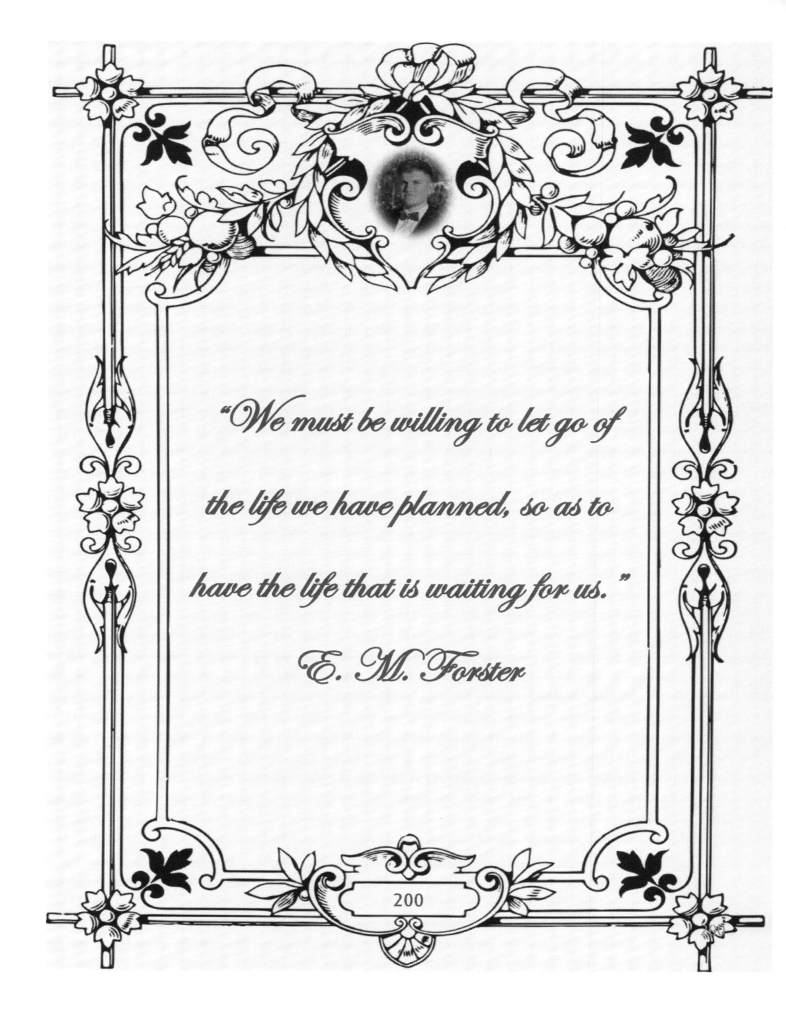

"We must be willing to let go of
the life we have planned, so as to
have the life that is waiting for us."

E. M. Forster

200

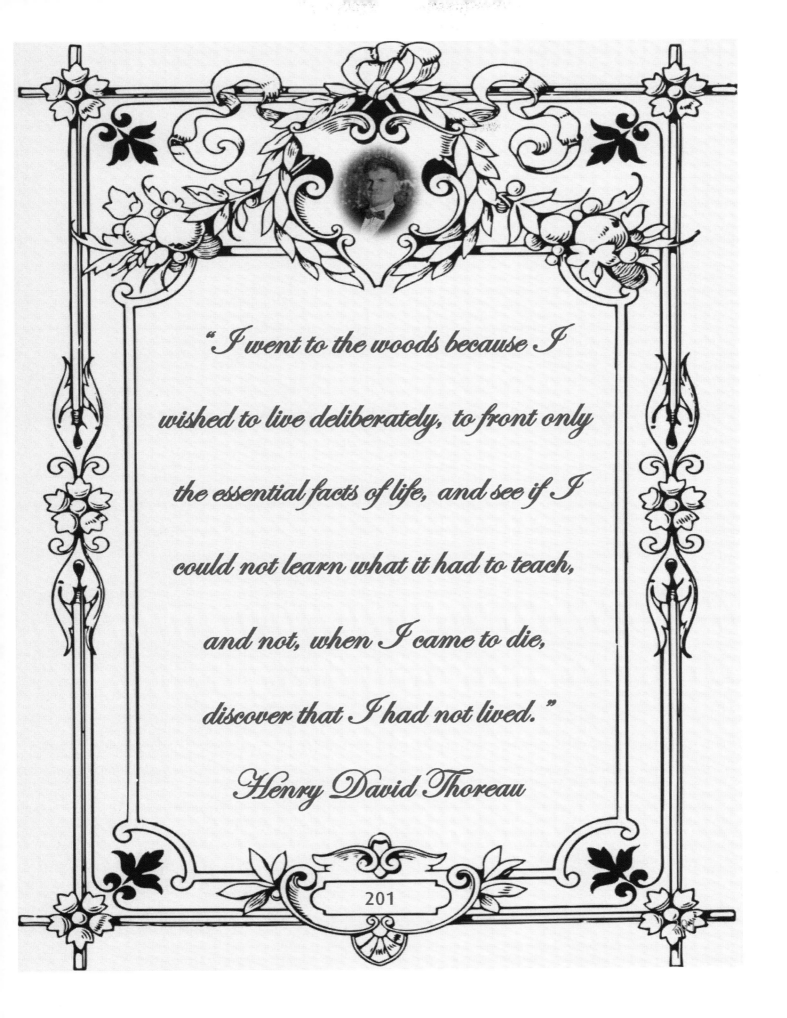

"I went to the woods because I wished to live deliberately, to front only the essential facts of life, and see if I could not learn what it had to teach, and not, when I came to die, discover that I had not lived."

Henry David Thoreau

"*No matter what anybody tells you, words and ideas can change the world.*"

Tom Schulman

202

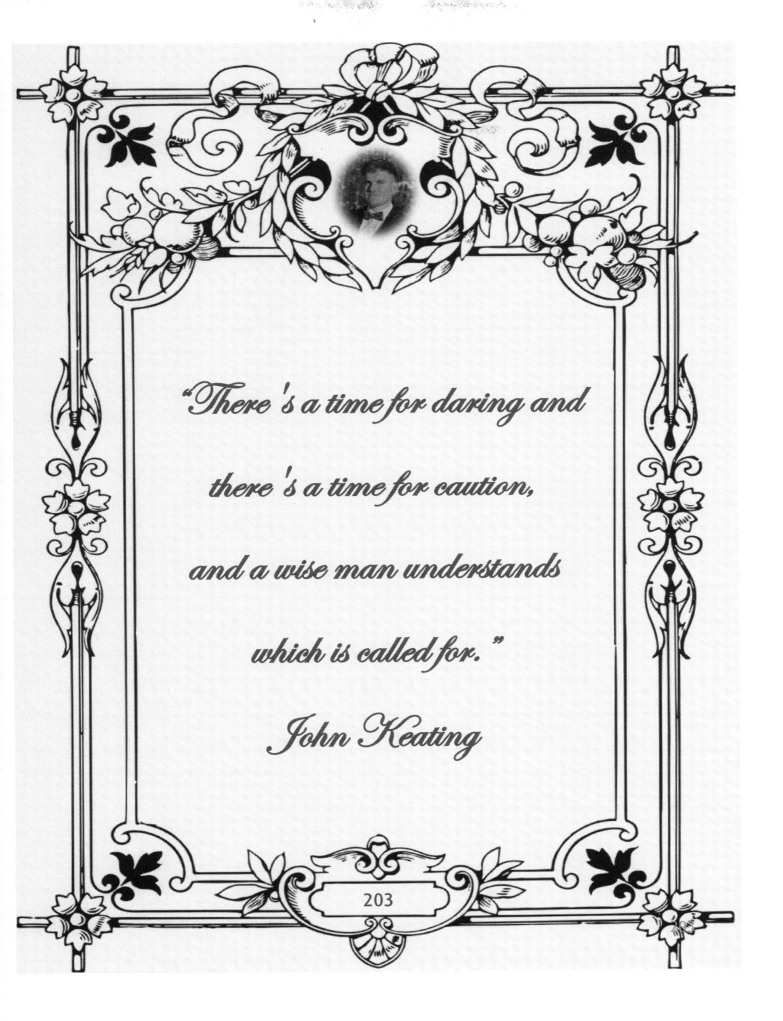

"There's a time for daring and

there's a time for caution,

and a wise man understands

which is called for."

John Keating

203

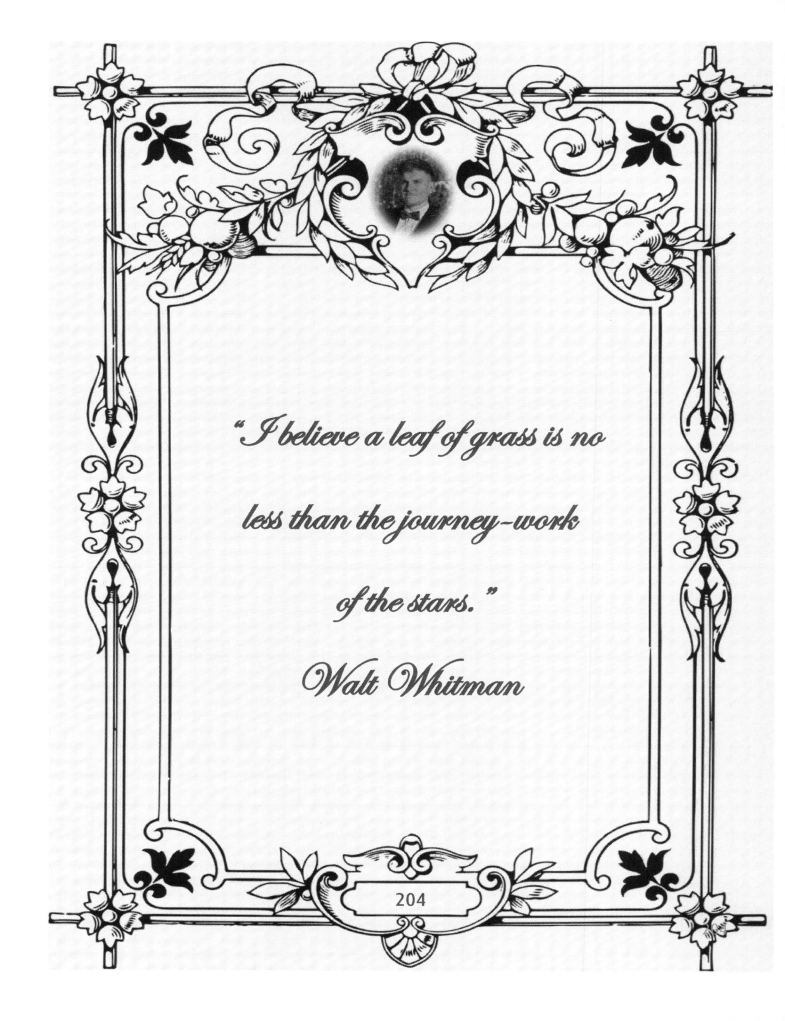

"I believe a leaf of grass is no

less than the journey-work

of the stars."

Walt Whitman

204

"You don't see something

until you have the right

metaphor to perceive it."

Robert Shaw

205

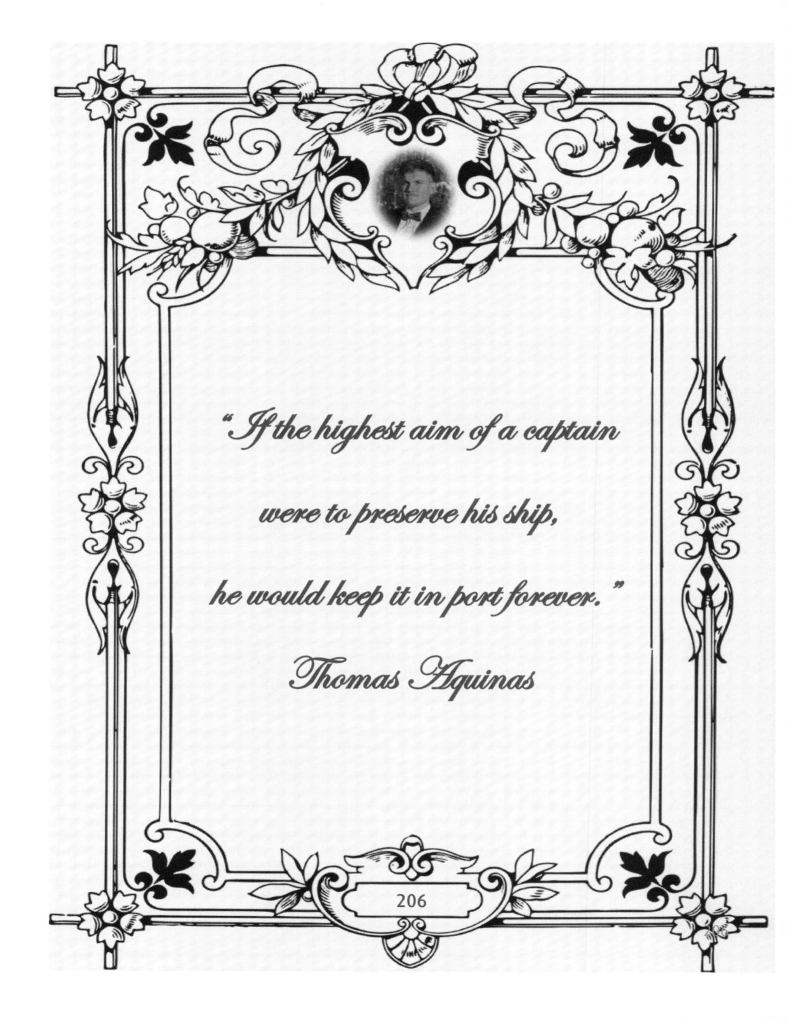

"If the highest aim of a captain

were to preserve his ship,

he would keep it in port forever."

Thomas Aquinas

"I've lived an amazing life. There's no reason to focus on the bad. They teach you that in racing school. Keep your eye where you want your front tire to be. You don't want to be stuck in the rut? Then don't look at the rut. Always look at where you want to go."

Francesco Quinn

"You don't see something until you have the right metaphor to perceive it."

Robert Shaw

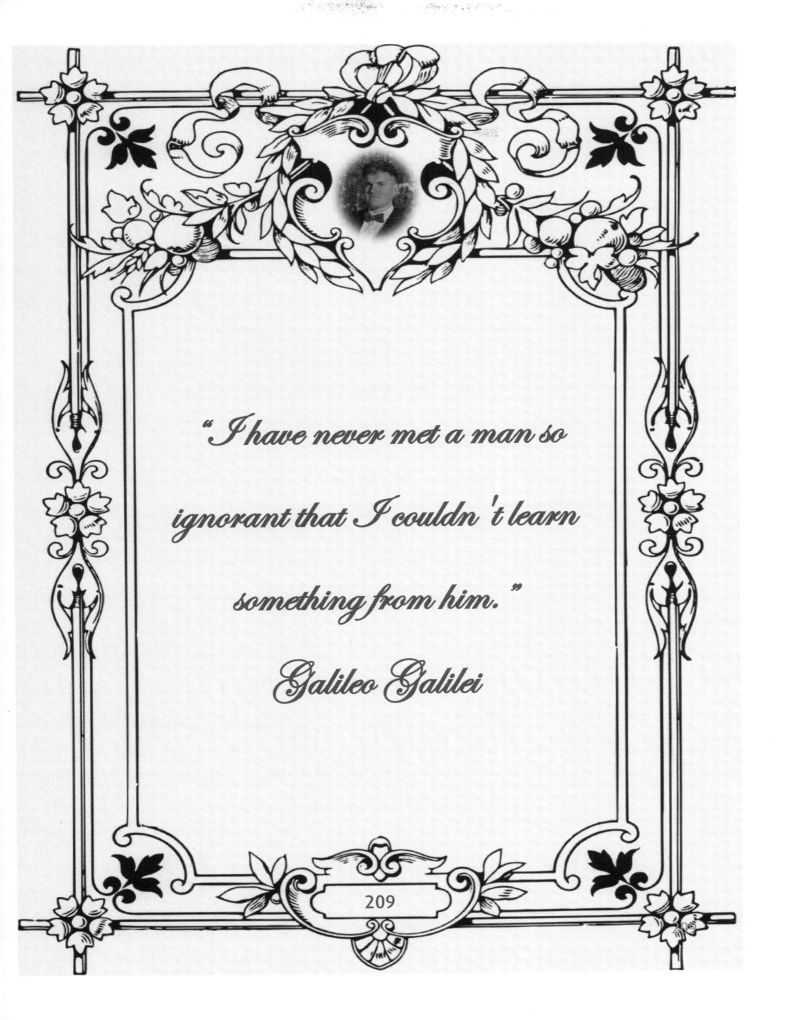

"I have never met a man so ignorant that I couldn't learn something from him."

Galileo Galilei

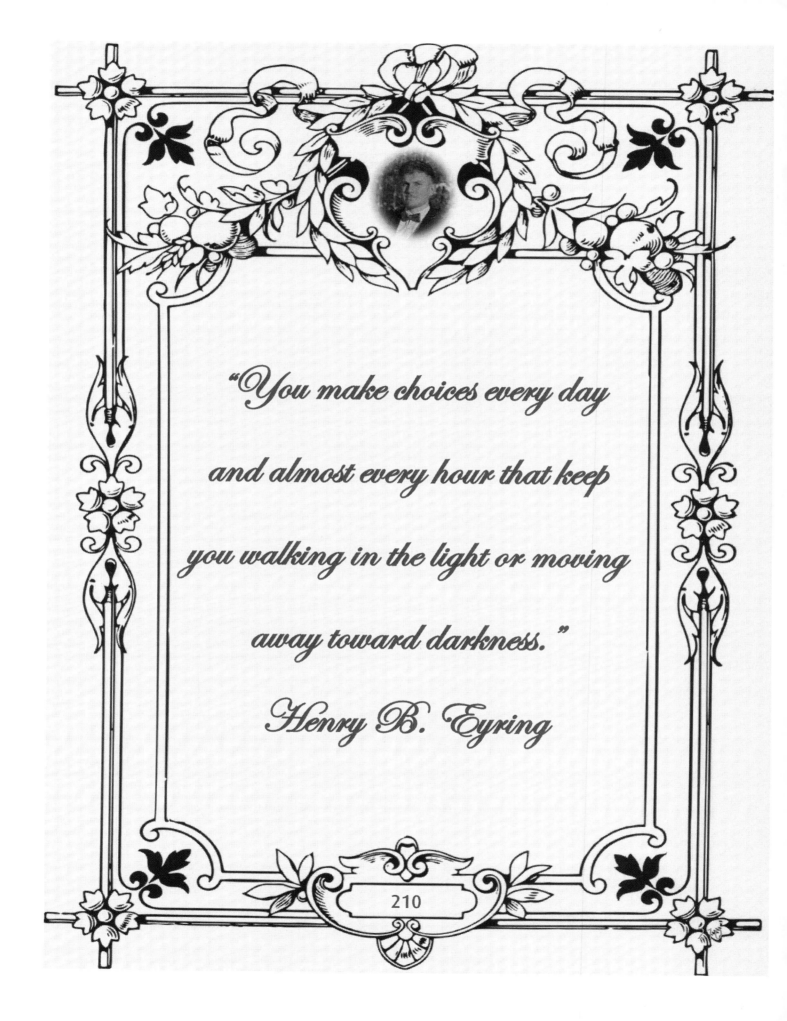

"You make choices every day

and almost every hour that keep

you walking in the light or moving

away toward darkness."

Henry B. Eyring

"With pride,

there are many curses.

With humility,

there come many blessings."

Ezra Taft Benson

211

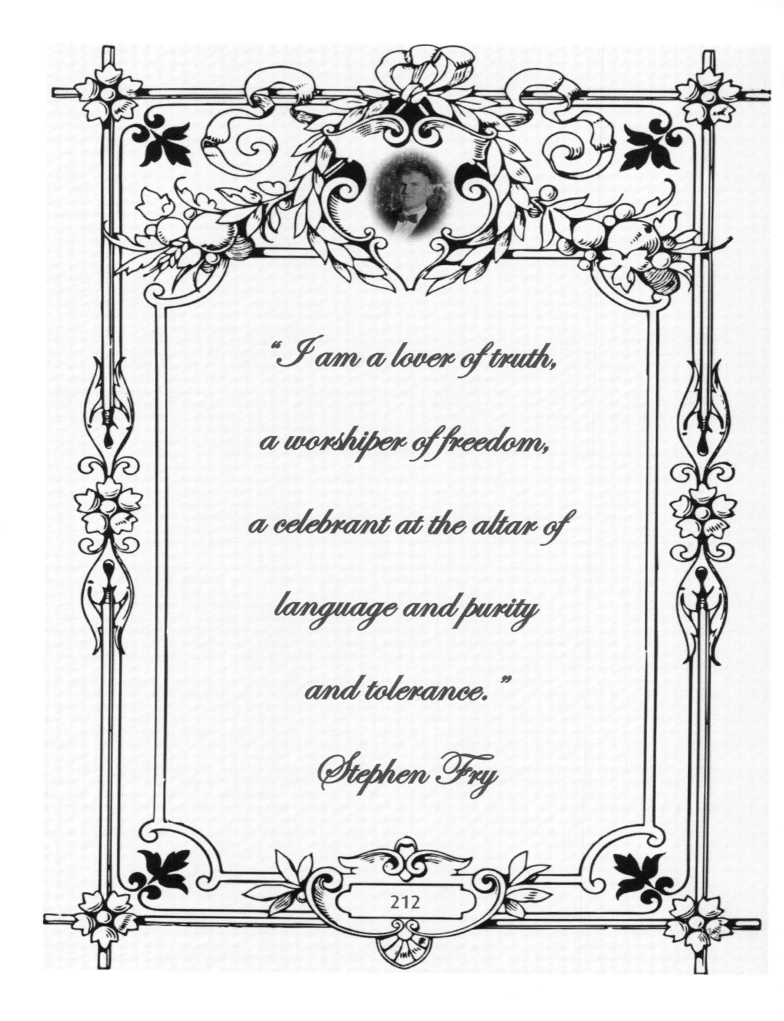

"*I am a lover of truth,*

a worshiper of freedom,

a celebrant at the altar of

language and purity

and tolerance."

Stephen Fry

"Then you get into it, especially if you start talking about football, fighting and Muhammad Ali. Then the ladies get very bored and start delivering ultimatums."

Oliver Reed

213

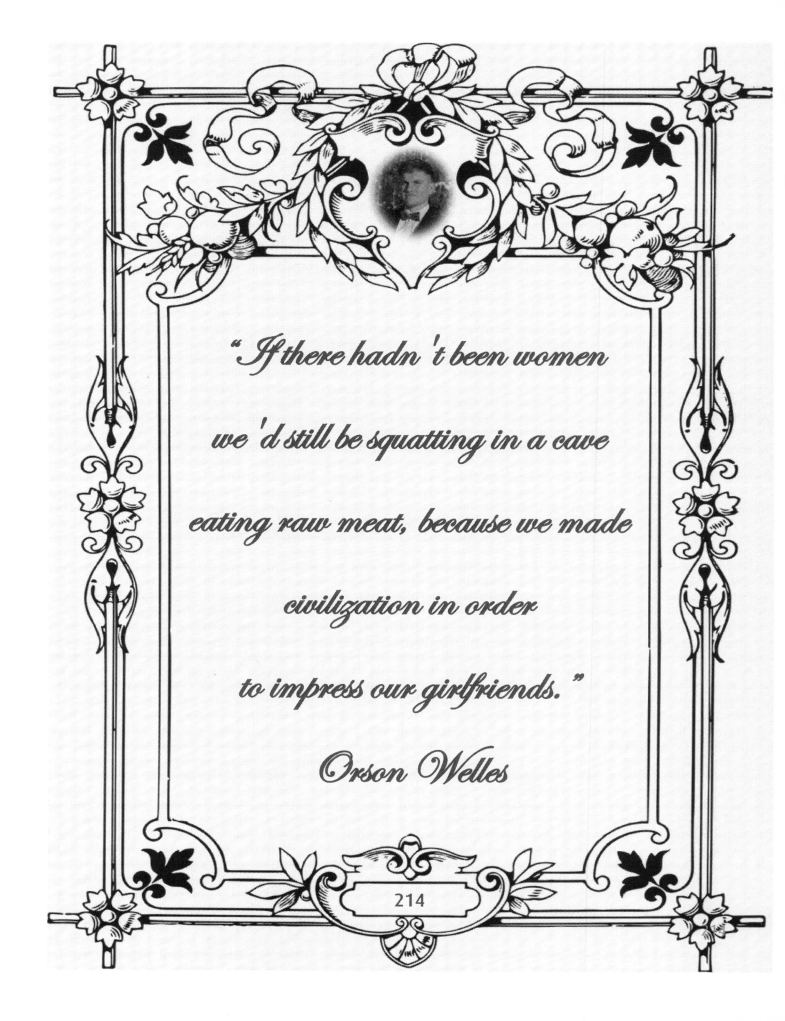

"*If there hadn't been women we'd still be squatting in a cave eating raw meat, because we made civilization in order to impress our girlfriends.*"

Orson Welles

214

"*Style is knowing who you are, what you want to say, and not giving a damn.*"

Gore Vidal

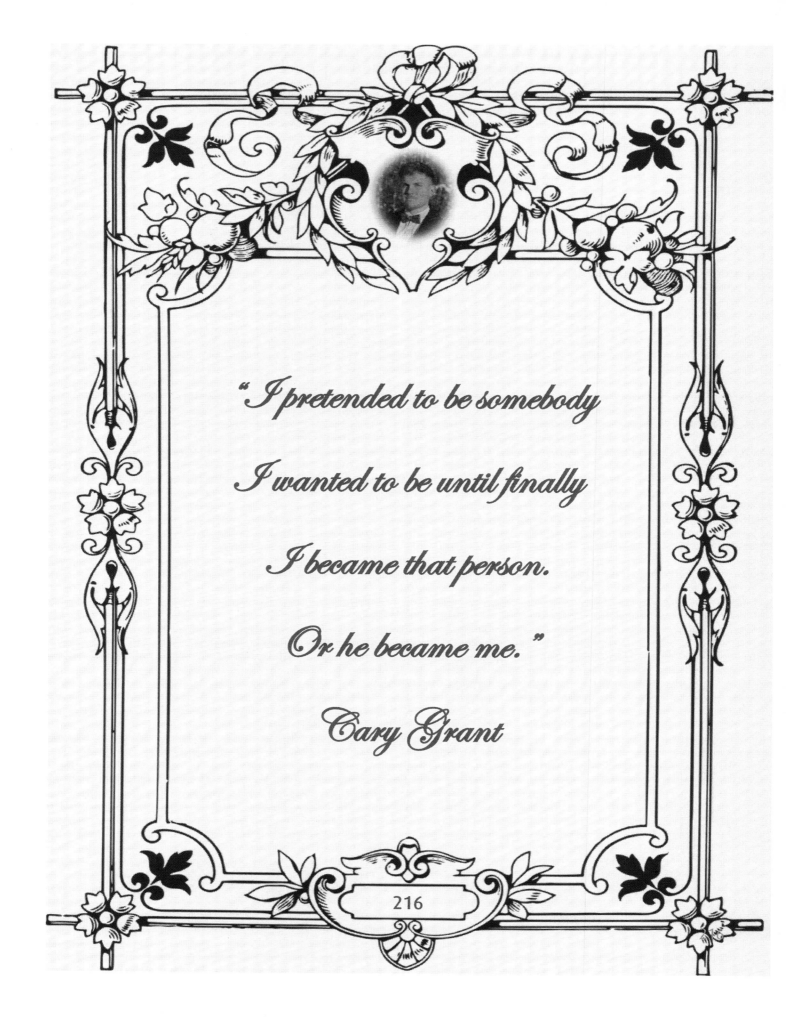

"I pretended to be somebody

I wanted to be until finally

I became that person.

Or he became me."

Cary Grant

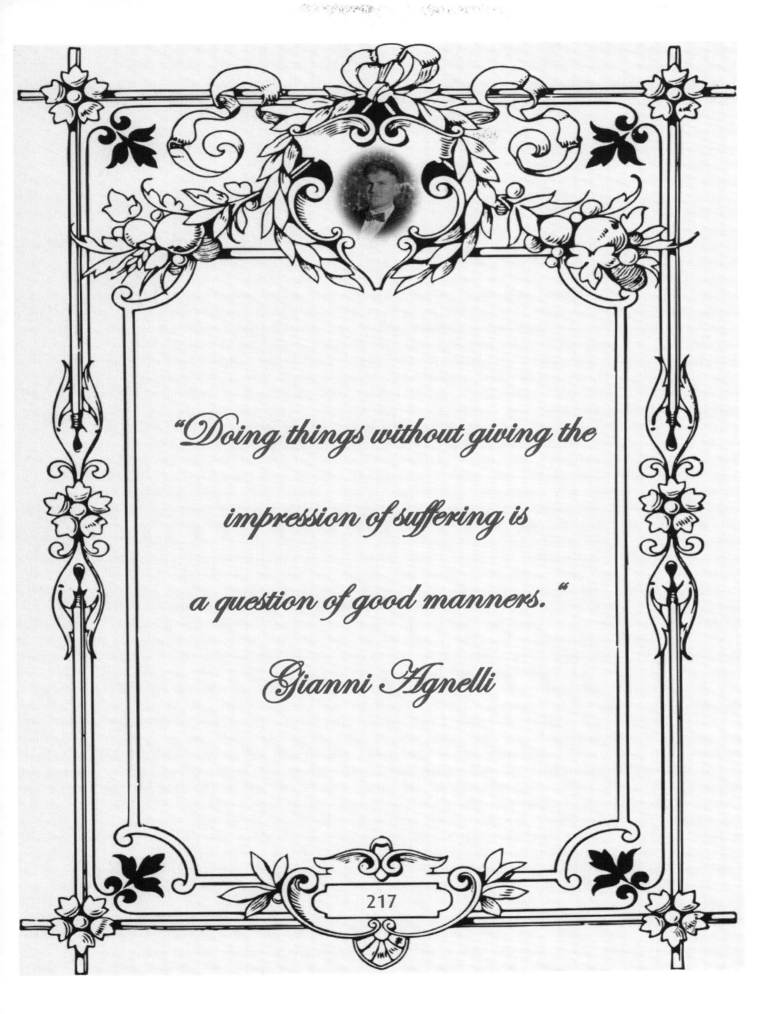

"Doing things without giving the

impression of suffering is

a question of good manners. "

Gianni Agnelli

217

" I live for myself and

answer to nobody. "

Steve McQueen

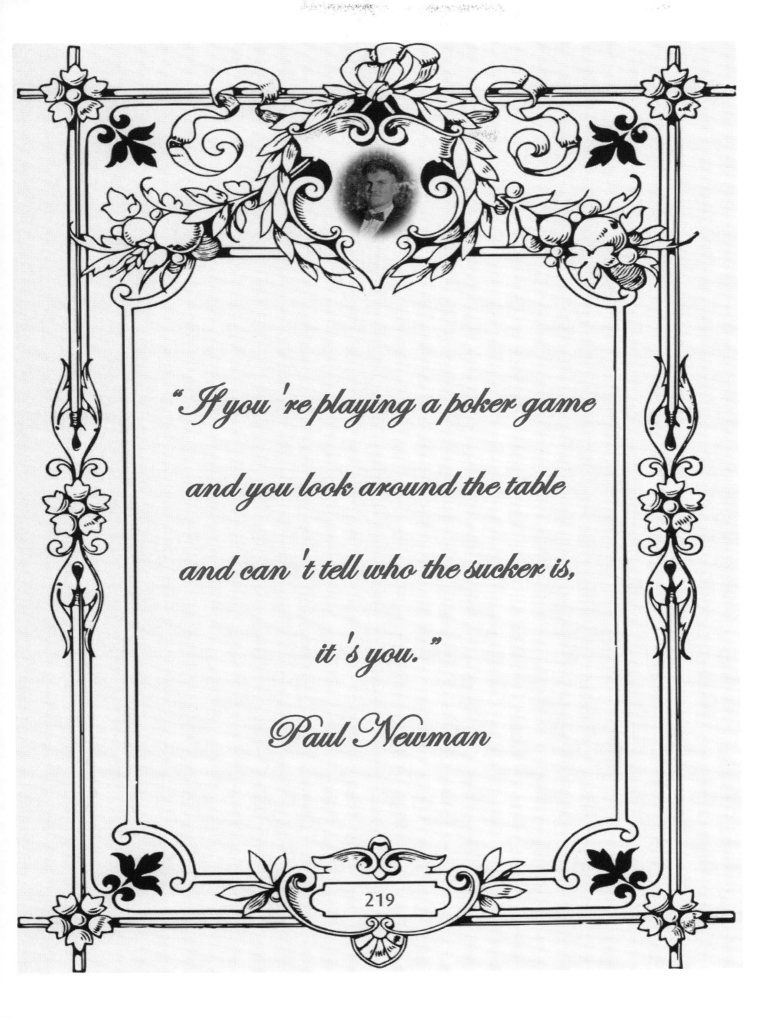

"If you're playing a poker game

and you look around the table

and can't tell who the sucker is,

it's you."

Paul Newman

219

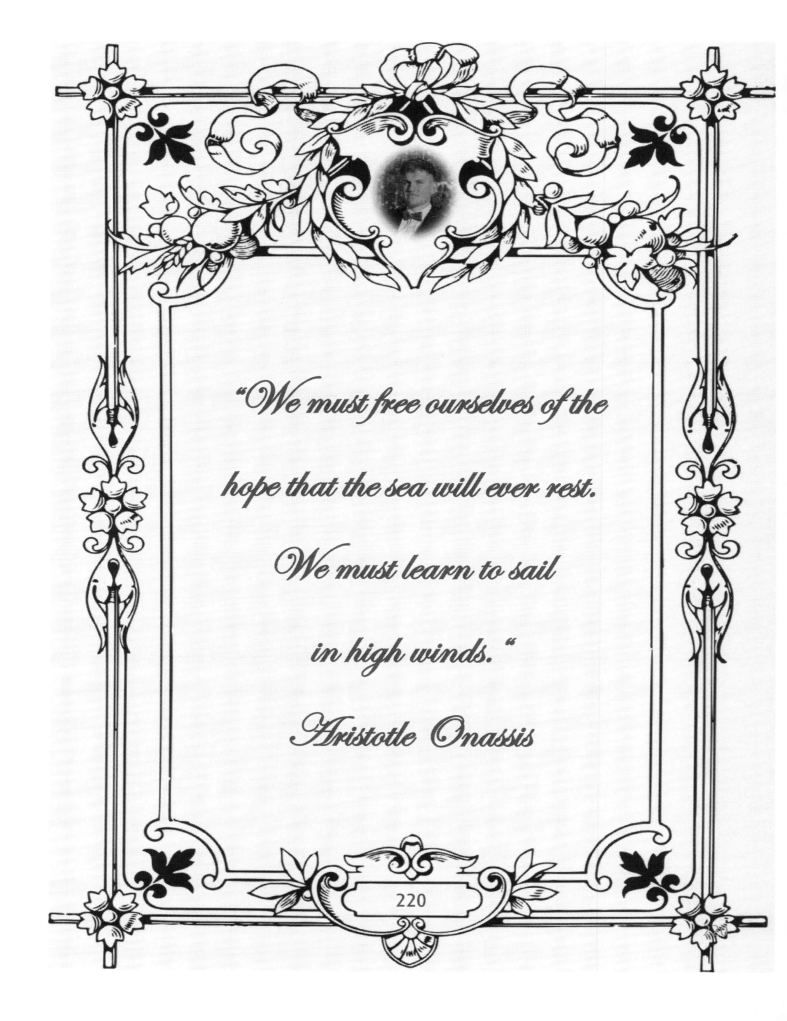

"We must free ourselves of the

hope that the sea will ever rest.

We must learn to sail

in high winds."

Aristotle Onassis

220

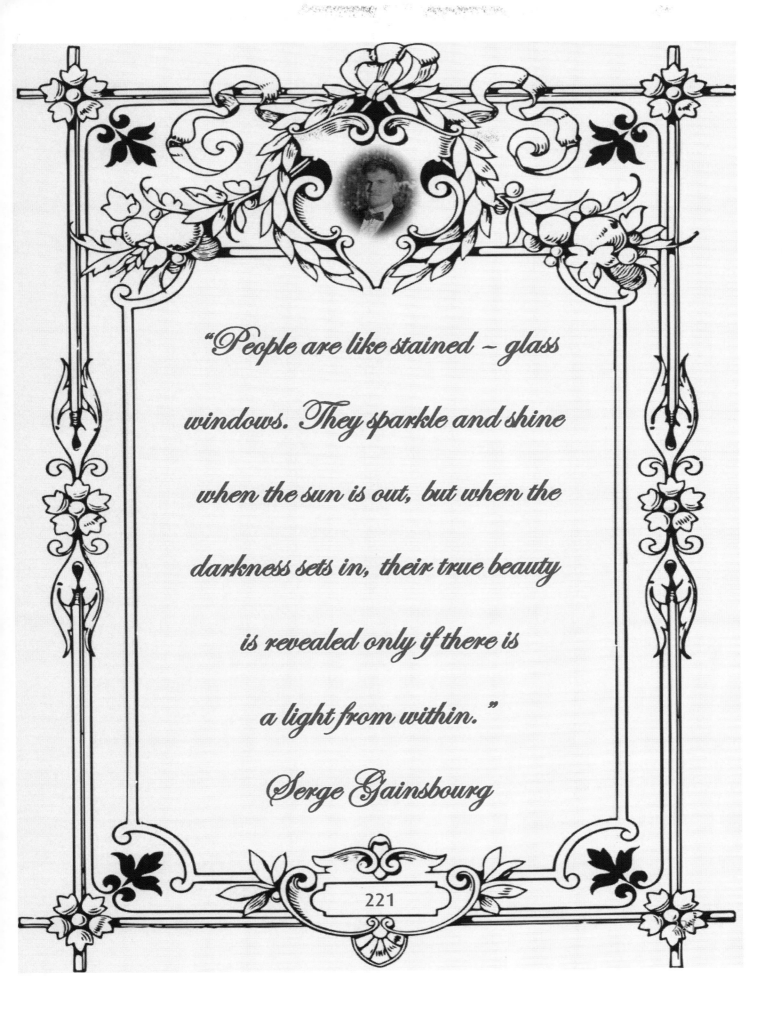

"People are like stained – glass windows. They sparkle and shine when the sun is out, but when the darkness sets in, their true beauty is revealed only if there is a light from within."

Serge Gainsbourg

221

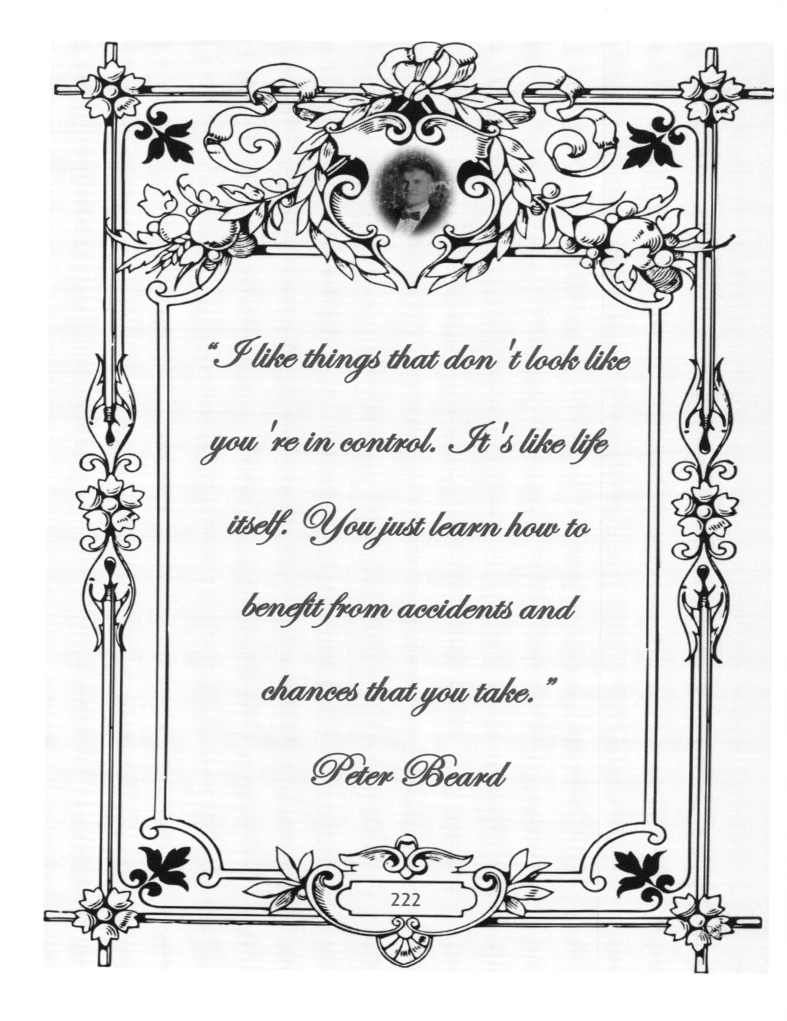

"*I like things that don't look like you're in control. It's like life itself. You just learn how to benefit from accidents and chances that you take.*"

Peter Beard

222

"We do not own this place,

we are just passengers."

Robert Redford

"Dressing is a way of life."

Yves Saint Laurent

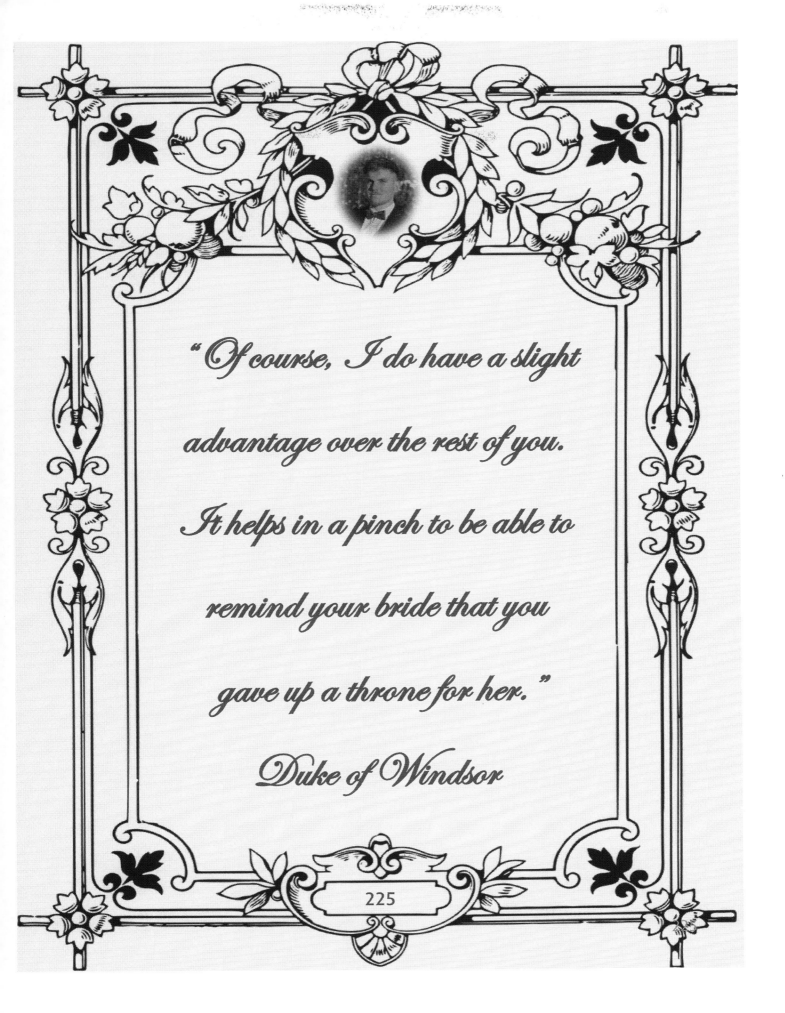

"*Of course, I do have a slight advantage over the rest of you. It helps in a pinch to be able to remind your bride that you gave up a throne for her.*"

Duke of Windsor

225

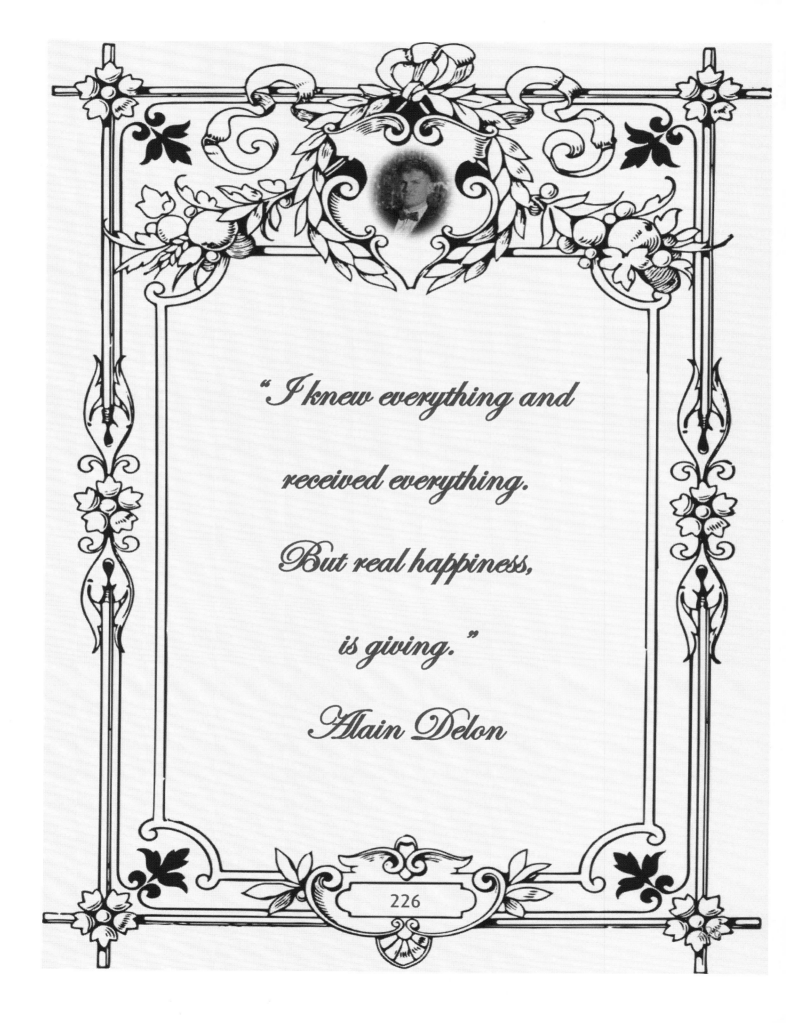

"*I knew everything and*

received everything.

But real happiness,

is giving."

Alain Delon

"The problem with the world is that

everyone is a few drinks behind."

Humphrey Bogart

I sincerely hope you have enjoyed my favourite and finely selected gentleman quotes. Now go on and keep up with the world and your drinks.

The End